Microsoft®
OFFICE 97
INTEGRATION

Step by Step

Other titles in the *Step by Step* series:

*Microsoft Access 97 Step by Step

*Microsoft Excel 97 Step by Step

*Microsoft Excel 97 Step by Step, Advanced Topics

*Microsoft FrontPage 97 Step by Step

  Microsoft Internet Explorer 3.0 Step by Step

*Microsoft Outlook 97 Step by Step

*Microsoft PowerPoint 97 Step by Step

  Microsoft Team Manager 97 Step by Step

  Microsoft Windows 95 Step by Step

  Microsoft Windows NT Workstation version 4.0 Step by Step

*Microsoft Word 97 Step by Step

*Microsoft Word 97 Step by Step, Advanced Topics

Step by Step books are also available for the Microsoft Office 95 programs.

* These books are approved courseware for Certified Microsoft Office User (CMOU) exams. For more details about the CMOU program, see page xviii.

Microsoft®
OFFICE 97
INTEGRATION

Step by Step

Microsoft Press

PUBLISHED BY
Microsoft Press
A Division of Microsoft Corporation
One Microsoft Way
Redmond, Washington 98052-6399

Library of Congress Cataloging-in-Publication Data
Microsoft Office 97 integration step by step / Catapult, Inc.
      p.   cm.
    Includes index.
    ISBN 1-57231-317-X
     1. Microsoft Office. 2. Business--Computer programs.
3. Integrated software I. Catapult, Inc.
HF5548.4.M525M523 1997
005.369--dc21   96-44274
                                              CIP

Printed and bound in the United States of America.

1 2 3 4 5 6 7 8 9 Rand–T 2 1 0 9 8 7

Distributed to the book trade in Canada by Macmillan of Canada, a division of Canada
Publishing Corporation.

A CIP catalogue record for this book is available from the British Library.

Microsoft Press books are available through booksellers and distributors worldwide. For further
information about international editions, contact your local Microsoft Corporation office. Or
contact Microsoft Press International directly at fax (206) 936-7329.

For Catapult, Inc.
Managing Editor: Diana Stiles
Writer: Michele M. Gordon
Contributing Writer: Eric J. Hansen
Project Editor: Karen A. Deinhard
Technical Editor: Vincent J. Abella
Production/Layout: Jeanne Hunt, Editor;
   Carolyn Thornley
Indexer: Jan Wright

For Microsoft Press
Acquisitions Editor: Susanne Freet
Project Editors: Laura Sackerman;
   Maureen Williams Zimmerman

Catapult, Inc. & Microsoft Press

Microsoft Office 97 Integration Step by Step has been created by the professional trainers and writers at Catapult, Inc., to the exacting standards you've come to expect from Microsoft Press. Together, we are pleased to present this self-paced training guide, which you can use individually or as part of a class.

Catapult, Inc., is a software training company with years of experience in PC and Macintosh instruction. Catapult's exclusive Performance-Based Training system is available in Catapult training centers across North America and at customer sites. Based on the principles of adult learning, Performance-Based Training ensures that students leave the classroom with confidence and the ability to apply skills to real-world scenarios. *Microsoft Office 97 Integration Step by Step* incorporates Catapult's training expertise to ensure that you'll receive the maximum return on your training time. You'll focus on the skills that can increase your productivity the most while working at your own pace and convenience.

Microsoft Press is the book publishing division of Microsoft Corporation. The leading publisher of information about Microsoft products and services, Microsoft Press is dedicated to providing the highest quality computer books and multimedia training and reference tools that make using Microsoft software easier, more enjoyable, and more productive.

Table of Contents

Table of Contents

Appendixes

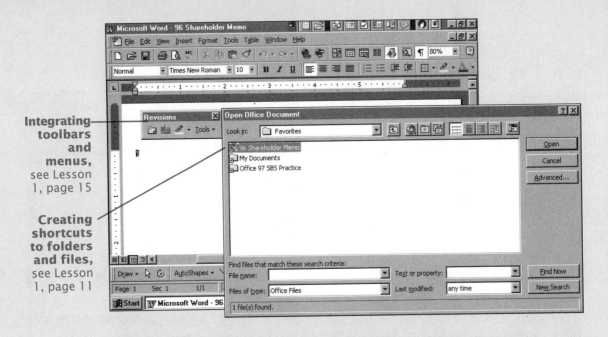

Integrating toolbars and menus, see Lesson 1, page 15

Creating shortcuts to folders and files, see Lesson 1, page 11

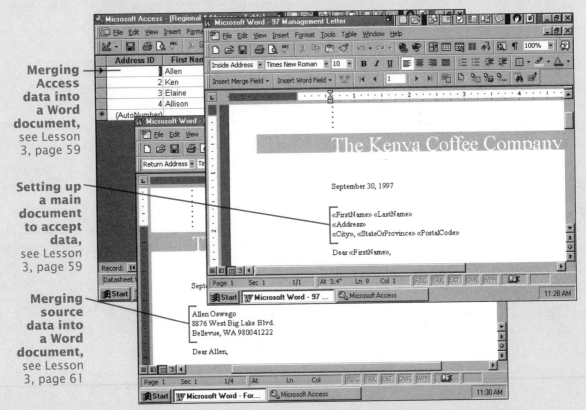

Merging Access data into a Word document, see Lesson 3, page 59

Setting up a main document to accept data, see Lesson 3, page 59

Merging source data into a Word document, see Lesson 3, page 61

Organizing related files with Office Binder, see Lesson 2, page 28

Embedding or linking objects from another program, see Lessons 4, 5, 7, 9, and 10

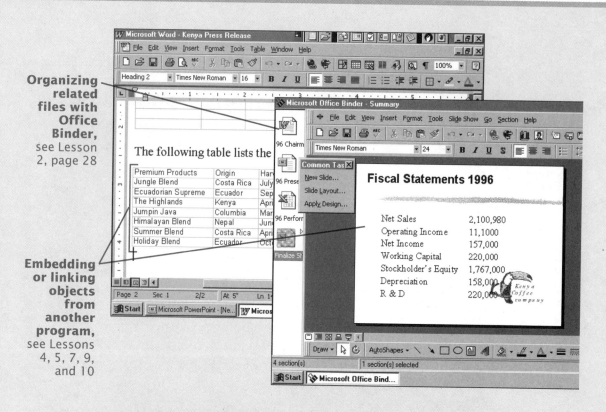

Creating and tracking a Journal entry in Outlook, see Lesson 4, page 86

Creating tasks in Outlook, see Lesson 5, page 105

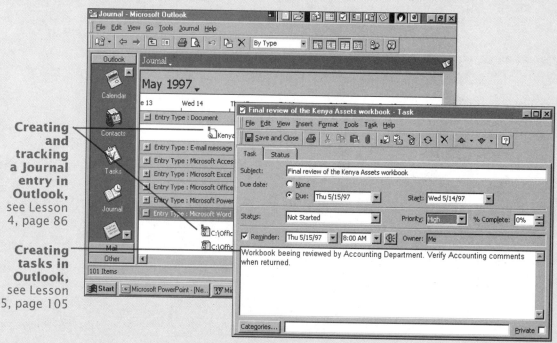

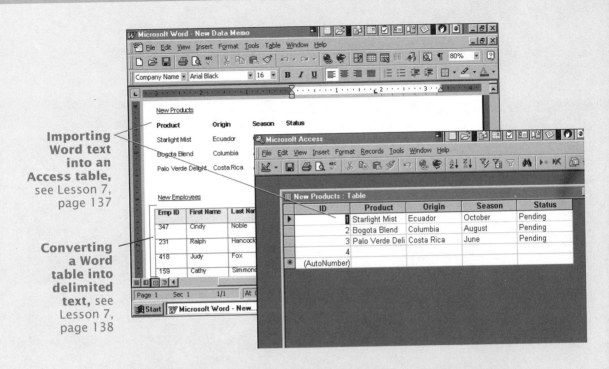

Importing Word text into an Access table, see Lesson 7, page 137

Converting a Word table into delimited text, see Lesson 7, page 138

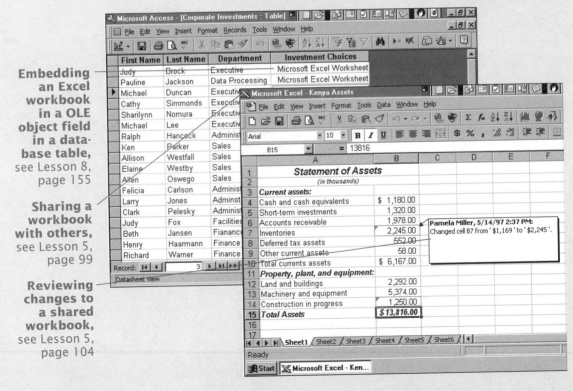

Embedding an Excel workbook in a OLE object field in a database table, see Lesson 8, page 155

Sharing a workbook with others, see Lesson 5, page 99

Reviewing changes to a shared workbook, see Lesson 5, page 104

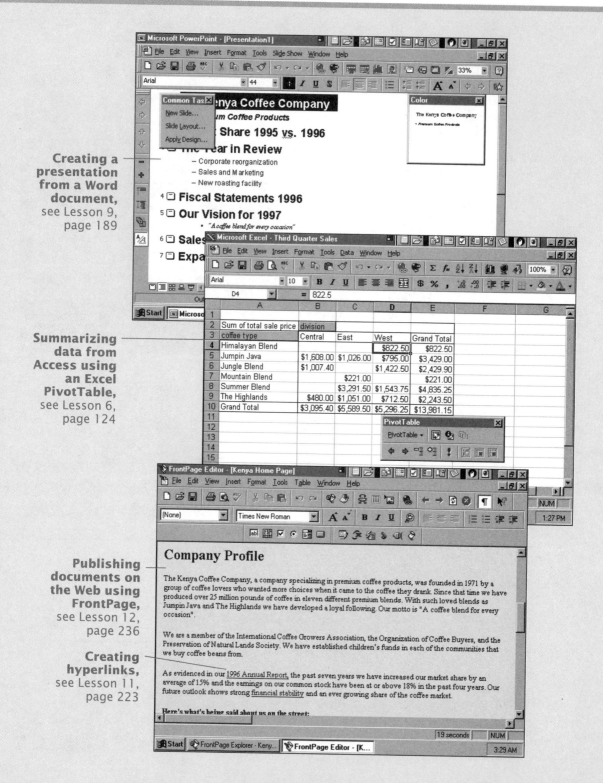

Creating a presentation from a Word document, see Lesson 9, page 189

Summarizing data from Access using an Excel PivotTable, see Lesson 6, page 124

Publishing documents on the Web using FrontPage, see Lesson 12, page 236

Creating hyperlinks, see Lesson 11, page 223

Finding Your Best Starting Point

Microsoft Office 97 is a powerful family of integrated programs that you can use to produce sophisticated documents. With Microsoft Office 97 Integration Step by Step, you'll quickly and easily learn how to integrate information from more than one program to get your work done.

 IMPORTANT This book is designed for use with Microsoft Office 97 Professional Edition for the Windows 95 and Windows NT version 4.0 operating systems. To find out what software you're running, you can check the product package or you can start the software, click the Help menu, and click About Microsoft for the Office 97 program you are using. If your software is not compatible with this book, a Step by Step book for your software is probably available. Many of the Step by Step titles are listed on page ii of this book. If the book you want isn't listed, please visit our World Wide Web site at http://www.microsoft.com/mspress/ or call 1-800-MSPRESS for more information.

Finding Your Best Starting Point in This Book

 IMPORTANT This book is designed for use with Microsoft Office 97 Professional Edition. If you are working with Microsoft Office 97 Standard Edition, you will be unable to complete some of the exercises in Lessons 3, 6, 7, 8 and Review & Practice 2 and 3. In addition, in order to work through Lesson 12, you must have Microsoft FrontPage installed. This book is also designed to work with the Microsoft Mail information service in Outlook. If you do not have a mail delivery system, you will be unable to complete some of the exercises in Lessons 2, 6, 8, 9, 11, and Review & Practice 3.

This book is designed for readers who are learning the integration techniques of Office 97 for the first time and for more experienced readers who want to learn and use methods of integration. Use the following table to find your best starting point in this book.

If you are	Follow these steps
New...	
to computers	**1** Install the practice files as described in "Installing and Using the Practice Files."
to graphical (as opposed to text-only) computer programs	**2** Become acquainted with the Windows 95 or Windows NT operating system and how to use the online Help system by working through Appendix A, "If You Are New to Windows 95, Windows NT, or Office 97."
to Windows 95 or Windows NT	
to Microsoft Office programs	**3** Learn basic skills for integrating Microsoft Office 97 programs by working sequentially through Lessons 1 through 12.

If you are	Follow these steps
Switching...	
from Lotus SmartSuite	**1** Install the practice files as described in "Installing and Using the Practice Files."
from Corel Office	**2** Learn basic skills for integrating Microsoft Office 97 programs by working sequentially through Lessons 1 through 12.

If you are	Follow these steps
Upgrading... from Microsoft Office 95 from a previous version of Microsoft Word, Microsoft Excel, Microsoft PowerPoint, or Microsoft Access	**1** Install the practice files as described in "Installing and Using the Practice Files." **2** Complete the lessons that cover the topics you need. You can use the table of contents and the *Quick*Look Guide to locate information about general topics. You can use the index to find information about a specific topic or a feature from Microsoft Office 95.

If you are	Follow these steps
Referencing... this book after working through the lessons	**1** Use the index to locate information about specific topics, and use the table of contents and the *Quick*Look Guide to locate information about general topics. **2** Read the Lesson Summary at the end of each lesson for a brief review of the major tasks in the lesson. The Lesson Summary topics are listed in the same order as they are presented in the lesson.

New Features in Office 97

The following table lists the major new features in Microsoft Office 97 that are covered in this book. The table shows the lesson in which you can learn how to use each feature. You can also use the index to find specific information about a feature or a task you want to do.

To learn how to use	See
Integrated toolbars and menus	Lesson 1
Office Assistant	Lesson 1 sidebar
Outlook	Lessons 1, 2, 4, 5, 8, and 9
Hyperlinks	Lessons 11 and 12
Web toolbar	Lesson 11
Track shared workbook changes	Lesson 5
Merge shared workbooks	Lesson 5
FrontPage (standalone program)	Lesson 12

Certified Microsoft Office User Program

The Certified Microsoft Office User (CMOU) program is designed for business professionals and students who use Microsoft Office 97 products in their daily work. The program enables participants to showcase their skill level to potential employers. It benefits accountants, administrators, executive assistants, program managers, sales representatives, students, and many others. To receive certified user credentials for a software program, candidates must pass a hands-on exam in which they use the program to complete real-world tasks.

The CMOU program offers two levels of certification: Proficient and Expert. The following table indicates the levels available for each Microsoft Office 97 program.

Software	Proficient level	Expert level
Microsoft Word 97	✔	✔
Microsoft Excel 97	✔	✔
Microsoft Access 97		✔
Microsoft PowerPoint 97		✔
Microsoft Outlook 97		✔
Microsoft FrontPage 97		✔

Microsoft Press offers the following books in the *Step by Step* series as approved courseware for the CMOU exams:

Proficient level:

Microsoft Word 97 Step by Step, by Catapult, Inc. ISBN: 1-57231-313-7
Microsoft Excel 97 Step by Step, by Catapult, Inc. ISBN: 1-57231-314-5

Expert level:

Microsoft Word 97 Step by Step, Advanced Topics by Catapult, Inc.
    ISBN: 1-57231-563-6
Microsoft Excel 97 Step by Step, Advanced Topics by Catapult, Inc.
    ISBN: 1-57231-564-4
Microsoft Access 97 Step by Step, by Catapult, Inc. ISBN: 1-57231-316-1
Microsoft PowerPoint 97 Step by Step, by Perspection, Inc. ISBN: 1-57231-315-3
Microsoft Outlook 97 Step by Step, by Catapult, Inc. ISBN: 1-57231-382-X
Microsoft FrontPage 97 Step by Step, by Catapult, Inc. ISBN: 1-57231-336-6

Candidates may take exams at any participating Sylvan Test Center, participating corporations, or participating employment agencies. Exams have a suggested retail price of $50 each.

To become a candidate for certification, or for more information about the certification process, please call 1-800-933-4493 in the United States or visit the CMOU program World Wide Web site at http:/www.microsoft.com/office/train_cert/

Corrections, Comments, and Help

Every effort has been made to ensure the accuracy of this book and the contents of the practice files disk. Microsoft Press provides corrections and additional content for its books through the World Wide Web at

http://www.microsoft.com/mspress/support/

If you have comments, questions, or ideas regarding this book or the practice files disk, please send them to us.

Send e-mail to

mspinput@microsoft.com

Or send postal mail to

Microsoft Press

Attn: Step by Step Series Editor

One Microsoft Way

Redmond, WA 98052-6399

Please note that support for Office 97 programs is not offered through the above addresses. For help using Office 97, you can call Microsoft Office 97 AnswerPoint at (206) 635-7056 on weekdays between 6 a.m. and 6 p.m. Pacific time.

Visit Our World Wide Web Site

We invite you to visit the Microsoft Press Word Wide Web site. You can visit us at the following location:

http://www.microsoft.com/mspress/

You'll find descriptions of all of our books, information about ordering titles, notices of special features and events, additional content for Microsoft Press books, and much more.

You can also find out the latest in software developments and news from Microsoft Corporation by visiting the following World Wide Web site:

http://www.microsoft.com/

We look forward to your visit on the Web!

Installing and Using the Practice Files

The disk inside the back cover of this book contains practice files that you'll use as you perform the exercises in the book. For example, when you're learning how to merge addresses with a letter, you'll use the Mail Merge Helper to insert merge fields in the letter, identify the data source, and then merge the two to create personalized letters. By using the practice files, you won't waste time creating the samples used in the lessons—instead, you can concentrate on learning how to integrate information between Office 97 programs. With the files and the step-by-step instructions in the lessons, you'll also learn by doing, which is an easy and effective way to acquire and remember new skills.

IMPORTANT Before you break the seal on the practice disk package, be sure that this book matches your version of the software. This book is designed for use with Microsoft Office 97 Professional Edition for the Windows 95 and Windows NT version 4.0 operating systems. To find out what software you're running, check the product package or start the software, and on the Help menu, click About Microsoft for the Office 97 program. If your program is not compatible with this book, an appropriate Step by Step book is probably available. Many of the Step by Step titles are listed on page ii of this book. If the book you want isn't listed, please visit our World Wide Web site at http://www.microsoft.com/mspress/ or call 1-800-MSPRESS.

Install the practice files on your computer

Follow these steps to install the practice files on your computer's hard disk so that you can use them with the exercises in this book.

 NOTE If you are new to Windows 95 or Windows NT, you might want to work through Appendix A, "If You Are New to Windows 95, Windows NT, or Office 97," before you install the practice files.

1 If your computer isn't on, turn it on now.

In Windows 95, you will also be prompted for a username and password when starting Windows 95 if your computer is configured for user profiles.

2 If you're using Windows NT, press CTRL+ALT+DEL to display a dialog box asking for your username and password. If you are using Windows 95, you will see this dialog box if your computer is connected to a network. If you don't know your username or password, contact your system administrator for assistance.

3 Type your username and password in the appropriate boxes, and then click OK. If you see the Welcome dialog box, click the Close button.

4 Remove the disk from the package inside the back cover of this book.

5 Insert the disk in drive A or drive B of your computer.

Close

6 On the taskbar at the bottom of your screen, click the Start button.

The Start menu opens.

Click Start...  ...and then click Run.

7 On the Start menu, click Run.

The Run dialog box appears.

For best results in using the practice files with this book, accept these preselected settings.

8 In the Open box, type **a:setup** (or **b:setup** if the disk is in drive B). Click OK, and then follow the directions on the screen.

9 When the files have been installed, remove the disk from your drive and put it back in the package inside the back cover of the book.

A folder called Office 97 SBS Practice has been created on your hard disk, and the practice files have been put in that folder.

Microsoft
Press
Welcome

Camcorder
Files On The
Internet

NOTE In addition to installing the practice files, the Setup program has created two shortcuts on your Desktop. If your computer is set up to connect to the Internet, you can double-click the Microsoft Press Welcome shortcut to visit the Microsoft Press Web site. You can also connect to this Web site directly at http://www.microsoft.com/mspress/

You can double-click the Camcorder Files On The Internet shortcut to connect to the *Microsoft Office 97 Integration Step by Step* Camcorder files Web page. This page contains audiovisual demonstrations of how to do a number of tasks in Office, which you can copy to your computer for viewing. You can connect to this Web site directly at http://www.microsoft.com/mspress/products/351/

Using the Practice Files

Each lesson in this book explains when and how to use any practice files for that lesson. When it's time to use a practice file, the book will list instructions for how to open the file. The lessons are built around scenarios that simulate a real work environment, so you can easily apply the skills you learn to your own work. For the scenarios in this book, imagine that you're an employee of The Kenya Coffee Company. In this book, you'll learn how to integrate information between the Office 97 programs to accomplish various tasks for the company.

Some of the exercises in this book might not work as indicated, depending on how your computer has been set up. To better perform the exercises in this book, follow the instructions in Appendix B, "Adding Microsoft Office 97 Components."

For those of you who like to know all the details, here's a list of the files included on the practice disk:

Filename	Description
Kenya Coffee Company	A database for The Kenya Coffee Company.
Lesson 1	
Financial Highlights	A workbook of financial data for 1993–1996.
Fiscal	A presentation for the 1996 Shareholders' meeting
Shareholder Memo	A memo to shareholders.
Lesson 2	
Public Information	A folder used to post a shared file.
96 Chairman Letter	A letter to shareholders from the company chairman.
96 Performance	A workbook detailing product revenue.
96 Presentation	A fiscal presentation from the previous year.

Filename	Description
Review & Practice 1	
Assistance Plan	A letter to new employees.
Investment Illustration	A workbook containing the five-year rate of return for the employee investment plan.
New Employee Memo	A memo about the employee investment plan.
Lesson 3	
97 Financial Health	A financial letter to regional managers.
Kenya Contact List	A list of company contacts.
Lesson 4	
Availability	A workbook of products and quantities available.
Blends	An organization chart of new products.
Future Products	A workbook of future products and their origin.
Highlands	A document describing a product.
Kenya Organization	A presentation slide with an organization chart.
Kenya Products	A presentation describing new products.
Lesson 5	
Asset Changes JS	A copy of a shared workbook with changes by JS.
Asset Changes MD	A copy of a shared workbook with changes by MD.
Assets	A workbook containing a statement of assets.
Income	A workbook of income figures for 1995–1997.
Shared Assets	A workbook that has been shared.
Vision	A letter to shareholders.
Review & Practice 2	
Coffee Inventory	A workbook of product inventory.
Employee Addresses	A workbook of employee addresses.
Final Inventory	A memo on the final product inventory.
Kenya Inventory	A letter about the product inventory task.
Sales	A workbook of third-quarter sales figures.
Surplus Coffee	A workbook of surplus product.
Lesson 6	
Sales	A workbook of third-quarter sales figures.
Lesson 7	
Inter-office Memo	A memo listing product and employee information.

Filename	Description
Lesson 8	
Employee Data	A workbook of employees, positions, and benefits.
Review & Practice 3	
Company Picnic Summary	A memo on the expenses for the company picnic.
Corporate Signoff	A workbook of expense authorization levels.
Satellite	A workbook of satellite branch expenses.
Lesson 9	
Kcclogo	The Kenya Coffee Company logo.
Preliminary Report	A preliminary version of the shareholders' report.
Lesson 10	
Finalize Shareholders'	The shareholders' presentation ready to be finalized.
Financial	A workbook of financial data and charts.
Product Information	A workbook detailing product revenue, availability, and products under development.
Summary	A binder for related files on the annual report.
Review & Practice 4	
Coffee Popularity	A workbook on product popularity.
Orientation	A new employee orientation document.
Lesson 11	
96 Financials	A workbook of financial data for 1993–1996.
Kenya Intranet	A memo introducing the company intranet.
Lesson 12	
FP Web	A folder for creating a Web site without access to a Web server.
Annual Report 96	The completed annual report.
Kcclogo	The Kenya company logo.
Press Release Excerpts	Excerpts from a recent company press release.
Supporting Financials	A workbook of financial information.
Review & Practice 5	
Dis	A folder for creating a Web site without access to a Web server.
Employee Handbook	The employee handbook document.
Forum Welcome	A letter about the discussion forum.

Creating a User Profile

When using Outlook, you can create a user profile, which contains information about customized options that you can use while you are working in Outlook, including your password and a list of the available information services. Your default profile will probably be set up for you by your system administrator.

Before you begin the lessons in this book, it is strongly recommended that you perform the following steps to create a profile for a fictional person, Pamela Miller. Creating this profile will give you a clean environment in which you can practice performing tasks.

Change the mailbox profile settings

1   Double-click the Microsoft Outlook shortcut icon on the Desktop.

Outlook starts.

2   On the Tools menu, click Options.

The Options dialog box appears.

3   Click the General tab, select the Prompt For A User Profile To Be Used option button, and then click OK.

Each time you start Outlook, you will be prompted to select a profile.

4   On the Outlook window, click the Close button.

Create a practice user profile

1   Double-click the Microsoft Outlook shortcut icon on the Desktop.

The Choose Profile dialog box appears.

2   Click New.

The Inbox Setup wizard starts.

If you are not sure what the primary information service used by your organization is, ask your system administrator.

3   Be sure that the Use The Following Information Services option button is selected, and only the check box for your mail delivery service is selected.

Either Microsoft Mail or Microsoft Exchange Server should be the only information service selected for purposes of this book, depending on which one your organization uses as its primary information service. If any other check boxes are selected, click them to clear them.

Depending on your mail delivery system, steps 4 through 10 may vary. Microsoft Mail was used in this example.

4   Click Next. In the Profile Name box, type **Pamela Miller** and click Next.

5   Click Browse.

6   Select the path to the postoffice location for your mail delivery system, and then click OK. Click Next.

7   Select your name from the list of postoffice names, or the name Pamela Miller if you have created a dummy postoffice box for purposes of this book, and then click Next.

8   Type your password or the password of the dummy postoffice in the Password box, and then click Next.

Create a practice personal address book and personal folder file

In this exercise, you create a practice personal address book associated with the Pamela Miller profile so that entries you add to the practice personal address book are not mixed up with your real personal address book. You also create a practice personal folder file, or set of Outlook folders, for the same reason.

1   Select the text "mailbox.pab," type **pamelam.pab** and then click Next.

2   Select the text "mailbox.pst," type **pamelam.pst** and then click Next.

3   Click Finish.

4   Click Cancel to close the Choose Profile dialog box.

You will use the Pamela Miller profile to start Outlook for exercises in this book using Outlook.

Need Help with the Practice Files?

Every effort has been made to ensure the accuracy of this book and the contents of the practice files disk. If you do run into a problem, Microsoft Press provides corrections for its books through the World Wide Web at

http://www.microsoft.com/mspress/support/

We also invite you to visit our main Web page at

http://www.microsoft.com/mspress/

You'll find descriptions of all of our books, information about ordering titles, notices of special features and events, additional content for Microsoft Press books, and much more.

Deleting the Practice Files

Use the following steps to delete the shortcuts added to your Desktop and the practice files added to your hard drive by the Step by Step Setup program.

1   Click Start, point to Settings, and then click Control Panel.

2   Double-click the Add/Remove Programs icon.

3   Select Microsoft Office 97 Step by Step Practice, and click Add/Remove.

4   Click Yes.

The practice files are uninstalled.

5   Click OK to close the Add/Remove Programs Properties dialog box.

6   Close the Control Panel window.

Conventions and Features in This Book

You can save time when you use this book by understanding, before you start the lessons, how instructions, keys to press, and so on are shown in the book. Please take a moment to read the following list, which also points out helpful features of the book that you might want to use.

 NOTE If you are unfamiliar with Windows, Windows NT, or mouse terminology, see Appendix A, "If You Are New to Windows 95, Windows NT, or Microsoft Office 97."

Conventions

- Hands-on exercises for you to follow are given in numbered lists of steps (1, 2, and so on). An arrowhead bullet (➤) indicates an exercise that has only one step.

- Text that you are to type appears in **bold**

- A plus sign (+) between two key names means that you must press those keys at the same time. For example, "Press ALT+TAB" means that you hold down the ALT key while you press TAB.

- The following icons identify the different types of supplementary material:

	Notes labeled	Alert you to
	Note *or* Tip	Additional information or alternative methods for a step.
	Important	Essential information that you should check before continuing with the lesson.
	Troubleshooting	Possible error messages or computer difficulties and their solutions.
	Warning	Possible data loss and how to proceed safely.
	Demonstration	Skills that are demonstrated in audio-visual files available on the World Wide Web.

Other Features of This Book

- You can learn about techniques that build on what you learned in a lesson by trying the optional One Step Further exercise at the end of the lesson.

- You can get a quick reminder of how to perform the tasks you learned by reading the Lesson Summary at the end of a lesson.

- You can quickly determine what online Help topics are available for additional information by referring to the Help topics listed at the end of each lesson. The Help system provides a complete online reference to Microsoft Office. To learn more about online Help, see Appendix A, "If You Are New to Windows 95, Windows NT, or Office 97."

- You can practice the major skills presented in the lessons by working through the Review & Practice sections at the end of each part.

- If you have Web browser software and access to the World Wide Web, you can view audiovisual demonstrations of how to perform some of the more complicated tasks in Office by downloading supplementary files from the Web. Double-click the Camcorder Files On The Internet shortcut that was created on your Desktop when you installed the practice files for this book, or connect directly to http://www.microsoft.com/mspress/products/351/. The Web page that opens contains full instructions for copying and viewing the demonstration files.

Introducing Integration with Microsoft Office

Understanding the Microsoft Office Environment

Estimated time
30 min.

In this lesson you will learn how to:

- Start, switch between, and close different Office 97 programs.
- Integrate toolbar buttons and menu commands.
- Manage files and documents on your hard disk using Microsoft Outlook.

If you are experienced with Windows 95 and Office 97, you might want to review the Lesson Summary table at the end of this lesson. If you are proficient in the topics covered in this lesson, you can skip to Lesson 2.

When you move into a new neighborhood, one of the first things you do is become familiar with your new environment. You learn who your neighbors are, where your mailbox is, and what's the quickest route to the grocery store. In short, you learn the most efficient way to get around in your new environment. In much the same way, Microsoft Office 97 is a new environment. This lesson will provide you with an overview of this environment, as well as the Microsoft Windows 95 environment and its shared components. You'll also be introduced to the tools and shortcuts that will help you navigate efficiently within the Office 97 environment.

Office 97 is a family of powerful business *software* that is designed to work together as one integrated *program*. With Office 97, you can concentrate on what's really important—getting your work done efficiently and sharing your information with others. The following programs comprise the Office 97 environment:

Program	Description
	Microsoft Word is a word processing program that you can use to write letters, memos, reports, and all the *documents* your organization needs.
	Microsoft Excel is a spreadsheet program that you can use to organize, calculate, and analyze data in *worksheets*, charts, and reports.
	Microsoft Access is a *database* program that you can use to *link* data in useful ways, perform queries, and create forms and reports. Access helps you manage your data efficiently.
	Microsoft PowerPoint is a *presentation* program that you can use to create professional slide shows and handouts. You can enhance the appeal of your presentations by adding charts, graphics, sound, and animation.
	Microsoft Outlook is a desktop information manager that you can use to manage personal items such as your *electronic mail* (e-mail), contacts, tasks, and *files* on your computer.

In today's workplace, it's likely that you need to do more than simply create a document in Word or manage data in Access. When you work with Office 97, you'll notice that the programs have been designed to work together in an integrated environment, giving you the ability to go beyond the limits of the individual programs. With Office 97, you can do the following:

- *Embed* information from one file type into another, to allow *editing* without altering the *source* information.
- Create links between files so when information is updated in one file it is automatically updated in the other file.
- Merge an address database in Access with a form letter in Word to quickly create a large-volume mail merge.
- Store and organize related documents in a single electronic location using Microsoft Binder.
- Manage your messages, plan your schedule, schedule tasks, and share information in a variety of ways using Outlook.
- Collaborate efficiently with co-workers by reviewing documents online, working together in shared *workbooks*, and exchanging information electronically.

Setting the Scene

As a new employee of The Kenya Coffee Company, which specializes in premium coffee products, you will develop informative literature for both the employees and customers of the company. For example, you will create a form letter that will be sent to customers. Using Office 97, you will update and then combine existing documents and information, and you will share files with your co-workers using e-mail, the *Internet*, and the company's *intranet*. Occasionally, you will help your co-workers use specific features of Office 97 to automate routine tasks and make complex tasks easier. These exercises will give you the skills you need to adapt Office 97 to your own work.

In this lesson, you will learn how to work with Office 97 programs and files using the Office Shortcut Bar and Windows 95 tools. You will also take advantage of the productivity tools in each Office program and customize them so that you can work efficiently.

Working with Programs and Files Using Microsoft Office

In your new neighborhood, there might be several routes you can take to get to your local grocery store; regardless, you probably want to determine the most efficient and comfortable one. Similarly, Office 97 and Windows 95 provide a variety of ways to accomplish the same task and, as you become familiar with the Office 97 environment, you will determine the most comfortable method for getting your work done.

With Office 97, you can use the Office Shortcut Bar to quickly open a file or create a new Outlook item. You can also use the Windows 95 Start menu to start your Office programs. You can then use the Windows 95 *taskbar* to switch between your open programs. Additionally, you can use the Outlook Bar to find and open files in the Office suite of programs.

In these exercises, you will explore the different methods for starting programs and opening files. You will use these files throughout this lesson to learn about using the Office 97 and Windows 95 productivity tools.

Starting Programs and Opening Files

After you install Office 97, you can use the Start menu to start an Office 97 program or open an existing file from the Windows 95 *Desktop*. One of the most powerful features of Windows 95 is its ability to have multiple programs running at the same time. After a program is running, you can use the taskbar on the Desktop to switch to any open program with a single click. All open programs, windows, and documents are represented by a button on the taskbar. In these exercises, you will use the Start menu to start programs, and then switch between open programs using the taskbar.

IMPORTANT   If you have not yet installed the practice files, refer to "Installing and Using the Practice Files" earlier in this book before continuing with this exercise.

Start Word and open a document file

Suppose you're new to the Office 97 and Windows 95 environment. You'd like to find the quickest way to start a program. You decide to experiment using the Start menu. In these exercises, you start Word and Excel using different techniques.

When you start an Office 97 program for the first time, you may be prompted to enter user information. Verify the information you entered when you installed Office 97, making any necessary changes before continuing.

IMPORTANT If the Office Assistant appears, click the Start Using Microsoft Word option. If the User Name dialog box appears, fill in your name and initials, and then click OK. On the Office Assistant, click the Close button.

For the purposes of this book, the Office Assistant will not appear in the illustrations. If you want to match the illustrations, any time the Office Assistant appears, use the right mouse button to click the Office Assistant, and then click Hide Assistant. If you want to leave the Office Assistant on top to help guide you, but if it is in your way, simply drag it to another area on the screen.

1 On the taskbar, click the Start button. On the Start menu, point to Programs, and then click Microsoft Word.

2 On the Standard toolbar in Word, click the Open button.

Open

The Open dialog box appears. In the Open dialog box, you can select the folder and the file you want to open. The Look In box shows the folder that is currently selected.

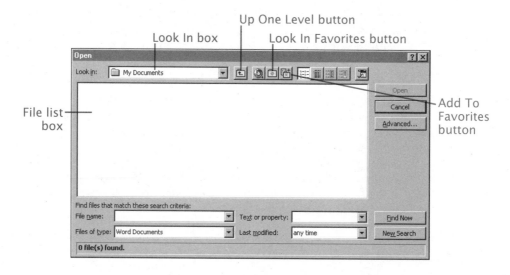

**Look In
Favorites**

*You will learn
more about
the Favorites
folder later in
this lesson.*

Maximize

3 Click the Look In Favorites button.

The folders and files that are contained within your Favorites folder are listed in the File list box.

4 In the File list box, double-click the folder named Office 97 SBS Practice, and then double-click the folder named Lesson 1.

The Word practice file for Lesson 1 appears.

5 Be sure that the file named Shareholder Memo is selected, and then click Open.

The Open dialog box closes and the Shareholder Memo file opens in the Word window. The file is a memo to the shareholders of The Kenya Coffee Company.

6 If the Word window and the document window are not maximized to fill the entire screen, click the Maximize button on the Word window.

Your screen should look similar to the following illustration.

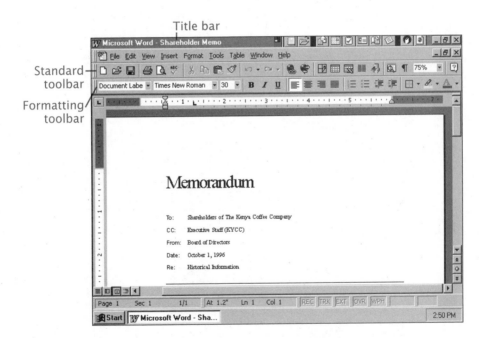

7 On the File menu, click Save As.

The Save As dialog box appears. By saving the document with a new name, you create a copy of the file that you can modify during the lesson.

8 Be sure that the Lesson 1 folder appears in the Save In box. If it does not, follow steps 3 and 4 to select the folder.

9 Be sure that the entire text in the File Name box is selected, and then type **96 Shareholder Memo**

10 Click Save.

The document is saved with the filename 96 Shareholder Memo in the Office 97 SBS Practice\Lesson 1 folder. The new name appears in the *title bar* of the Word window.

Start Excel and open a workbook file

In this exercise, you open the Financial Highlights practice file using the Windows 95 Start menu to start Excel.

1 On the taskbar, click Start. On the Start menu, click Open Office Document.

The Open Office Document dialog box appears.

Look In Favorites

2 Click the Look In Favorites button, double-click the Office 97 SBS Practice folder, and then double-click the Lesson 1 folder.

The practice files for Lesson 1 appear.

3 Click the Financial Highlights file, and then click Open.

The file opens, displaying a workbook with information about last year's financial projections.

You can also double-click a file to open it.

4 If the Excel window and the workbook window are not maximized to fill the entire screen, click the Maximize button on the Excel window.

Your screen should look similar to the following illustration.

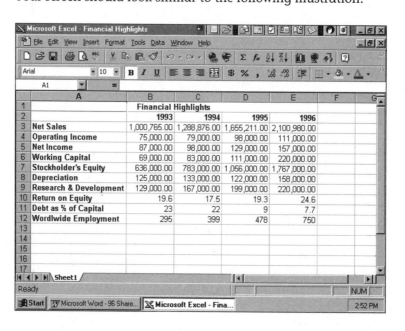

5   On the File menu, click Save As.

6   Click the Look In Favorites button, double-click the Office 97 SBS Practice folder, and then double-click the Lesson 1 folder.

7   Select the entire text in the File Name box, and then type **96 Financial Highlights**

8   Click Save.

Switch between the open programs

In a typical day, you might work on two or three projects at the same time. Or, you might refer to one project while working on another project. Suppose that you're using Excel, but you need to verify a date in a Word document. You can use the Windows 95 taskbar to toggle between open programs.

1   On the taskbar, click the Microsoft Word button.

The Word window opens. Excel is still open, and is running in the background.

2   On the taskbar, click the Microsoft Excel button.

The Excel window appears. Word is still open, and is running in the background.

Close the open programs

Now that you've verified your information, you close Excel and Word.

Close

1   On the Excel window, click the Close button.

If you see the Save As dialog box, click No to not save any changes to the file.

2   Be sure that the Word window is visible.

If the Word window is not visible, click the Microsoft Word button on the taskbar.

3   On the Word window, click the Close button.

If you see the Save As dialog box, click No.

An Introduction to the Office Assistant

While you are working with Office 97, an animated character called the *Office Assistant* pops up on your screen to help you work productively. The Office Assistant offers help messages as you work. You can ask the Office Assistant questions by typing your question, then clicking Search. The Office Assistant then shows you the answer to your question.

You will sometimes see a light bulb next to the Office Assistant—clicking the light bulb displays a tip about the action you are currently performing. You can view more tips by clicking Tips in the Office Assistant balloon when the Office Assistant appears. In addition, the Office Assistant is tailored to how you work—after you master a particular skill, the Office Assistant stops offering tips.

You can also click Exit on the File menu to close a program.

You can close any Office Assistant tip or message by pressing ESC.

Clippit, an Office Assistant, in action

The Office Assistant appears in the following situations:

- When you click the Office Assistant button on the Standard toolbar.
- When you choose Help on the Help menu or when you press F1 in any of the Office 97 programs.
- When you use the Mail Merge Helper for the first time.

The Office Assistant is a shared application—any settings that you change will affect the Office Assistant in other Office 97 programs. You can customize the Office Assistant in two ways.

Determining under what circumstances you want to see the Office Assistant

You can use the right mouse button to click the Office Assistant and click Options to open the Office Assistant dialog box. You can then define when you want the Office Assistant to appear, and what kind of help you want it to offer.

Change your Office Assistant character

You can use the right mouse button to click the Office Assistant and click Options to open the Office Assistant dialog box. Click the Gallery tab to select a different Office Assistant character.

Office Assistant

Creating Shortcuts to Programs and Files

The Office Shortcut Bar can help you with basic tasks such as creating a new document, opening an existing document, and sending messages. Ordinarily, if you decided to open an existing document, you would start the program first and then open the document. Using the Office Shortcut Bar, you can open a document, and the corresponding program starts automatically.

The Office Shortcut Bar will appear each time you start your computer and can be hidden or displayed as needed. The Office Shortcut Bar appears as a series of buttons in the upper-right corner of the Windows 95 Desktop. Much like using the Windows 95 Start menu, you can use the Office Shortcut Bar to quickly create or open a document. This can be particularly useful when you are sharing information between programs.

 NOTE If you do not see the Office Shortcut Bar on your screen, refer to Appendix B, "Adding Microsoft Office 97 Components."

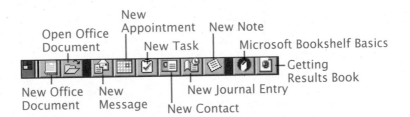

You can easily customize the Office Shortcut Bar to suit your needs by changing its location on the screen, and by adding or removing buttons. For example, you can add a button to provide direct access to your screen savers or printers.

Office 97 also comes with six other shortcut bars you might want to use, including the Programs Shortcut Bar and the Favorites Shortcut Bar. When multiple shortcut bars are open at the same time, they are layered on top of one another so that only one shortcut bar is visible at a time. As each shortcut bar is opened, a button is added to the current shortcut bar that can be used to switch between open shortcut bars.

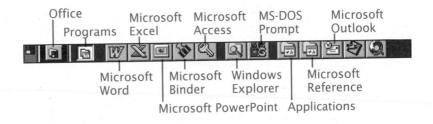

Start PowerPoint using the Office Shortcut Bar

Suppose you are beginning a new project and you want to gather information to use as reference material. A co-worker informs you that a presentation that was given last year could provide you with critical information. In this exercise, you start PowerPoint and open the Fiscal Presentation practice file all at once.

*Open Office
Document*

1 On the Office Shortcut Bar, click the Open Office Document button.

The Open Office Document dialog box appears.

2 Be sure that the Lesson 1 folder appears in the Look In box.

3 Double-click the Fiscal presentation file to open it.

PowerPoint starts, and the presentation file opens.

4 If the PowerPoint window and the presentation window are not maximized to fill the entire screen, click the Maximize button on the PowerPoint window.

Your screen should look similar to the following illustration.

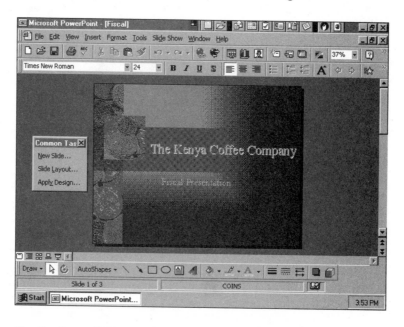

5 On the PowerPoint window, click the Close button.

TIP To temporarily hide a Shortcut Bar, use the right mouse button to click a blank area on the Shortcut Bar, and then click Auto Hide. To use the Shortcut Bar when it is hidden, point to the screen where the Shortcut Bar was last displayed and it will appear. When you move the pointer away from the area, the Shortcut Bar will disappear. If the Auto Hide command is dimmed, use the right mouse button to click a blank area on the Shortcut Bar, and then click Customize. On the View tab, clear the Auto Fit Into Title Bar Area check box, and then click OK. The Auto Hide command will now be available.

Use the Programs Shortcut Bar to start a program

To close the Programs Shortcut Bar, use the right mouse button to click a blank area on the Programs Shortcut Bar, and then click Programs.

In addition to the Office Shortcut Bar, Office 97 provides a Programs Shortcut Bar that enables you to start an Office 97 program at the click of a button. The Programs Shortcut Bar contains a button for each Microsoft program listed on the Programs menu when you click Start. For example, you can quickly open Excel by clicking the Microsoft Excel button on the Programs Shortcut Bar. In this exercise, you learn to start and use the Programs Shortcut Bar.

1 Use the right mouse button to click a blank area on the Office Shortcut Bar.

2 On the shortcut menu, click Programs.

The Programs Shortcut Bar is layered on top of the Office Shortcut Bar. You can only see the contents of one shortcut bar at a time. A button for the Office Shortcut Bar is added to the Programs Shortcut Bar.

Windows Explorer

3 On the Programs Shortcut Bar, click the Windows Explorer button.

The Exploring window opens. You can use Windows Explorer to browse through, open, and manage the *disk drives*, folders, and files on your computer. The Exploring window should look similar to the following illustration.

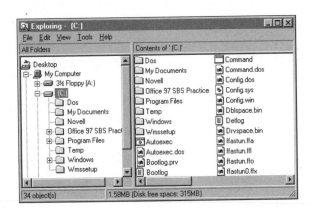

4 On the Exploring window, click the Close button.

5 On the Programs Shortcut Bar, click the Office button.

The Office Shortcut Bar is layered on top of the Programs Shortcut Bar.

Office

Storing and Retrieving Frequently Used Files

When you work with multiple files, it's easy to forget where each file is saved. You might find it helpful to have one location where you can store your files for easy retrieval.

Windows 95 provides a Favorites folder, in which you can store a *shortcut* to a file or folder that you use frequently. If you add a file or folder to the Favorites folder, the original file or folder stays in its original location, and a shortcut to the file is added to the Favorites folder. A shortcut is similar to a pointer that directs you to a specific location. When you want to revisit the file, the shortcut provides you with quick access to the file without having to remember where the file is stored.

NOTE With Office 97, you can also store a frequently used file in the My Documents folder. By default, each time you start an Office 97 program the My Documents folder will appear in the Open dialog box and the Save dialog box.

Save a shortcut in the Favorites folder

Suppose that you're reviewing a memo with a co-worker, and it takes you several moments to find the location of your file. You decide to create a shortcut to the memo in your Favorites folder, so you don't have to remember the location each time you want to open the file. In this exercise, you create a shortcut to a Word document.

Open Office Document

1 On the Office Shortcut Bar, click the Open Office Document button.

The Open Office Document dialog box appears.

2 Be sure that the Lesson 1 folder appears in the Look In box.

3 Click 96 Shareholder Memo, and then click the Add To Favorites button.

A shortcut menu appears.

Add To Favorites

4 On the shortcut menu, click Add Selected Item To Favorites.

A shortcut for the 96 Shareholder Memo file is added to the Favorites folder.

Look In Favorites

5 Click the Look In Favorites button.

The contents of your Favorites folder appear. Your screen should look similar to the following illustration.

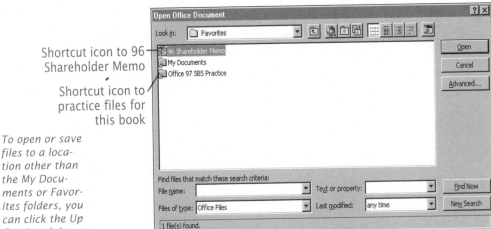

Shortcut icon to 96
Shareholder Memo

Shortcut icon to
practice files for
this book

To open or save
files to a loca-
tion other than
the My Docu-
ments or Favor-
ites folders, you
can click the Up
One Level down
arrow or the
Look In down
arrow to move
through your
computer's
filing system.

6 Be sure that 96 Shareholder Memo is selected in the Favorites folder, and
then click Open.

The 96 Shareholder Memo opens.

Integrating Toolbars and Menus

For a demon-
stration of how
to integrate
toolbars and
menus, double-
click the
Camcorder Files
On The Internet
shortcut on your
Desktop or con-
nect to the Inter-
net address
listed on p. xxx.

Office 97 programs share a consistent design and common tools, such as
toolbars and shortcut menus, which make learning these programs easier. For
example, users who are familiar with Word will find it easy to work with Excel.
The toolbars in Office 97 programs provide you with quick access to frequently
used *commands* and procedures. For example, in every Office 97 program, the
Standard toolbar contains buttons used for creating a new file, opening an existing file, and saving a file. Each toolbar button has a yellow *ToolTip* that describes what the button does. To view a ToolTip, you place the mouse pointer
over a button and the ToolTip appears.

ToolTip

After you are familiar with the Office 97 work environment, you might try cus-
tomizing toolbars and menus to streamline your work environment. For example, you can add menu commands to an existing menu or to a menu that
you create. You can also customize toolbars by adding or deleting toolbar buttons, and assigning commonly used buttons to an existing toolbar.

In addition, Office 97 enables you to add toolbar buttons to menus and add
menus to toolbars to create your own customized toolbars. You can create custom toolbars to provide fast access to frequently used commands. By default,

toolbars are stored in the Normal *template*, and are available for all files. You can also store toolbars in specialized templates. If a custom toolbar is stored in a template other than the Normal template, that toolbar will be available only in files created from that specialized template.

In these exercises, you will create a custom toolbar to simplify the routine task of editing company correspondence.

Create a custom toolbar

Let's assume that you've noticed editing errors in your organization's correspondence. To simplify editing the correspondence, you create a custom toolbar that incorporates several of the Reviewing toolbar buttons and the Tools menu. The Reviewing toolbar has tools for adding and reviewing comments on a document while the Tools menu has commands such as Spelling, Grammar, and AutoCorrect. By creating a custom toolbar, you can put all your editing tools in one convenient location.

1 On the View menu, point to Toolbars, and then click Customize.

   The Customize dialog box appears. The Toolbars tab should be selected.

2 Click New.

   The New Toolbar dialog box appears.

3 In the Toolbar Name box, type **Revisions**

4 Be sure that Normal appears in the Make Toolbar Available To box.

   The Revisions toolbar will be stored with the Normal template.

5 Click OK.

   A blank toolbar, called Revisions, appears on the screen.

Place reviewing buttons on a toolbar

In this exercise, you add the Insert Comment, Delete Comment, and Highlight buttons to the Revisions toolbar.

1 Drag the Revisions toolbar to the left of the Customize dialog box.

   You can now work with both the Customize dialog box and the Revisions toolbar at the same time. Your screen should look similar to the following illustration.

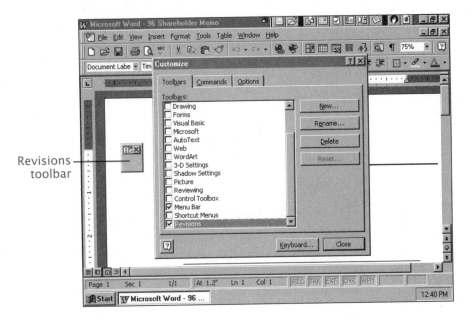

Revisions toolbar

2   Click the Commands tab.

3   In the Categories box, click Insert.

The toolbar buttons available in the Insert category appear under Commands.

When you drag a command button onto a toolbar, an I-beam will appear to indicate where the button will be placed.

4   In the Commands box, drag the Comment button onto the Revisions toolbar.

5   In the Commands box, drag the Delete Comment button onto the Revisions toolbar.

6   In the Categories box, click Format, and then drag the Highlight button onto the Revisions toolbar.

Place a menu on a toolbar

In this exercise, you add the Tools menu to the Revisions toolbar.

1   In the Categories box, click Built-In Menus.

2   In the Commands box, drag the Tools menu onto the Revisions toolbar.

3   On the Customize dialog box, click Close.

The Customize dialog box closes, and the Revisions toolbar is complete.

Edit a document using a custom toolbar

In this exercise, you edit the Shareholders Memo using the Revisions toolbar.

1 Be sure that the Shareholder Memo is displayed.

2 Select the text "Executive Staff (KYCC)" on the CC line of the memo.

3 On the Revisions toolbar, click the Insert Comment button.

The Revisions toolbar can be displayed again by using the right mouse button to click a blank area on the toolbar, and then clicking Revisions.

The Comments window opens in the lower portion of your screen, and the selected text is highlighted in yellow.

4 Type **Please list all Executive Staff members.**

Your initials and the comment text appear in the Comments window.

5 On the Comments window, click the Close button.

The Comments window closes, and the selected text remains highlighted but in pale yellow.

6 Place the pointer over the highlighted text.

A yellow note appears with your name and the comment you inserted about the text. When the 96 Shareholder Memo is revised, your comments can be incorporated.

7 On the Revisions toolbar, click the Close button.

The Revisions toolbar closes.

8 On the Standard toolbar, click the Save button.

9 On the Word window, click the Close button.

Save

Managing Files on Your Computer

Outlook is a desktop information management program that helps you manage your e-mail, plan your schedule, monitor tasks, maintain a list of contacts, keep notes, and manage your electronic folders and files. In addition, you can share your information with others by using shared folders on a network or even on the Internet.

All of the functionality of My Computer is built into Outlook, so you never have to leave Office 97 to find files or start programs. With Outlook, you can view or open any of the files on your computer, as well as any files that are located on a network system. You can view files as *icons* or in a detail list, and quickly open, *copy*, *move*, or print them.

You can think of Outlook as the starting point when you work on your computer. Whether your documents are stored in different folders, on different disks, or even on different computers on your network system, you can use Outlook to find your files.

In these exercises, you will start Outlook from the Windows 95 Desktop and search for a specific file on your computer.

> **IMPORTANT** If you haven't set up the practice user profile, refer to "Creating a User Profile" earlier in this book.

Start Outlook

In this lesson, you start Outlook using the practice user profile.

Programs

Microsoft Outlook

1 On the Office Shortcut Bar, click the Programs button.

The Programs Shortcut Bar is displayed.

2 On the Programs Shortcut Bar, click the Microsoft Outlook button.

The Choose Profile dialog box appears.

3 Click the Profile Name down arrow.

A list of user profiles appears.

4 Select Pamela Miller, and then click OK.

5 Follow the logon procedures for your mail system.

The Outlook Inbox appears. You can use the Outlook Bar on the left side of your screen to navigate to other parts of Outlook, to your e-mail folders, or to network folders. Your Inbox should look similar to the following illustration.

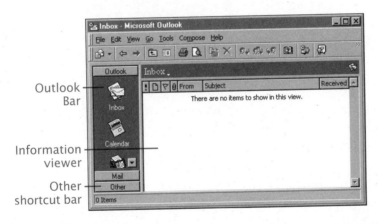

Maximize

6 On the Outlook window, click the Maximize button.

Find files on your computer

Let's assume that you're searching for a specific document that describes a new product called Himalayan Blend. Unfortunately, you don't remember the name of the document. Using Outlook, you search all the files on your computer for the word "Himalayan."

1   On the Outlook Bar, click the Other shortcut bar.

Icons for the folders in the Other group, including My Computer, appear on the Outlook Bar. The contents of your Inbox are still displayed in the Information viewer because you have not selected a different folder yet.

My Computer

2   On the Outlook Bar, click the My Computer icon.

The available drives for your computer appear in the Information viewer. You can use this window to browse through, open, and manage the disk drives, folders, and files on your computer.

3   On the Tools menu, click Find Items.

The Find window opens.

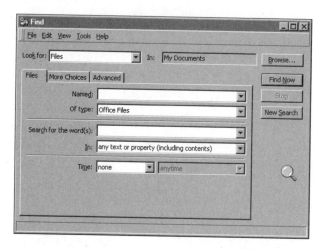

4   Click Browse.

The Select Folders dialog box appears.

5   Clear the My Documents check box, and then select the Office 97 SBS Practice check box.

A search can be made case-sensitive by clicking the More Choices tab, and then clicking the Match Case check box.

6   Click OK.

The Find window opens.

7   Click in the Search For The Words box, and then type **Himalayan**

You search all files on your computer for the word "Himalayan." By default, the search is not case-sensitive.

The Find Command will search all files and folders in your Office 97 SBS Practice folder.

8   On the Find dialog box, click Find Now.

When you use the Find window to locate files on your computer, you can sort, group, or change the search results. The search is performed, and all files that contain the word "Himalayan" are listed. Your screen should look similar to the following illustration.

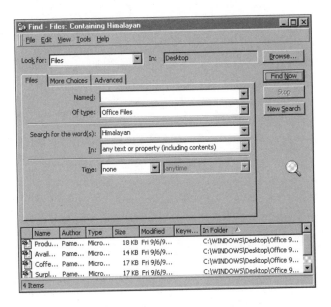

Open a file from the Find window

You may need to drag the Find window up so you can view the find results.

1 Double-click the Availability file in the Find window.

The Availability file opens in Excel.

2 On the Excel window, click the Close button.

3 On the Find window, click the Close button.

TIP You can use the Outlook Find window while in another program even if you are not running Outlook. Click the Start button on the Windows 95 Desktop, point to Find, and then click Using Microsoft Outlook.

Manage your hard disk

Suppose you want to delete a file or a shortcut that you have created in order to keep your *hard disk* well organized. You can use Outlook to delete items on your hard disk as well as to copy and move items. In this exercise, you delete the Shareholder Memo shortcut in the Favorites folder.

Favorites

1 On the Outlook Bar, click the Favorites icon.

The contents of the Favorites folder appear.

Delete

2 Click the 96 Shareholder Memo shortcut to select it.

3 On the Standard toolbar, click the Delete button.

The Confirm File Delete message appears.

4   Click Yes.

The shortcut to the 96 Shareholders Memo is deleted from the Favorites folder.

5   On the Outlook window, click the Close button.

Outlook closes.

 NOTE   If you'd like to build on the skills that you learned in this lesson, you can do the One Step Further. Otherwise, skip to "Finish the lesson."

One Step Further: Customizing the Office Shortcut Bar

You can customize the Office Shortcut Bar to simplify frequently used tasks in Office 97, as well as in Windows 95. You can add, remove, and rearrange buttons on the Office Shortcut Bar to give you direct access to frequently used commands or to a specific program.

Add a button to the Office Shortcut Bar

Suppose you've recently reviewed a memo that you want to present at an upcoming meeting. You want to print a quality copy of the memo to distribute at the meeting. In addition, you need to print a copy of the Fiscal Presentation files for your reference only, so it's not important to use a high-quality printer. To quickly switch between the printers in your office, you add the Printers button to the Office Shortcut Bar.

Office

1   On the Programs Shortcut Bar, click the Office button.

The Office Shortcut Bar is displayed.

2   Use the right mouse button to click a blank area on the Office Shortcut Bar.

3   On the shortcut menu, click Customize.

The Customize dialog box appears.

4   Click the Buttons tab.

The Customize dialog box should look like the following illustration.

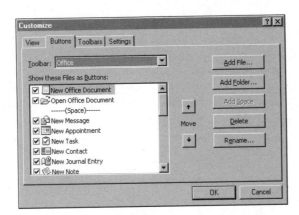

5 In the Show These Files As Buttons box, scroll down and select the Printers check box.

The Printers button will appear on the Office Shortcut Bar.

6 Click OK.

The Customize dialog box closes.

7 On the Office Shortcut Bar, click the Printers button.

The Printers window opens.

Printers

8 On the Printers window, click the Close button.

Remove a button on the Office Shortcut Bar

In this exercise, you remove the Printers button you added to the Office Shortcut Bar.

1 Use the right mouse button to click a blank area on the Office Shortcut Bar.

2 On the shortcut menu, click Customize.

3 Click the Buttons tab.

4 In the Show These Files As Buttons box, clear the Printers check box.

The Printers button is removed from the Office Shortcut Bar.

5 Click OK.

Finish the lesson

1 Close all open windows.

2 Use the right mouse button to click a blank area on the Office Shortcut Bar, and then click Programs.

The Programs Shortcut Bar closes.

Lesson Summary

To	Do this	Button
Start an Office 97 program	On the taskbar, click the Start button, point to Programs, and then click the appropriate program. *or* Be sure that the Programs Shortcut Bar is displayed. Click the appropriate program button.	
Open an Office 97 file	Click the Start button, and then click Open Office Document. Select a file, and then click Open. *or* On the Office Shortcut Bar, click the Open Office Document button, select a file, and then click Open.	
Switch to an open program	On the taskbar, click a program button.	
Quit an Office 97 program	Click the Close button on the program window. *or* On the File menu, click Exit.	
Save a file in the Favorites folder	In the Save As dialog box, click the Add To Favorites button, and then click Add Selected Items To Favorites.	
Create a custom toolbar	On the View menu, point to Toolbars, and then click Customize. Click New, and then type the name of the custom toolbar. Select the template you want to make the custom toolbar available in, and then click OK. Click the category that contains the command or button you want to add to the custom toolbar. Drag each command or button to the new custom toolbar, and then click OK.	
Manage files on disk using Outlook	Click the Other shortcut bar, and then double-click My Computer.	

For online information about	On the Help menu, click Contents And Index, click the Index tab, and then type
Starting programs	*Windows 95*: Start menu
Opening documents	*Windows 95*: opening
Switching between programs	*Windows 95*: switching
Using the Office Shortcut Bar	*Office Shortcut Bar*: displaying Shortcut Bar
Using custom toolbars	toolbars
Managing files using Outlook	*Outlook*: files
Customizing the Office Shortcut Bar	*Office Shortcut Bar*: customizing Shortcut Bar

Organizing Related Files

Estimated time
35 min.

In this lesson you will learn how to:

- Create a binder to organize and store related files.
- Enhance consistency between common projects by creating a binder template.
- Share a binder with others by posting it to a shared folder on a network.
- Store information using notes.

If you're familiar with assembling printed documents in, for example, a three-ring binder for collection and distribution, then you're familiar with the limitations that go along with it. Paper binders take up space, you can lose pages, and the material is hard to keep organized. By using Microsoft *Office Binder* to create a binder, however, you can organize documents electronically in a single location, similar to using a binder clip to keep printed documents together. You can also think of an Office Binder file as a three-ring binder used to store related documents that are created using more than one Microsoft Office 97 program. The electronic documents always remain in the order that you place them, and they can be moved, saved, or printed as a single file. For example, if you need to bring together documents from several different departments to create a single report, an Office Binder can help you organize the documents, distribute them for review, and print them as an integrated report.

In this lesson, you will gather together several existing company files that you will use in your year-end report. To work with these files more easily, you will store and organize all the related files in an Office Binder. You will then make the binder available to your co-workers by posting it on the company network.

Assembling Related Files in a Binder

An Office Binder is an unique tool that provides you with the flexibility to assemble and share information between Office 97 programs. Let's say, for example, that you have a Microsoft Excel workbook, a Microsoft Word document, and a Microsoft PowerPoint presentation that together make up a single report. By placing the files in a binder, you can work on the files together in one location. For example, you can check spelling, apply a consistent style, and print the files as a single document.

Using a binder, you can integrate documents created by Office 97 programs, as well as by other Microsoft programs, into a single file that is divided by *sections*. Each file in a binder is an independent copy—there is no relationship between the original file and the copy that is placed in the binder. Because of this, you can save the Office Binder file to a disk or post it to a shared network location without having to worry about unexpected changes or updates from external files.

If you're interested in sharing an Office Binder file with your co-workers, you'll be glad to know that a binder can be posted to a shared folder on your company's network to enable your co-workers to work on specific sections of the binder file, one at a time. The Office Binder file will reflect those changes that your co-workers have made.

Creating a Binder Using Existing Files

An Office Binder is most effectively used as a place to assemble finished documents that are related in some way. Let's say, for example, that you have an Office Binder file that contains a Word document and an Excel workbook. The document and workbook comprise the *sections* that are stored within the binder file. The left pane of the binder file will display icons that represent the sections in the binder—in this case Word and Excel. The right pane of the binder file will display the currently open section. For example, if the Word icon is selected in the left pane, the Word document, or section, will be displayed in the right pane. The menus and toolbars that are specific to the open section, in this case Word, will appear in the binder file, as shown in the following illustration.

Click here to display or hide the left pane.

Active binder section

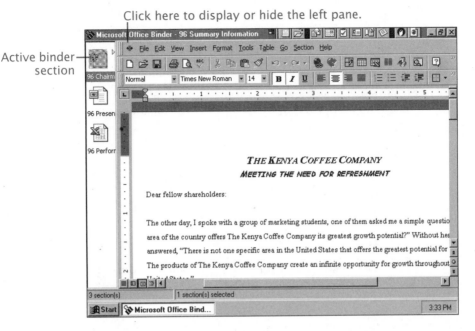

When you work in sections in an Office Binder, the menus are somewhat different from the menus you use when you work in specific Office 97 programs such as Word or Excel. For example, the File menu will include file management commands that affect all sections of the binder file, such as printing the entire binder file. Additionally, a new Section menu is available on the menu bar that you can use to work on individual sections in a binder.

When editing sections in an Office Binder, you should be aware of some limitations. You cannot add Microsoft Access database information as a separate binder section. You can *export* or copy Access information to other documents, workbooks, and presentations, and then store those documents as sections in your binder.

While researching and gathering information for your upcoming report, you continue to review the information that was included in last year's report for content and structure. In the following exercises, you will create an Office Binder, add existing files to the binder, and then add a blank section to create a placeholder for a file that has not yet been created.

Create an Office Binder

In this exercise, you create an Office Binder that will contain information from last year's annual report.

29

*New Office
Document*

1   On the Office Shortcut Bar, click the New Office Document button.

The New Office Document dialog box appears, and the General tab is selected.

2   Click the Blank Binder icon, and then click OK.

A blank binder file opens.

3   Click the Maximize button on the Office Binder window.

4   On the File menu, click Save Binder.

The Save Binder As dialog box appears.

5   Be sure that the text in the File Name box is selected, and then type
96 Summary Information

6   Click the Look In Favorites button, double-click the Office 97 SBS Practice folder, and then double-click the Lesson 2 folder.

7   Click Save.

The binder is saved with the name 96 Summary Information in your Office 97 SBS Practice\Lesson 2 folder. The binder name appears in the title bar of the Office Binder window.

 TIP   You can also create Office 97 documents from the Desktop. For example, to create a new binder, you use the right mouse button to click the Desktop, point to New, and then click Microsoft Office Binder. You can then rename the new binder and move it to a folder or leave it on the Desktop.

Add existing files to the binder

In this exercise, you add existing files from last year's annual report to the 96 Summary Information binder.

1   On the Section menu, click Add From File.

The Add From File dialog box appears.

2   Click the Look In Favorites button, double-click the Office 97 SBS Practice folder, and then double-click the Lesson 2 folder.

3 Click 96 Chairman Letter, and then click Add.

A copy of the 96 Chairman Letter document is added to your binder. The file in the binder is an independent copy of the original file. Your screen should look like the following illustration.

Word menus and toolbars

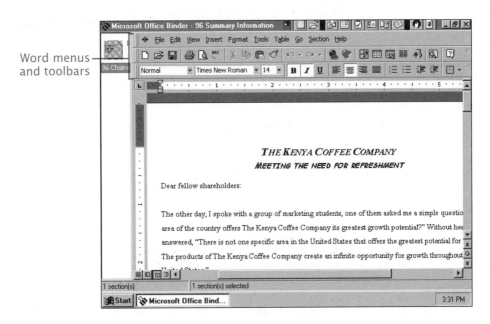

4 On the Section menu, click Add From File.

5 In your Office 97 SBS Practice\Lesson 2 folder, click 96 Performance, and then click Add.

A copy of the 96 Performance workbook is added to your new binder. You now have two sections in your binder.

6 On the Section menu, click Add From File.

7 In your Office 97 SBS Practice\Lesson 2 folder, click 96 Presentation, and then click Add.

A copy of the 96 Presentation is added to your new binder. You now have three sections in your binder. Your screen should look like the following illustration.

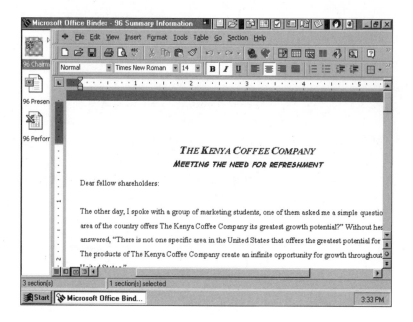

Add a new section to your binder

As you continue to bring together the elements of your report, you realize that you are still waiting for an additional PowerPoint presentation file. You add a blank section to your binder to serve as a placeholder for the presentation file.

The blank binder section will be inserted after the selected section.

1   Be sure that the 96 Chairman Letter is displayed.

2   On the Section menu, click Add.

The Add Section dialog box appears, and the General tab is selected.

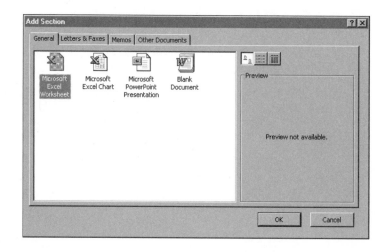

3 Click the Microsoft PowerPoint Presentation icon.

By selecting the Blank Presentation icon, you identify the new section as a placeholder for a PowerPoint presentation.

4 Click OK.

A blank presentation section is added to the 96 Summary Information binder. You will insert the presentation file in Lesson 9, "Integrating Documents for an Informative Presentation." Your screen should look similar to the following illustration.

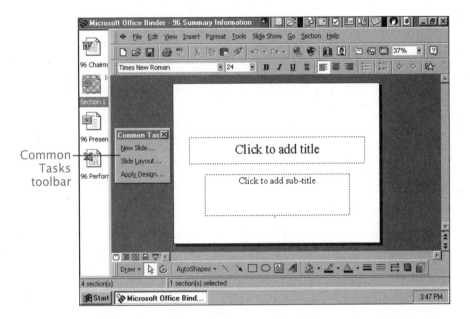

Common —
Tasks
toolbar

> **TIP** If you want to preserve specific information in a binder section as a separate file, you can save the section as a separate document. On the Section menu, click Save As File, and then type the new name and location for the file. By saving a section as a separate document, the section is copied as a separate file. It is not removed from the binder, and the binder section is not updated if you modify the separate document.

Viewing and Arranging Binder Contents

When you work with files in a binder, you can easily view and rearrange the sections. For example, you can move Section 1 below Section 2 or vice versa. If you decide to change the order of sections in your binder, you can use *drag-and-drop* editing to rearrange the program icons in the left pane, or you can use the Rearrange command on the Section menu. Additionally, if you're unsure of how the sections in your binder will look when they are printed, you can *preview* the sections using the Print Preview command on the File menu.

Suppose you need to organize the sections in the 96 Summary Information binder in a more logical order. To do this, you will switch between sections in your binder to review the structure, and then rearrange the sections in your binder. You will also make a few changes to the contents of your binder, and then preview and print a copy of your binder.

Switch between sections in your binder

In this exercise, you switch between the different sections you added to your new binder to review the order that you placed them in.

1   In the left pane of the binder, click the Excel icon, which is labeled 96 Performance.

    The workbook section appears in the binder. The menu, toolbars, and other screen controls change to those of Excel.

2   In the left pane, click the Word icon, which is labeled 96 Chairman Letter.

    The document section appears in the binder. The menu, toolbars, and other screen controls change to those of Word.

3   In the left pane, click the PowerPoint icon, which is labeled 96 Presentation.

    The presentation section appears in the binder. The menu, toolbars, and other screen controls change to those of PowerPoint.

Rearrange sections in your binder

Now that you have reviewed the section contents in your binder, you rearrange the order of the sections to create a logical progression of documents. In this exercise, you rearrange the sections using different techniques.

1   Be sure that the PowerPoint icon, 96 Presentation, appears in the right pane.

2   On the Section menu, click Rearrange.

    The Rearrange Sections dialog box appears.

3 Click Move Down, and then click OK.

The 96 Presentation file is moved. The document is positioned as the last section in the binder file.

4 In the left pane, click the PowerPoint Presentation icon, which is labeled Blank Presentation.

The presentation section appears in the binder.

5 Click and hold down the left mouse button on the PowerPoint section icon until a paper icon appears on the pointer.

6 Drag the icon down in the left pane until a black arrow appears below the 96 Presentation icon. Release the mouse button.

The Blank Presentation icon is repositioned below the 96 Presentation. Your screen should look similar to the following illustration.

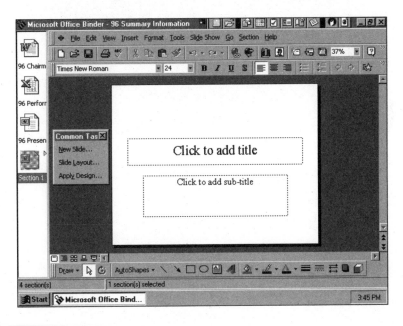

Edit the contents of your binder

In this exercise, you edit the contents of a binder section and check the spelling.

1 In the left pane, click the Excel icon, which is labeled 96 Performance.

The workbook appears in the right binder pane. The menu, toolbars, and other screen controls change to those of Excel.

2 In the Excel workbook, click cell A12. Type **We exceeded our 1996 coffee bean revenue by 29%.** and then press ENTER.

3 On the File menu, click Save Binder.

The workbook and the binder are saved.

Clicking the Save button on the Standard toolbar will only save the current section file, not the entire binder.

4 On the Tools menu, click Spelling, and then click Yes.

The Excel workbook is checked for spelling errors from the beginning.

5 Complete the spell check as needed. When a dialog box appears informing you that the spell check is complete, click OK.

 TIP   The spell checker will check only the current section in a binder. To check the spelling of each section in your binder file, click the section icon in the left pane of the binder window, and then click Spelling on the Tools menu for each section.

Preview and print the binder

Now that you've created, rearranged, and edited the contents of your binder file, you're ready to print it. First you want to see how your binder file will look before it's printed. In this exercise, you preview and then print all the sections in the binder.

1 On the File menu, click Binder Print Preview.

The Binder Print Preview toolbar and the 96 Chairman Letter preview appear. Your screen should look similar to the following illustration.

Binder Print
Preview
toolbar

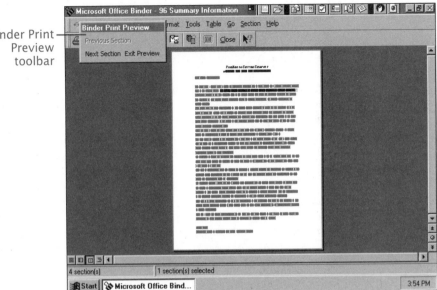

2 On the Binder Print Preview toolbar, click Next Section.

   The next section in the binder, the 96 Performance workbook, appears.

3 On the Binder Print Preview toolbar, click Exit Preview.

   The Print Preview window closes.

4 On the File menu, click Print Binder.

   The Print Binder dialog box appears.

5 Be sure that the All Visible Sections option button under Print What is
   selected, and then click OK.

   All the sections in the Office Binder are printed.

6 On the File menu, click Save Binder.

7 On the Office Binder window, click the Close button.

   The 96 Summary Information binder closes.

Using Binder Templates for Consistency

Office 97 comes with ready-to-use binder *templates* that incorporate template files from Excel, Word, and PowerPoint. A binder template is a predesigned document that you can use as a model for creating new documents. Templates can save you time when you create a set of documents in a binder. For example, the Report template included with Office Binder provides a cover letter, invoice, executive summary letter, slide show, analysis letter, and report data spreadsheet. If the binder templates provided do not meet your organizational needs, you can create a binder template of your own.

Although several templates are available in Office Binder, you can create your own binder template to act as a "master copy" for a set of documents in a binder. By basing new binder files on a binder template, you can create a blueprint for consistent binders. In addition, binder templates include all of the related documents you need to complete a specific project.

Open an existing binder template

While gathering the information for your upcoming report, you notice an inconsistent format in several binders that contain financial reports. In each binder file, the information appears in different formats and is placed in different locations, making the information difficult to review. To establish a consistent format, you create a binder template for future financial reports. As a first step, you review the Report binder template to determine whether it could be used by the company.

New Office Document

1   On the Office Shortcut Bar, click the New Office Document button.

The New Office Document dialog box appears.

2   Click the Binders tab.

The available binder templates appear.

3   Click the Report icon, and then click OK.

The Report binder template appears. Your screen should look similar to the following illustration.

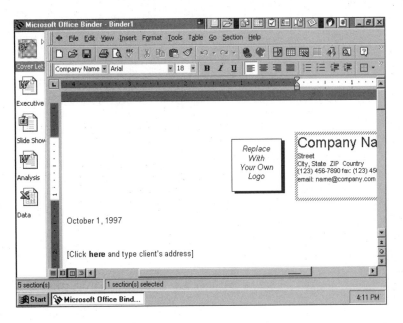

4 Preview each section in the Report binder template.

Create a binder template

While reviewing the Report template, you are informed that a slide show will not be necessary for every financial report. You delete the Slide Show from the Report template and then save the template with a new name to create a new binder template. This will preserve the original Report template with the Slide Show, which you might want to use for another project.

 WARNING Although you can modify the binder templates that come with Office Binder, you should make copies of the templates before you modify them so that you retain the original templates. For example, if you alter the Excel templates that perform calculations or automated tasks, they may not work properly in the future.

---

1   In the left pane of the binder, click the PowerPoint icon, which is labeled Slide Show.

The Report Slide Show template appears.

2   On the Section menu, click Delete.

The Microsoft Office Binder dialog box appears, confirming that you'd like to delete the binder document.

3   In the Microsoft Office Binder dialog box, click OK.

The binder document is removed from the binder template.

4   On the File menu, click Save Binder As.

The Save Binder As dialog box appears.

5   Click the Save As Type down arrow, and then click Binder Templates.

A list of folders and files appears.

6   In the list of folders and files, double-click the Binders folder.

7   Select the text in the File Name box, and then type **Kenya Financial Reporting**

8   Click Save.

The binder is saved as a template with the name Kenya Financial Reporting. All departments can now use this binder as a template.

9   On the Office Binder window, click the Close button.

 IMPORTANT When you save binder templates in the Templates folder, the templates will appear on the Binder tab in the New Binder dialog box and the New Office Document dialog box.

Sharing Binders with Others

You can use Office 97 tools to share the contents of your binder file with your co-workers. By doing so, your information can be reviewed by members of your project team. Let's assume that you met the target date for the research phase of the upcoming annual report. Your co-workers, who will also be working on the annual report, want quick access to the information you gathered. You decide to post your binder to the company network to make the information available to your co-workers.

It can be a frustrating experience searching through shared folders for a particular binder file. Using Microsoft Outlook, you can create a shortcut to your shared folder on a network. The shortcut can be stored on the Outlook Bar in the Other Folders group so you can jump directly to your folder.

In the following exercises, you will create a shared folder called Public Information on The Kenya Coffee Company network and create a shortcut to the shared folder so you can reference it quickly. You will also move the 96 Summary Information binder file to the shared folder to make it available to your co-workers.

 NOTE If the Sharing command is not available on the shortcut menu, you need to enable your file and print sharing services. Contact your network administrator or see your Windows 95 documentation for more information.

Start Outlook and locate a folder

In this exercise, you start Outlook and locate a folder.

To view the entire name of a folder or file, you may need to resize the Name column in the Information Viewer. To resize a column, place the pointer on the right side of the column heading and drag to the right.

1   Start Outlook using the Pamela Miller profile.

You can start Outlook by double-clicking the Microsoft Outlook shortcut icon on the Desktop, through the Start menu, or from the Programs Shortcut Bar.

2   On the Outlook Bar, click the Other shortcut bar.

3   On the Outlook Bar, click the Favorites Folder icon.

The contents of Favorites folder appear.

4   In the Favorites window, double-click the shortcut to Office 97 SBS Practice folder.

5   In the Office 97 SBS Practice window, double-click the Lesson 2 folder.

The contents of the Office 97 SBS Practice\Lesson 2 folder appear.

Create a shared folder

In this exercise, you designate the Public Information folder on your Desktop as a shared folder.

1   Use the right mouse button to click the Public Information folder.

2   On the shortcut menu, click Sharing.

The Public Information Properties dialog box appears. The Sharing tab is selected.

3 Click the Shared As option button.

The Shared As options become available.

4 Click in the Share Name box, type **KenyaPublic** and then click Add.

The Add Users dialog box appears.

5 Be sure that The World is highlighted in the Name list, click Read Only, and then click OK.

6 Click OK.

The Public Information folder on your Desktop is now accessible to your co-workers.

Create a shortcut to a shared folder on a network

In this exercise, you create a shortcut to the Public Information folder and add the shortcut to the Other shortcut bar for easy access.

1 In your Office 97 SBS Practice\Lesson 2 window, double-click the Public Information folder.

2 On the File menu, click Add To Outlook Bar.

The Add To Outlook Bar dialog box appears.

You can open the Public Information folder by clicking the Public Information folder icon.

3 Be sure that the Public Information folder is selected in the Folder list, and then click OK.

The Public Information folder icon is added to the Outlook Bar.

Move a binder file to a shared folder

In this exercise, you move the 96 Summary Information binder file to the shared Public Information folder.

Up One Level

1 On the Standard toolbar, click the Up One Level button.

2 Drag the 96 Summary Information file from the Information Viewer to the Public Information folder on the Outlook Bar.

The 96 Summary Information binder file is moved to the shared Public Information folder.

3 On the Outlook Bar, click the Public Information folder.

Your screen should look similar to the following illustration.

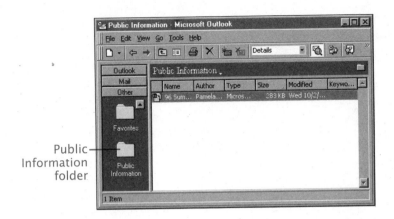

Public Information folder

TIP You can easily remove a shortcut icon from the Outlook Bar. Use the right mouse button to click the shortcut icon on the Outlook Bar, and then click Remove From Shortcut Bar. In the Microsoft Outlook dialog box, click Yes.

Creating Notes to Store Information

From time to time, you probably store bits and pieces of extraneous information on a paper pad or post-it notes. You might jot down questions, ideas, phone numbers, Internet addresses, or simple reminders. However, paper notes can be misplaced or accidentally thrown away.

Notes in Outlook are the electronic equivalent of paper sticky notes. Notes can be displayed on the screen while you work, and you can change the size, color, location, or content of a note. You can also save and store notes to preserve important information. Notes remain until you deliberately delete them, which makes it impossible to lose them or throw them away accidentally.

Create a note

Suppose you need to verify a piece of information with the Marketing department before your report goes out for final printing. In this exercise, you create a reminder note using Outlook.

1   On the Outlook Bar, click the Outlook shortcut bar.

Notes

2 On the Outlook Bar, click the Notes icon.

The Notes window appears. Your screen should look similar to the following illustration.

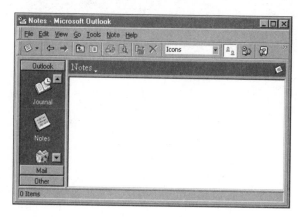

New Note

You can reposition the note by dragging the title bar of the Note window to a new location.

3 On the toolbar, click the New Note button.

A blank note appears.

4 In the note, type **Verify holiday projections with Marketing.**

5 Click outside of the new note.

A Note icon and its contents are added to the Notes window, as well as to the taskbar. The note icon on the taskbar is a reminder to verify the holiday projections. Notes that are not displayed on the screen can be viewed from the Notes window.

Delete a note

In this exercise, you delete the note after verifying the holiday projections.

1 On the taskbar, click the Untitled-Note button.

The note is displayed on the screen.

Close

2 On the note, click the Close button.

The note is no longer displayed on the taskbar. The Note icon and its contents appear in the Notes window.

3 Use the right mouse button to click the Verify holiday projections with Marketing note.

A shortcut menu appears. You can use this shortcut menu to change the color of the note, print the note, or delete the note.

4 On the Notes shortcut menu, click Delete.

The note and its contents are removed.

5   On the Outlook window, click the Close button.

Outlook closes.

NOTE   If you'd like to build on the skills that you learned in this lesson, you can do the One Step Further. Otherwise, skip to "Finish the lesson."

One Step Further: Applying Headers and Footers to a Binder

Headers and footers contain information repeated at the top or bottom of the pages in a document. You can use a header or footer to provide the reader with useful information. For example, a header or footer can contain the document's title, a company logo, the author's name, or the time and date the file was last saved or printed. Using Office 97, you can apply a header and footer across the sections in a binder. You can choose from a list of predefined headers and footers, or you can define custom headers and footers.

Apply a custom header and footer to a binder section

Suppose you want the name of the binder file to appear in the header and the binder section number to appear in the footer when you print the 96 Summary Information binder. In this exercise, you apply a custom header and footer to the binder file.

Open Office Document

1   On the Office Shortcut Bar, click the Open Office Document button.

2   From your Office 97 SBS Practice\Lesson 2\Public Information folder, open the 96 Summary Information binder.

3   On the File menu, click Binder Page Setup.

The Binder Page Setup dialog box appears.

4   Be sure that the Header/Footer tab is selected.

5   In the Apply Binder Header/Footer To area, click the All Supported Sections option button.

The header/footer will be applied to all sections in the binder.

6   In the Header area, click the Header down arrow.

A list of predefined headers appears.

7   Click the 96 Summary Information header.

8   In the Footer area, click the Footer down arrow.

A list of predefined footers appears.

9 Click the Section 1 Of 4 footer.

Your screen should look similar to the following illustration.

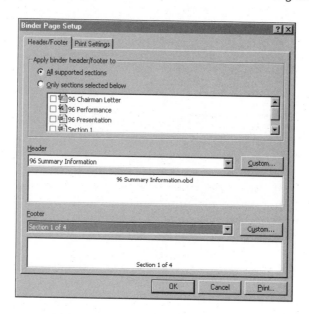

10 Click OK.

The custom header and footer are applied to all sections in the binder file. The 96 Summary Information header are dimmed at the top of the 96 Chairman Letter document.

11 On the File menu, click Save Binder.

12 On the Office Binder window, click the Close button.

Finish the lesson

1 Close all open windows.

2 Delete the Kenya Financial Reporting binder template.

Lesson Summary

To	Do this	Button
Create a binder	On the Office Shortcut Bar, click the New Office Document button, click the Blank Binder icon, and then click OK.	

To	Do this	Button
Add an existing file as a new section in a binder	On the Section menu, click Add From File. Find and click the appropriate file. Click Add.	
Add a blank document as a new section in a binder	On the Section menu, click Add. Click the type of document, and then click OK.	
Open an existing binder template	On the Office Shortcut Bar, click the New Office Document button. Click the Binder tab. Click the binder template you want, and then click OK.	
Create a binder template	Create a new binder or edit an existing binder template. On the File menu, click Save Binder As. Type the new name of the binder template. Click the Save As Type down arrow, click Binder Templates, and then click Save.	
Share a folder with others	In Outlook, locate the folder to share. Using the right mouse button, click the folder to share. On the shortcut menu, click Sharing, and then click the Shared As option button. Select sharing options, and then click OK.	
Create a shortcut to a shared folder	In Outlook, locate the folder you want to create the shortcut to. Double-click the folder. On the File menu, click Add To Outlook Bar.	
Create a note	Click the Outlook shortcut bar, and then click the Note icon. Click the New Note button, and then type the contents of the note.	
Delete a note using Outlook	Use the right mouse button to click the note. On the shortcut menu, click Delete.	

For online information about	On the Help menu, click Contents And Index, click the Index tab, and then type
Creating a binder file	*Office Binder*: binder
Adding sections to a binder	*Office Binder*: binder

For online information about	On the Help menu, click Contents And Index, click the Index tab, and then type
Previewing a binder	*Office Binder*: viewing
Using binder templates	*Office Binder*: templates
Creating notes in Outlook	*Outlook*: notes
Applying headers and footers to binder sections	*Office Binder*: headers and footers

Review & Practice

You will review and practice how to:

Estimated time
35 min.

- Store information using notes.
- Start programs and open files.
- Review and save documents.
- Organize related files in a binder.
- Work with binder templates.

Before you move on to Part 2, you can practice the skills you learned in Part 1 by working through the steps in this Review & Practice section. You store information using notes, start Microsoft Office 97 programs and open files with the Office Shortcut Bar, integrate a project with Office Binder, and create a binder template.

Scenario

You have been asked to streamline the process of information management at The Kenya Coffee Company. You are responsible for reviewing documents, organizing documents electronically, and creating a binder template to use as a model for creating new binder files.

Step 1: Store Information Using Notes

You have been asked to review a memo and a packet of information that will be distributed to all new employees of The Kenya Coffee Company. This needs to be done as soon as possible, so you decide to create a note as a reminder instead of adding the task to your schedule.

1 Using Microsoft Outlook, create a note and type the following information: **Review new employee memo and supporting information**

2 Move the note to the lower-right corner of the Desktop.

For more information about	See
Creating notes to store information	Lesson 2

Step 2: Start Programs and Open Files

Later that day, the note on your desktop reminds you to review the memo and the packet of information that will be distributed to the new employees of The Kenya Coffee Company.

1 Using the Office Shortcut Bar, open the New Employee Memo from your Office 97 SBS Practice\Review & Practice 1 folder.

2 Start Microsoft Excel using the Programs Shortcut Bar.

3 From your Office 97 SBS Practice\Review & Practice 1 folder, open the Microsoft Excel workbook called Investment Illustration.

4 Use the taskbar to switch to Microsoft Word.

5 From your Office SBS Practice\Review & Practice 1 folder, open the Microsoft Word document called Assistance Plan.

6 Delete the note.

For more information about	See
Creating notes to store information	Lesson 2
Creating shortcuts to programs and files	Lesson 1

Step 3: Review and Save Your Open Documents

Before you edit the information in the documents that you'll be reviewing, you save the files with new names to preserve the original information.

1 Save the Assistance Plan document as **Employee Assistance** in the Office 97 SBS Practice\Review & Practice 1 folder.

2 Save the New Employee memo as **Employee Savings** in the Office 97 SBS Practice\Review & Practice 1 folder.

3 Save the Investment Illustration worksheet as **Income Deferral** in the Office 97 SBS Practice\Review & Practice 1 folder.

For more information about	See
Storing and retrieving frequently used files	Lesson 1

Step 4: *Organize Related Files in a Binder*

You are now ready to assemble the files in an Office Binder so that they can be distributed as a single file.

1 Create a new binder file.

2 From your Office 97 SBS Practice\Review & Practice 1 folder, add the Employee Savings document, Income Deferral workbook, and Employee Assistance document to a new binder file using the Add From File command on the Section menu.

3 Switch to the workbook and review the information.

4 Rearrange the sections in the binder making the workbook the first section.

5 Save the binder file as **New Hire Information** in your Office 97 SBS Practice\Review & Practice 1 folder.

For more information about	See
Assembling related files in a binder	Lesson 2

Step 5: *Create a Binder Template*

After reviewing the binder, you find that the documents need updating to reflect current information. To make sure that the documents maintain a consistent format and structure, you create a binder template using the existing binder.

1 Save the binder file as a template.

2 Name the new template **New Hire**

For more information about	See
Using binder templates	Lesson 2

Finish the Review & Practice

Follow these steps to complete the Review & Practice.

1 Close all open windows.

2 Delete the New Hire binder template.

3 Hide the Programs Shortcut Bar.

Getting Results with Office Integration

Merging Information with a Form Letter

Estimated time
25 min.

In this lesson you will learn how to:

- Set up a form letter to accept information from a database table.
- Add placeholders to a form letter that specify where to insert personalized data.
- Merge a mailing list with a form letter.

Standardized letters and large mailings have become commonplace in today's business world. Addressing each of these letters individually can be time consuming, and sending a "to whom it may concern" letter is impersonal. If you keep names and addresses in a database or some other form of list, you can merge them with a form letter to create a personalized letter for each person on the list. For example, if you need to send a letter to all your clients informing them of their current account balance, you can write a form letter and then merge the letter with a list containing each client's name, address, and account balance.

The Mail Merge Helper can guide you through the process of creating personalized letters from a mailing list. It will help you create a form letter and identify the data to be merged into the form letter. Your merge data can come from a Microsoft Access database table, a Microsoft Excel worksheet, a Microsoft Word data source document, or your Microsoft Outlook contacts *folder*. Whether you mail only a few letters a day, or hundreds of letters a week, you can use the Mail Merge Helper to automate the task of addressing and personalizing form letters.

In this lesson, you will use an existing form letter and database table to create a mail merge. In the form letter you will identify the areas for personalized information and then merge the letter and the data. You will also merge the form letter with your contact list.

Starting a Mail Merge

A mail merge is the combining of a *main document* and a *data source* to create multiple personalized letters or documents. A form letter, containing the basic text to be used in each recipient letter, is often your main document. A database table containing names and addresses can be used as a data source.

Using the Mail Merge Helper, which is unique to Word, you can easily specify the main document and data source to be used in a mail merge. The Mail Merge Helper consists of a series of dialog boxes, similar to a wizard, that guide you through the three steps in creating a mail merge. In addition to creating merged form letters, you can create other merged documents, such as labels, name tags, and phone lists. You can think of the Mail Merge Helper as centrally coordinating the merging of the main document with a data source. The three steps in a mail merge are:

- Creating or identifying the main document and adding merge fields to it.
- Creating or identifying the data source, such as an Access database table or an Excel worksheet.
- Merging the data source into the main document.

Specifying a Main Document

A main document contains the text and merge fields that remain the same in each version of a merged document, such as a form letter. You can create a form letter from scratch or by using a Letter wizard, a letter template, or a letter format that's unique to your organization. When you create a form letter, or any main document, to be used in a mail merge, you generally do not include names, addresses, or personalized information—this information is added automatically from your data source based on data placeholders you insert into the main document.

Using Word, you can create two types of form letters: those that are filled in manually and those that are filled in automatically. The first type of form letter is ideal in a situation where you need to include information that is different for each recipient. When you use this type of form letter, it's similar to being prompted for information that is not included in your data source. The second type of form letter is generated automatically by merging information directly from a data source. In this lesson, you will create and use the latter type of form letter.

Open a form letter

In this exercise, you open a form letter to the regional managers of The Kenya Coffee Company.

Open Office Document

1　On the Office Shortcut Bar, click the Open Office Document button.

　　The Open Office Document dialog box appears.

2　From your Office 97 SBS Practice\Lesson 3 folder, open the 97 Financial Health document.

　　This document will be the main document for your mail merge.

3　Save the file as **97 Management Letter** in your Office 97 SBS Practice\ Lesson 3 folder.

Specify a form letter as the main document

In this exercise, you specify the 97 Management Letter as the main document for a mail merge.

1　On the Tools menu, click Mail Merge.

　　The Mail Merge Helper dialog box appears. The three steps for creating a mail merge are displayed.

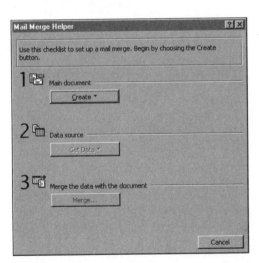

2　In the Mail Merge Helper dialog box, click Create, and then click Form Letters.

　　This identifies the format of the main document for your mail merge.

3　Click Active Window.

　　This indicates that the 97 Management Letter will be the main document source for the mail merge.

Specifying a Data Source

For a demonstration of how to insert merge fields into a document, double-click the Camcorder Files On The Internet shortcut on your Desktop or connect to the Internet address listed on p. xxx.

Now that you have specified the main document, you can merge a list of names and addresses (data source) with the form letter to create personalized letters. For example, you can store each individual's name, address, and other detailed information in an Access database. In this case, the database is the data source for the merge, even though it's in a separate program. Mail merge enables you to merge information from the data source into specific areas of the main document. The end result is a personalized letter addressed to all persons on your mailing list.

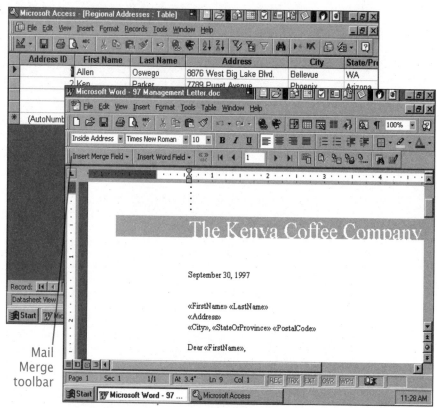

Mail Merge toolbar

Using an Access database table as the data source for a mail merge is the best technique to use when your project meets one or more of the following criteria:

- You want to personalize a letter with a mail merge.
- You already have an Access database table that includes the information you need for the mail merge.
- You need to create a database, and you want to use the mail merge data source as the foundation for a larger database.

If your mailing list is short and you won't need to update it frequently, you might want to create the data source in Word. If your list requires frequent updates, you could also use a Excel worksheet or an Outlook Contact List, depending on your needs.

Specifying an Access table as the data source

In this exercise, you identify an existing Access database table as the data source for a mail merge.

1   In the Mail Merge Helper dialog box, click Get Data, and then click Open Data Source.

    The Open Data Source dialog box appears.

2   Be sure that the Office 97 SBS Practice folder appears in the Look In box.

3   Click the Files Of Type down arrow, and then click MS Access Databases.

4   Click Kenya Coffee Company, and then click Open.

Other data sources include Excel workbooks and other Word files.

TROUBLESHOOTING If your database was created in a previous version of Access, you will be prompted to convert the database or open the database as a previous version. When you convert a database, it will be unusable with previous versions of Access.

---

5   In the Microsoft Access dialog box, be sure that the Tables tab is selected.

6   Click the Regional Addresses table, and then click OK.

    The Regional Addresses table is now identified as the data source for the mail merge. A message appears informing you that there are no merge fields in the main document.

When you open a document containing merge fields, the Mail Merge toolbar automatically appears.

7   Click Edit Main Document.

    The 97 Management Letter appears with the Mail Merge toolbar displayed. You can now insert merge fields in the main document using the Mail Merge toolbar.

Setting Up a Main Document to Accept Data

Now that you have attached the data source to your main document, you need to insert *merge fields* into the document. Merge fields serve as placeholders—in a merge document, the specific data from the data source is inserted in the merge fields. For example, merge fields might include placeholders for names, titles, addresses, or product information.

Insert merge fields into a form letter

Be sure to press ENTER or the SPACEBAR and type the appropriate punctuation, as indicated in the steps for this exercise.

1 Click the insertion point above the text "Dear Regional Manager," and then on the Mail Merge toolbar, click the Insert Merge Field button.

All the data source fields from the Regional Addresses table appear. (The field names are taken from the header row in your data source.) Your screen should look similar to the following illustration.

Insert Merge Field list

Click here to insert the merge field in the main document.

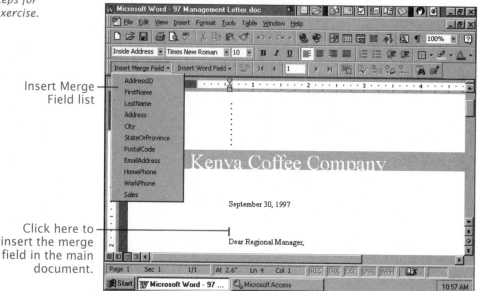

2 From the Insert Merge Field list, click FirstName.

The <<FirstName>> field appears in the form letter at the insertion point.

It's important to leave a space before or after a merge field, just as you would if you were typing the information.

3 Press the SPACEBAR, and then click the Insert Merge Field button.

4 Click LastName, and then press ENTER to insert a new line for the address information.

5 On the Mail Merge toolbar, click the Insert Merge Field button.

6 Click Address, and then press ENTER to insert a new line for the following information.

7 Follow the same process to insert the City, StateOrProvince, and PostalCode merge fields on the current line. Press ENTER after inserting the PostalCode field.

Be sure to type a comma between the City field and the StateOrProvince field.

8 In the salutation, select the text "Regional Manager" (but don't select the comma), and then, from the Insert Merge Field list, click FirstName.

Your screen should look similar to the following illustration.

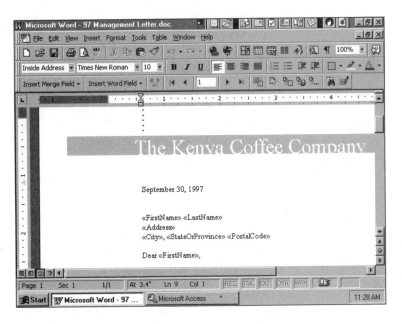

Save

9 On the Standard toolbar, click the Save button.

Your letter is saved with the merge fields.

Merging a Data Source into a Main Document

When you're satisfied with your main document, you can merge it with the data source by clicking one of the three merge buttons on the Mail Merge toolbar. These buttons and their functions are described in the following table.

Button	Button name	Function
	Merge To New Document	Merges the letters to a new document. The merged form letters are placed in a single document and are separated by *section breaks*.
	Merge To Printer	Prints a personalized form letter for each address retrieved from the data source.
	Mail Merge	Displays the Merge dialog box so that you can choose from a variety of merge options.

You can also initiate a mail merge from Access using the OfficeLinks button and the Merge It With MS Word command on the Database toolbar. Regardless of the program from which you initiate the mail merge, the result will be identical. Choose whichever method is convenient for you. If you're currently working in Access, it might be more convenient to initiate the mail merge there. If you're working in Word, it might be easier to start the mail merge there.

Now that your form letter includes all the necessary merge fields, you're ready to merge the Access database information with the form letter. In the next exercise, you will use the first merge option in the previous table, which will result in a new document containing all the personalized mail-merged letters, ready for you to print and mail.

Start the mail merge from Word

In this exercise, you initiate the mail merge from Word.

Merge To New Document

1   On the Mail Merge toolbar, click the Merge To New Document button.

The information from the Access database merges into the form letter at the appropriate fields. A new document is created that contains a separate letter for each record in the database table, as shown in the following illustration.

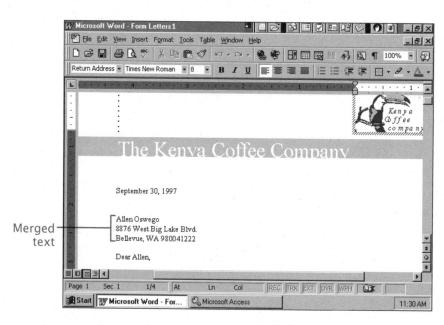

Merged text

2   Scroll through and review the merged document.

Each letter is separated by a section break. Your original form letter is still intact, so you can use it again later.

Save

3 On the Standard toolbar, click the Save button.

4 Save the merged document as **Merged Regional Letters** in your Office 97 SBS Practice\Lesson 3 folder.

5 On the File menu, click Close.

 TIP You can also perform a merge by clicking the Merge To Printer button on the Mail Merge toolbar. The results are sent directly to the printer, one for each name and address retrieved from the mailing list.

Using a Contact List

You can maintain extensive information about your contacts in the Contacts folder in Outlook. A *contact* is a person or organization with whom you correspond. Using the Contacts folder, you can store information such as job titles, addresses, phone numbers, and notes.

There are several ways to obtain address information to use as your data source. In Outlook, you can use address lists in your Address Book, including the global address book and your own personal address book, as data sources. The global address book is created and maintained by the system administrator for your organization and contains the names and e-mail addresses of all the users in the system. The personal address book is created by you. The personal address book is best used for personal distribution lists, such as a list of everyone on a project team, in a workgroup, or in a department.

Create a contact list

In this exercise you will create a contact in Outlook.

Contacts

New Contact

1 Start Outlook using the Pamela Miller profile.

2 On the Outlook Bar, click the Contacts icon.

The Contacts window appears.

3 On the Standard toolbar, click the New Contact button.

The Untitled Contact window opens.

4 Be sure that the insertion point is in the Full Name box, type **Lynn Martinez** and then press TAB.

The insertion point moves to the Job Title box.

5 Type **Regional Manager** and then press TAB.

6 Type **Espresso and Go,** and then click Address.

The Check Address dialog box appears.

7 Type **2200 West Sound Avenue,** and then press TAB.

8 Type **Seattle,** press TAB, type **Washington,** press TAB, type **98444,** and then click OK.

Your screen should look similar to the following illustration.

 9 On the Standard toolbar, click the Save And Close button.

The new contact is added to the Kenya Contact List.

 TIP To delete a contact, select the contact that you want to remove and then click the Delete button on the Standard toolbar.

Add more contacts

In this exercise, you add two additional contacts to your contact list.

1 Create new contacts using the following table.

	Contact No. 1	Contact No.2
Full Name	Jim Partner	Susie Ross
Job Title	Owner	Buyer
Company	A Cup Full	Giant Market
Street	555 Market Way	1635 132nd Pl SE
City	Kirkland	Portland
State/Province	Washington	Oregon
Zip/PostalCode	97654	90867

Your screen should look similar to the following illustration.

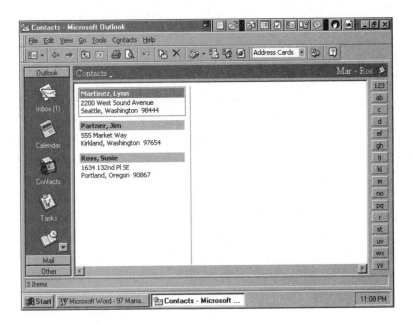

Export a contact list to Excel

In this exercise, you export your contact list to an Excel workbook for use as a mail merge data source.

1 On the File menu, click Import And Export.

The Import And Export Wizard dialog box appears.

2 In the Choose An Action To Perform box, click Export To A File, and then click Next.

The Export To A File dialog box appears.

3 In the Select Folder To Export From box, be sure that Contacts is selected, and then click Next.

The Export To A File dialog box appears.

4 In the Create A File Of Type box, click Microsoft Excel, and then click Next.

5 Click Browse.

The Browse dialog box appears.

6 In the File Name box, type **contacts**, select your Office 97 SBS Practice\Lesson 3 folder, click OK, and then click Next.

7 Click Finish.

The contact list is exported to an Excel workbook file named Contacts.

65

Close

8 On the Outlook window, click the Close button.

The 97 Management Letter appears in Word.

Use a contact list as your source data

In this exercise, you start Mail Merge Helper, and then identify your exported contact list as the data source for your mail merge.

Mail Merge Helper

1 On the Mail Merge toolbar, click the Mail Merge Helper button.

The Mail Merge Helper dialog box appears. Be sure that the main document merge type is set to Form Letters under step 1.

2 In the Mail Merge Helper dialog box, click Get Data, and then click Open Data Source.

The Use Address Book dialog box appears.

3 Click the Files Of Type down arrow, and then click MS Excel Worksheets.

4 From your Office 97 SBS Practice\Lesson5 folder, click Contacts, and then click Open.

The data source is now set to the exported contact list in Excel.

5 Click Contacts, and then click OK.

Merge an exported contact list with a form letter

In this exercise, you change the merge field names to reflect the appropriate merge field information in the exported contact list, and then you merge the exported contacts with the 97 Management Letter.

1 In the Mail Merge Helper dialog box, click Edit under step 1 Main Document, and then click Form Letter.

The 97 Management Letter appears.

2 Select the Address merge field in the 97 Management Letter.

This merge field will be replaced by a merge field from the Contact List.

3 On the Mail Merge toolbar, click the Insert Merge Field button, and then click BusinessStreet.

The BusinessStreet merge field replaces the Address merge field.

4 Replace the City merge field with BusinessCity, StateOrProvince with BusinessState, and Postal Code with BusinessPostalCode.

*Merge To New
Document*

5 On the Mail Merge toolbar, click the Merge To New Document button.

The records in the exported contact list are merged with the 97 Management Letter.

6 Save the merged document as **Contact List Letter** in your Office 97 SBS Practice\Lesson 3 folder.

7 Save and close all open Word files.

> **NOTE** If you'd like to build on the skills that you learned in this lesson, you can do the One Step Further. Otherwise, skip to "Finish the lesson."

One Step Further: Creating a New Data Source for a Mail Merge

If the amount of source data that you need to store is not extensive, and you don't need to share the data with other users, the easiest way to store and manage your data is in a Word document. You can create a data source document by typing the information in a blank document, or you can use the Mail Merge Helper to automate the process of creating a data source document. When you're prompted to specify the data source for the mail merge, you simply specify the Word document.

Create a data source using the Mail Merge Helper

In this exercise, you use the Mail Merge Helper to create a data source for a mail merge.

New

1 On the Standard toolbar, click the New button.

A new Word document opens.

2 On the Tools menu, click Mail Merge.

The Mail Merge Helper dialog box appears.

3 Click Create, and then click Form Letters.

4 Click Active Window.

5 Click Get Data, and then click Create Data Source.

The Create Data Source dialog box contains a list of commonly used field names. You can accept, add, or remove field names to create a customized header row for a data source. Your screen should look similar to the following illustration.

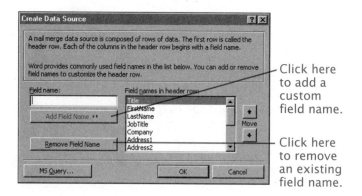

Click here to add a custom field name.

Click here to remove an existing field name.

6 In the Field Names In Header Row list, click Address2, and then click Remove Field Name.

The Address2 field name is removed from the Field Names In Header Row list and will not appear in the new data source.

7 Repeat steps 6 and 7 for the Country, HomePhone, and WorkPhone field names.

The remaining fields in the Field Names In Header Row list will appear in the new data source.

8 Click OK.

9 Save the file as **Private Contacts** in your Office 97 SBS Practice\Lesson 3 folder.

A message box appears, informing you that the data source you created contains no data records. You can add new records to your data source by clicking Edit Data Source, and you can add merge fields to your main document by clicking Edit Main Document in the Mail Merge Helper dialog box.

10 Click Edit Data Source.

The Data Form dialog box appears with fields that you selected.

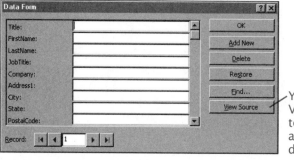

You can click the View Source button to display the data as a Word table in a document window.

11 In the Data Form dialog box, type information on the electronic address card that will be useful for you. Click Add New after typing the Postal Code of each record. When you are finished entering information, click OK.

12 On the Word window, click the Close button.

A message appears asking if you want to save changes to Private Contacts.

13 Click Yes, and then click No.

Document 1 does not need to be saved because it contains no information.

Finish the lesson

Close

1 On the Word window, click the Close button.

2 On the Outlook window, click the Close button.

3 Close all open windows.

Lesson Summary

To	Do this	Button
Specify a form letter	On the Tools menu, click Mail Merge, click Create, and then select the document type. Indicate if the document is active or is to be created.	
Specify the data source	In the Mail Merge Helper, click Get Data, and then click Open Data Source. Select the data source file, and then click Open.	
Insert mail merge fields into the form letter	Click in the source document. On the Mail Merge toolbar, click the Insert Merge Field button. Click the field to be inserted.	
Merge the data source with the form letter	On the Mail Merge toolbar, click the Mail Merge button, and then click Merge.	![button]
Open a contact list	On the Outlook Bar, click the Contacts icon, and then open the appropriate contact list.	
Add new contacts	Click the New Contact button. Type the contact information in the New Contact dialog box.	![button]

69

To	Do this
Use an Outlook contact list as a mail merge data source	In the Mail Merge Helper dialog box, click Get Data, and then click Use Address Book. Select Outlook contact list.

For online information about	On the Help menu, click Contents And Index, click the Index tab, and then type
Specifying a form letter	*Word*: main documents for mail merge
Specifying a data source	*Word*: data source for mail merge
Adding merge fields in a form letter	*Word*: merge fields
Merging the data source and form letter	*Word*: mail merge
Adding new contacts	*Outlook*: contacts
Using a contact list as a data source	*Outlook*: data sources

Integrating Information Between Programs

In this lesson you will learn how to:

■ Import and export information among different Office 97 programs.

■ Embed a document in another document.

■ Link information in different documents so that changes made to one document are automatically made to all the linked documents.

■ Edit and update embedded and linked information.

■ Record activities in your Journal folder.

Estimated time
40 min.

When working on reports, presentations, or documentation, you may have found yourself piecing together pages of information that you've gathered and printed from several different programs. This can lead to an inappropriate flow of information and large areas of unused space on the printed page. If you integrate information between programs, you can create a more cohesive, attractive document. For example, if you have a worksheet that contains a current pricing list for your company's products, you could integrate the worksheet table in a form letter to potential customers. Then, if you change any information in the worksheet, the form letter is automatically updated.

With Microsoft Office 97, you can efficiently import, embed, and link information between Office 97 programs. By sharing information between the programs, you can save time and effort by using existing information and by updating information contained in multiple documents in one place. All this leads to a more professional delivery of information.

In this lesson, you will combine information from different Office 97 programs to create a press release for The Kenya Coffee Company. You will create a new document based on an existing Microsoft PowerPoint presentation, and you will integrate Microsoft Excel workbook data with a Microsoft Word document. You will also learn to track your daily activities using the Journal folder in Microsoft Outlook.

Start the lesson

In this exercise, you start PowerPoint and open the Kenya Products presentation.

Open Office Document

1   On the Office Shortcut Bar, click the Open Office Document button.

   The Open Office Document dialog box appears.

2   From your Office 97 SBS Practice\Lesson 4 folder, open the Kenya Products presentation.

   This file consists of a presentation detailing the new products that will be released by The Kenya Coffee Company.

3   Save the file as **New Products** in your Office 97 SBS Practice\Lesson 4 folder.

Integrating Presentation Text and Organizational Charts in a Document

You can easily integrate information between Office 97 programs to create a single document. For example, you can integrate an Excel worksheet and a PowerPoint graphic into a Word document. The integrated information from the source document becomes an *object* in the destination document. The following are the three methods you can use to accomplish this:

Export or import   Converts a file created in one program into a format that another program can interpret. What is converted between the programs is the *file format*—the manner in which the file codes the information. When you export a file, you are saving the file in the file format of the destination program. When you import a file, you are saving the file in the file format of the source program.

Embed   Copies an object from a source document into a destination document even if the object was created in a different program. An *embedded object* maintains a relationship to the program in which it was embedded and not to the source document. To edit the embedded object, you double-click the object in the destination document, and the source program used to create that object opens. For example, if you embed an Excel chart in a Word document, you can edit the chart from the Word document. When you double-click the chart in Word, the menus and toolbars that are unique to Excel appear in the Word document. Embedding copies the object; the copy retains no link to the original document it was created in.

Link   Copies an object from a source document into a destination document, and retains a direct connection, or *link*, to the source document. If information in the source document is changed, the information in the destination document is automatically updated. For example, if you insert a linked Excel chart into a Word document, each time the information in the Excel chart changes, the linked chart in Word is automatically updated to reflect the change. A linked object requires less disk space than an embedded object.

> **NOTE**   To review integration methods in each Office 97 program, see Appendix C, "Integration Techniques."

The following table will help you determine which method to use to integrate information between Office 97 programs.

If your task meets these criteria	Use this method
You need to duplicate the entire contents of a file that was produced in one program in another program.	Export or import
You do not want any changes in the source object to be reflected in the destination object. Or, you want to make changes to the destination object, but you don't have access to the source object.	Embed
You want any changes made to the source object to be reflected in the destination object.	Link

Exporting Presentation Text to a Document

You can create a document based on an existing PowerPoint presentation by exporting the presentation into Word. This can be useful when you need documentation that offers more than a place to take notes and a thumbnail sketch of each slide. By exporting a presentation, the slide headings and bullets are recreated in a new document as an outline. The easiest way to export information from PowerPoint to Word is to use the Send To command in PowerPoint to export the presentation text to a file format that Word can interpret.

In this lesson, you will convert a PowerPoint presentation into *Rich Text Format (RTF)*, which is a format that Word can read. When you export a file, you are saving it in the file format of the destination program. After you've exported the information from PowerPoint, you can open the new Word document and the information will look as though it was created in Word.

Export a presentation to a document

Suppose you want a press release for The Kenya Coffee Company to correspond with the content and structure of an existing PowerPoint presentation. In this exercise, you export a PowerPoint presentation to a new Word document.

1   On the File Menu, point to Send To, and then click Microsoft Word.

     The Write-Up dialog box appears.

2   Click the Outline Only option button, and then click OK.

     Word starts. The presentation text appears as a new document in Normal View.

3   On the Word window, click the Maximize button.

     Your screen should look like the following illustration.

Maximize

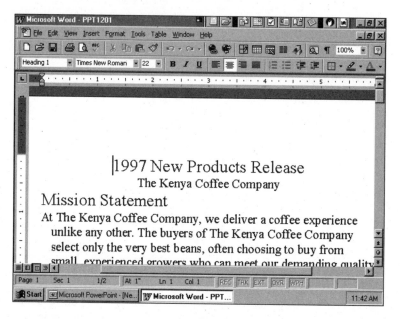

4   On the File menu, click Save As.

5   Click the Save As Type down arrow, and then click Word Document.

6   Save the file as **Kenya Press Release** in your Office 97 SBS Practice\ Lesson 4 folder.

     The file is saved as a Word document. You can now edit and format the document to create a press release for The Kenya Coffee Company.

Embedding an Organization Chart in a Document

Embedding an object is similar to copying an object from one program to another. When you embed information, the embedded object is integrated into the new document. You can edit the embedded object by double-clicking it. When you double-click an embedded object, the source program used to create the object is activated and the file opens within the destination program. You can then use the source program's menus and toolbars to edit the embedded object. For example, if you have a worksheet containing survey data and a document with text about how the data was gathered, you could embed the text on the worksheet instead of typing the text in the worksheet. Embedding the text eliminates the need to manipulate the text within the worksheet cells.

You can embed an existing file or object, or you can create and embed a new object in your document. Either way, you can use the full resources of the source program. A program called Microsoft Organization Chart is shared among the Office 97 programs and can be used to embed an organization chart in any of those programs.

Embedding is preferable to linking objects in the following instances:

- The information does not need to be updated frequently or automatically.

- You want to edit the information without affecting the source file.

- File size is not a concern.

 TIP If you want to work with a file or an embedded object for which you do not have the Microsoft application, you can obtain a free viewer that will allow you to view and print the file or object. Viewers are available for Word, Excel, and PowerPoint. For details, see http://microsoft.com/msoffice/

Embed an object from an existing file

In this exercise, you embed a copy of an organization chart created in PowerPoint into an existing Word document.

When working in Excel, you can also embed an object by copying it in its source program and pasting the object in Excel.

1 Click at the end of the text "The following organizational chart lists our new line of products:" and then press ENTER.

2 On the Insert menu, click Object.

  The Object dialog box appears.

3 Click the Create From File tab.

  Your screen should look similar to the following illustration.

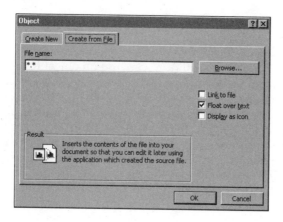

4 Click Browse.

The Browse dialog box appears.

5 From your Office 97 SBS Practice\Lesson 4 folder, click Blends, and then click OK.

The File Name box displays the file name of the object to be inserted.

6 Clear the Float Over Text check box.

7 Click OK.

Word embeds a copy of the Blends organization chart in the Word document. Your screen should look similar to the following illustration.

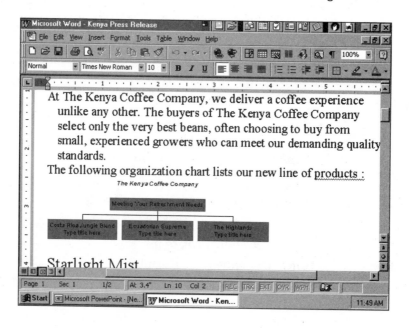

Edit and update an embedded object

You can use the Organization Chart shared program to create and insert an organization chart in any file. In this exercise, you activate the embedded organization chart to make some changes.

1 Double-click the embedded Blends organization chart.

The Organization Chart program starts. You can use the program's menus and toolbars to edit the embedded object. Your screen should look similar to the following illustration.

Menu and buttons unique to Organization Chart

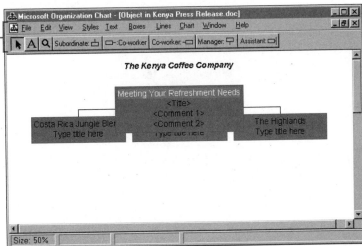

2 If necessary, double-click the Meeting Your Refreshment Needs text box to make it active.

3 Type **1997 New Products**

4 On the File menu in Organization Chart, click Exit And Return To Kenya Press Release.doc.

A message appears informing you that the object has changed and prompting you to save the changes before proceeding.

5 Click Yes.

Organization Chart closes, and the embedded organization chart is updated in the Word document.

Embedding a New Object

You can also use the resources from another program to create a new embedded object. For example, you might want to include a table in a Word document with figures that need periodic updating and recalculating. Because Excel handles this task best, you can embed the table as an Excel workbook. You can then open the workbook from within the Word document anytime you need to update it. The workbook exists only within the Word document, but it gives you all the capabilities of Excel.

Create and embed a new object

Suppose that you have new data on a line of coffee products. You'd like to present the information in an Excel worksheet within a Word document. In this exercise, you create a new workbook object and embed it in your document.

1   Press CTRL+END, click at the end of the text "The following table lists the pricing of our new products:" and then press ENTER.

2   On the Insert menu, click Object.

The Object dialog box appears. The Create New tab is selected.

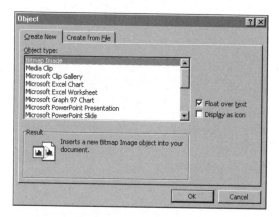

3   Click Microsoft Excel Worksheet, clear the Float Over Text check box, and then click OK.

A worksheet appears in the document as an embedded Excel object.

4   Enter the following information into the worksheet starting with cell A1.

Product Name	Price per lb.	Qty Discount	Qty Price
Starlight Mist	12.95	.21	
Bogota Blend	11.95	.15	
Palo Verde Delight	10.95	.09	

5   Double-click the column borders of columns A, B, and C to expand the columns and make all text visible.

Add cell calculations

In this exercise, you create calculations to show the quantity discount price.

1   Click in cell D2, type **=B2-C2** and then press ENTER.

The calculation for the quantity discount price is entered. The result is 12.74.

2   Be sure that cell D3 is selected, type **=B3-C3** and then press ENTER.

3   Be sure that cell D4 is selected, type **=B4-C4** and then press ENTER.

4   Click anywhere in the Kenya Press Release document.

Your screen should look similar to the following illustration.

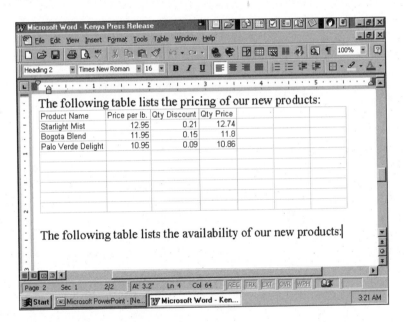

Save

5   On the Standard toolbar, click the Save button.

Integrating Worksheet Data in a Document

Perhaps you're familiar with linking cells within Excel. When the contents of the original cell are changed, the contents of the linked cell change automatically. Similarly, you can select information in one file, and then link it as an object in another program. When you change the contents of the source file, the contents of the linked object change automatically. Because the information in the destination file is a linked object, you cannot alter or change the object in the destination file as you can with an embedded object. The only way to change the linked object is to change the source information.

For example, suppose you are working on an annual report in Word and you need to include sales figures from an Excel workbook. Instead of copying the figures, you can link them to make sure that the figures in your Word document are always up to date. Then if the figures are modified in the workbook, they will be automatically updated in the linked Word document. The following illustration demonstrates how information is linked between files.

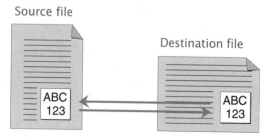

A linked object contains the same information as the source file.

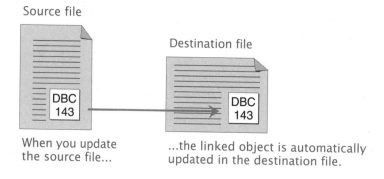

When you update the source file...   ...the linked object is automatically updated in the destination file.

Linking is preferable to copying in the following instances:

- You need a live link to information stored in other files.
- You don't want to increase the size of the destination file.
- You frequently update the source file.

If you rename or move the source file, the linked object will not be able to locate the source information. You can reestablish the link by updating the source file location.

Linking an Excel Table to a Document

You can link information between files that have been created in any Microsoft program. Linking allows you to update information in one file and automatically see the changes reflected in the linked files. You can link information in several ways.

If you want to	Use this command
Link selected information	On the Edit menu, use the Copy and Paste Special commands.
Link an entire file	On the Insert menu, use the Object command.

At The Kenya Coffee Company, the availability of products is updated on a weekly basis. To keep the information in the press release updated, you link the Availability worksheet in Excel to the Kenya Press Release document in Word.

Open a workbook

In this exercise, you open an Excel workbook containing the data you want to link to the Kenya Press Release.

Open Office Document

1 On the Office Shortcut Bar, click the Open Office Document button.

The Open Office Document dialog box appears.

2 From your Office 97 SBS Practice\Lesson 4 folder, open the Availability worksheet.

This file is a worksheet detailing the availability of the new products to be released by The Kenya Coffee Company.

3 If necessary, maximize the Excel window and the Availability window.

4 Save the file as **Product Availability** in your Office 97 SBS Practice\ Lesson 4 folder.

Link an object

In this exercise, you link an Excel worksheet that describes product availability for the new line of Kenya Coffee Company products to the Kenya Press Release document.

Copy

The file format for the worksheet will be converted to Rich Text Format (RTF), which is a file format that Word can read.

1 Select cells A1 through E8.

2 On the Standard toolbar, click the Copy button.

3 On the taskbar, click the Microsoft Word button.

4 Press CTRL+END.

The insertion point is positioned at the end of the document.

5 On the Edit menu, click Paste Special.

The Paste Special dialog box appears.

6 Be sure that Formatted Text (RTF) is selected in the As box, and then click the Paste Link option button.

The Paste Link option establishes a link between the source information in Excel and the destination Word file. Your screen should look similar to the following illustration.

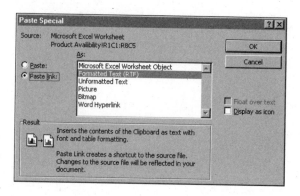

If necessary, use the sizing handles around the object frame to adjust the size of the worksheet.

7 Click OK.

The Excel information is inserted and linked to your Word document. Whenever the information changes in the Excel workbook, the linked information in the Word document is automatically updated. Your screen should look similar to the following illustration.

Linked Excel data in a Word document —

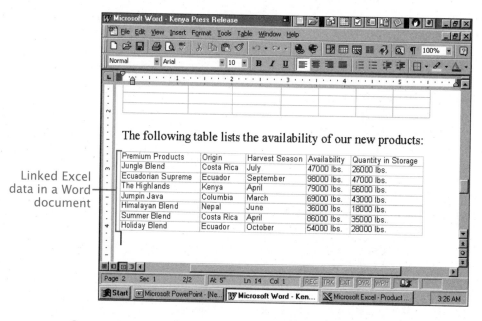

Save

8 On the Standard toolbar, click the Save button.

Change data in a linked table

Suppose a week has gone by and you have just received the new availability figures. In this exercise, you enter the figures in the original Excel worksheet. Then you see how the changes in the source worksheet affect the table in the destination Word document.

1 On the taskbar, click the Microsoft Excel button.

2 In the Availability column, type the following figures in cell D2 through cell D4: **37000 lbs.**, **88000 lbs.**, **69000 lbs.**

3 On the Standard toolbar, click the Save button.

4 On the Excel window, click the Close button.

Excel closes and Word appears. The figures that you typed in the Product Availability worksheet are updated automatically and appear in the Word document. Your screen should look similar to the following illustration.

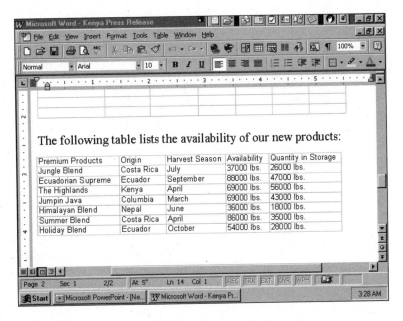

5 On the Standard toolbar, click the Save button.

6 Close the Kenya Press Release file.

IMPORTANT If the source filename or location changes, the link between the files will be broken. To reestablish the link, you must update the field code that creates the link to reflect the new filename or location. On the Edit menu, click Links, select the link that you need to reestablish, and then click Change Source. In the Change Links dialog box, select a new filename or location to reestablish the link.

Importing a Worksheet into a Document

Importing converts a file from the source program into a format that the destination program can interpret. When you import a file, you open it in the destination program. The file has all the functionality of a file created in the source program. As mentioned earlier, when you import a file, you convert its format to that of the destination program.

Importing a file to a different file format is the best technique to use when your project meets all the following criteria:

- You need all the information in a file created by another program.

- You want to bring the file from the other program into the current program.

- You need to edit the information without altering the original file, and you can do so by using the resources of the destination program.

When you import a file, you use the Open command, and then you select the file format in which the file was created. When you open the file, a copy is automatically converted and opened in the file format of the program you are opening the file in.

NOTE When you import a file, the source file still exists in its original file format. When you save the imported file, you can choose to save it either under its original file format or using the new file format. If you choose the latter, you have two versions of the file—the source file saved with the original file format and the new file saved with the destination file format.

The Marketing department has asked you to provide them with a copy of the Future Products worksheet to be included with the Kenya Press Release. The Marketing department would like help importing the Excel worksheet into a Word document, so they can evaluate how the information will look in a document.

Import a file

In this exercise, you import an Excel worksheet into a new Word document.

New

Open

1 On the Standard toolbar, click the New button.

A new Word document appears.

2 On the Standard toolbar, click the Open button.

The Open dialog box appears.

3 Click the Files Of Type down arrow, and then click All Files.

All files in the current folder are displayed, regardless of the program they were created in.

4 From your Office 97 SBS Practice\Lesson 4 folder, open the Future Products workbook.

The Open Worksheet dialog box appears.

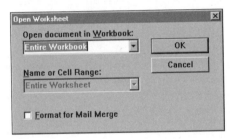

5 Click OK.

The Excel worksheet is imported into the Word document. The worksheet appears as if it had been created using Word. Your screen should look similar to the following illustration.

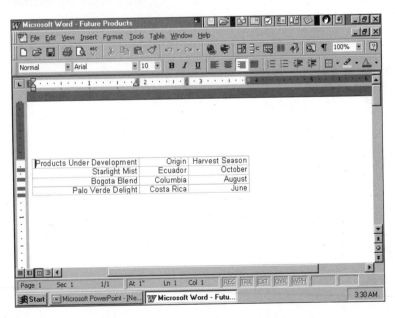

6 Save the document as **Imported Products** in your Office 97 SBS Practice\Lesson 4 folder.

7 Close the Imported Products file.

Creating and Tracking a Journal Entry

In Microsoft Outlook, you can use the Journal folder to record all your daily activities in a timeline format. A horizontal timeline enables you to track information in daily, weekly, or monthly increments. Using this information management tool, you can track the time you spend on any activity.

Your journal entries create a record of your interactions with important contacts and the time you spend working on documents. For example, if you are integrating documents from various sources and working on multiple projects, you can monitor project details as well as the time you spend on each project.

The Kenya Press Release has been completed using integrated information. The Marketing department must now review the information for content and accuracy before it can be distributed. You have also been notified that you must keep track of how much time you spend on each of your projects. You use your journal to track your tasks.

NOTE   By default, all Office 97 programs installed on your computer are automatically tracked in your journal. The date, along with the time you open, close, and save files in these programs, creates a journal entry. To change the default settings, on the Tools menu, click Options. On the Journal tab, clear the check boxes of the programs in which you do not want to record your actions.

Create a journal entry

In this exercise, you create a journal entry for reviewing the press release by the Marketing department.

1 Start Outlook using the Pamela Miller profile.

My Computer

2 On the Outlook Bar, click the Other shortcut bar, and then click the My Computer icon.

The contents of your computer filing system appear in the My Computer window.

3 In the My Computer window, double-click the Drive C icon, and then double-click the Office 97 SBS Practice folder.

4   In the Office 97 SBS Practice window, double-click the Lesson 4 folder.

The contents of your Office 97 SBS Practice\Lesson 4 folder are displayed.

5   On the Outlook Bar, click the Outlook shortcut bar icon.

Be sure that the Journal icon appears on the Outlook Bar.

Journal

6   Drag the Kenya Press Release icon from the Lesson 4 window to the Journal icon on the Outlook Bar.

The journal entry window appears. Kenya Press Release is the subject of the journal entry, Document is the journal entry type, and a shortcut to the Kenya Press Release document appears in the note area. Your screen should look similar to the following illustration.

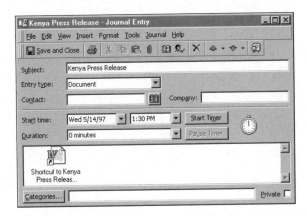

Add details to the journal entry

In this exercise, you add a note describing the task and its scheduled duration.

If the journal entry is scheduled to begin at a later date, you can click the Start Date down arrow to select the data the entry will occur.

1   Be sure that the insertion point appears in the note area, and then type **Marketing department to verify content and accuracy.**

The note further explains the journal entry.

2   Click the Duration down arrow, and then click 1 hour.

By selecting a duration of 1 hour, you're noting that it will take the Marketing department approximately 1 hour to review the Kenya Press Release for content and accuracy.

3   On the Standard toolbar, click the Save And Close button.

The journal entry window closes, and the Lesson 4 window opens.

Track your work

In this exercise, you view the work you've done with files.

1 Click the Journal icon on the Outlook Bar.

A timescale appears in the Journal window. The current date is shown.

2 Click the plus sign (+) next to the "Entry Type: Document" heading.

The category expands, and an icon for the Kenya Press Release appears on the timeline at the time the journal entry was created.

3 Click the plus sign (+) next to the "Entry Type: Microsoft Word" heading.

The category expands. All Word documents with which you have worked appear as icons. Your screen should look similar to the following illus-tration.

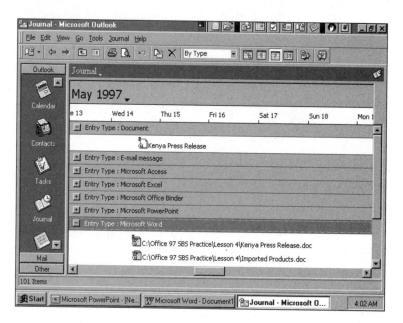

 NOTE If you'd like to build on the skills that you learned in this lesson, you can do the One Step Further. Otherwise, skip to "Finish the lesson."

One Step Further: Breaking an Object Link

If you find that you no longer need to have an object linked, you can break the link. When you break a link, the information remains in the destination document as a static object; it cannot be updated or edited. For example, perhaps you have created a link between sales figures in a worksheet and a report for an upcoming meeting. Once the report is finalized there is no need for the link to remain because the sales figures do not need to be updated.

The Kenya Press Release is ready to be distributed. To ensure that the current figures in the press release remain unchanged from this point forward, you will break the link between the Product Availability worksheet and the Kenya Press Release document.

Break a link to an object

In this exercise, you break the link to convert the object to a static object.

Open

1 On the taskbar, click the Microsoft Word button.

2 On the Standard toolbar, click the Open button.

The Open dialog box appears.

3 From your Office 97 SBS Practice\Lesson 4 folder, open the Kenya Press Release document.

4 On the Edit menu, click Links.

The Links dialog box appears.

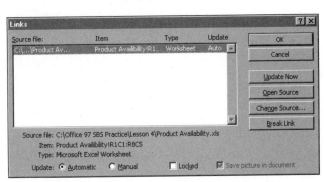

5 Be sure that the Product Availability source file is selected, and then click Break Link.

A message appears asking you to confirm the breaking of the link.

6 Click Yes.

The link is removed from the Links list, and the dialog box closes. The link between the Word document and the Excel worksheet is broken.

7   Press CTRL+END, and then click the Product Availability table.

Although the Product Availability table appears the same, it is now a static object. If the information in the Product Availability worksheet changes, the information in the Kenya Press Release document will not be updated.

Save

8   On the Standard toolbar, click the Save button.

9   On the Word window, click the Close button.

The Outlook window appears.

Finish the lesson

1   In the Journal window, click the Kenya Press Release icon under the Entry Type: Document heading.

Delete

2   On the Standard toolbar, click the Delete button.

The Kenya Press Release entry is deleted from your journal.

3   On the Outlook window, click the Close button.

4   On the PowerPoint window, click the Close button.

Lesson Summary

To	Do this
Export a file to Word from PowerPoint	Open the presentation. On the File menu, point to Send To, and click Microsoft Word. Click the Outline Only option button, and then click OK. On the File menu, click Save As. Click the Save As Type down arrow, and click Word Document.
Embed an object from an existing file	In the destination file, click where you want to insert the embedded object. On the Insert menu, click Object. Click the Create From File tab. Click Browse, and then locate the file to embed. Click OK. *or* In the source file, select the information to embed, and then click Copy. In the destination file, click where you want to insert the embedded object. On the Edit menu, click Paste Special, click Paste, and then click OK.

To	Do this	Button
Edit an embedded object	Double-click the embedded object to open the object's source program. Edit the object, and then click outside the object when you're finished.	
Embed a new object	Click where you want to embed the new object. On the Insert menu, click Object. On the Create New tab, click the type of object in the Object Type box, and then click OK. Edit and resize the object as needed. Click outside the object when you're finished.	
Link an object between two programs	In the source file, select the information to be linked, and then click Copy. In the destination file, click where you want to insert the linked object. On the Edit menu, click Paste Special, click the Paste Link option button, and then click OK.	
Import a file	In the Open dialog box of the current program, click the Files Of Type down arrow, and then select the file format of the file to be imported or select All Files. Click the filename you want to import, and then click OK.	
Create a journal entry from an existing file	On the Outlook Bar, click the My Computer icon, and then locate the file for the new entry. Click the Outlook shortcut bar, and then drag the file in the Information viewer to the Journal icon. Enter the journal entry details, and then click the Save And Close button on the Standard toolbar.	Save and Close

For online information about	On the Help menu, click Contents And Index, click the Index tab, and then type
Exporting presentation text to a Word document	*PowerPoint*: Microsoft Word, exporting data to
Embedding an object from another program	embedded objects
Linking an object between two programs	linked objects
Importing a file	*Word*: importing data
Creating a journal entry	*Outlook*: journal entries, archiving and then creating

Creating and Managing a Shared Workbook

Estimated time
35 min.

In this lesson you will learn how to:

- Integrate workbook data with other programs.
- Collaborate with your co-workers using a shared workbook.
- Use tasks to track project activities.

In the previous lesson, you created a workbook from files created in other Microsoft Office 97 programs. One advantage to this is the opportunity to collaborate with your co-workers. Using Office 97, you can give your co-workers full access to your files for review and editing. If your time is limited, they can even work on the same files simultaneously and see each other's changes. You can then review conflicting changes, view specific information about each change, and decide whether to keep or discard the changes. Using Microsoft Outlook, you can also manage your projects and assign tasks to track your progress.

In this lesson, you will create and manage a shared Microsoft Excel workbook to be included in The Kenya Coffee Company's annual report. You will share the workbook with others on a network resource, and you will update the workbook to reflect changes made by your co-workers. Finally, you will use Outlook to track your tasks and activities.

Start the lesson

In this exercise, you open an Excel workbook detailing this year's consolidated income statement for The Kenya Coffee Company. You also open a Word document that you will integrate with the workbook.

Open Office Document

1   On the Office Shortcut Bar, click the Open Office Document button.

The Open Office Document dialog box appears.

2   From your Office 97 SBS Practice\Lesson 5 folder, open the Income workbook.

The workbook consists of financial information detailing the consolidated income statement for The Kenya Coffee Company.

3   Save the file as **Net Income** in your Office 97 SBS Practice\Lesson 5 folder.

4   On the Office Shortcut Bar, click the Open Office Document button.

5   From your Office 97 SBS Practice\Lesson 5 folder, open the Vision document.

6   Save the document as **Kenya Vision** in your Office 97 SBS Practice\Lesson 5 folder.

Integrating Workbook Data and Document Text

As you work in Office 97, you will find many situations where it is advantageous to integrate information between programs. For example, you could include text from a Word document in a workbook or include an Excel chart in a Word document. You can link, embed, copy, or paste easily between Office 97 programs such as Word and Excel without having to learn new buttons or menu commands.

 NOTE To review integration methods in each Office 97 program, see Appendix C, "Integration Techniques."

Embedding Document Text in a Workbook

The previous lesson discussed how to embed information created in one file (the source file) into another file (the destination file). After you embed an object, you can edit it by clicking on it in the destination file. You can then use the resources of the source program to edit the embedded object.

You can embed an object by using the Object command on the Insert menu, specifying the file, and then embedding the file as an object. You can also use the Paste Special command on the Edit menu. Each method provides different options depending on your specific needs.

The Net Income workbook is to become part of The Kenya Coffee Company's annual report. To spice up the financial information, you include a quote from the Kenya Vision document in a worksheet in the Net Income workbook.

Embed document text in an Excel worksheet

In this exercise, you embed text from a Word document in a worksheet.

Copy

1 In the Kenya Vision document, scroll downward and select the text that begins with "Financial consistency does not" and ends with "universe of our business." in the fifth paragraph.

2 On the Standard toolbar, click the Copy button.

The selected text is copied to the Clipboard.

3 On the taskbar, click the Microsoft Excel button.

4 On the Consolidated Income Statement worksheet, click cell A15.

Cell A15 is selected.

5 On the Edit menu, choose Paste Special.

The Paste Special dialog box appears.

6 Be sure that Microsoft Word Document Object is selected in the As box, and that the Paste option button is selected.

Selecting the Paste option button ensures that the contents of the Clipboard will be embedded in the worksheet.

To change the size of an object and retain its proportions, hold down CTRL while dragging a sizing handle.

7 Click OK.

Excel embeds a copy of the Kenya Vision text in the worksheet. You can edit the embedded object at any time by double-clicking it. Your screen should look similar to the following illustration.

Word text embedded in Excel worksheet

95

Edit the embedded object

In this exercise, you use Word tools to format the quote you embedded in the worksheet.

1 Double-click the embedded Word text.

The menus and toolbars unique to Word appear at the top of the window. You can now use these to edit the embedded object. A ruler and sizing handles are also displayed. Your screen should look like the following illustration.

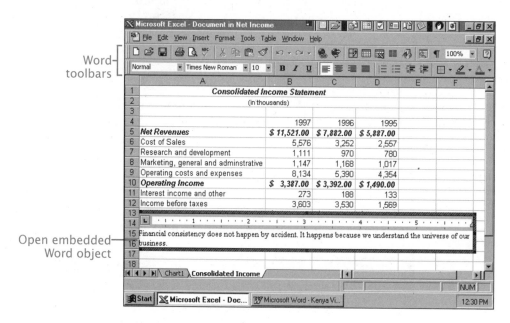

2 Drag to select the embedded text.

3 On the Formatting toolbar in Word, click the Bold button.

The embedded text is now formatted bold.

Bold

If necessary, use the sizing handles around the embedded object to adjust its size.

4 On the Formatting toolbar in Word, click the Font down arrow, and then click Arial.

5 In the embedded Word text, enclose the embedded text in quotation marks.

6 Click outside the embedded object.

The menus and toolbars change back to those of Excel.

7 On the Standard toolbar, click the Save button.

Save

Linking a Worksheet Chart to a Document

In the previous lesson, you learned how to link information created in the source file into the destination file. When you change the information in the source file, the linked object in the destination file is updated automatically. This is because you've established a link between the two files, even though they exist in different programs. To link pieces of information, use the Copy and Paste Special commands on the Edit menu. To link an entire file, use the Object command on the Insert menu.

The Consolidated Income Chart in the Net Income workbook needs to appear in the Kenya Vision document. The chart will be updated several times before the document is mailed. You link the chart to the document to ensure that it contains the most current information when it is mailed. You then find out that there is an error in the Consolidated Income Statement and update the information.

Link a chart in a document

In this exercise, you link a chart in a workbook to a document.

If the Copy button is not active, try clicking farther away from the chart body.

Copy

1 Click the Chart 1 worksheet tab.

   The Chart toolbar and Chart 1 appear.

2 Click the white area surrounding the chart.

   The entire Consolidated Income chart should be selected. Chart Area should appear on the Chart toolbar.

3 On the Standard toolbar, click the Copy button.

4 On the taskbar, click the Microsoft Word button.

5 In the document window, click the blank line below the sentence that begins "The following chart is a graphical representation."

6 On the Edit menu, click Paste Special.

   The Paste Special dialog box appears.

7 Be sure that Microsoft Excel Chart Object is selected in the As box, and then click the Paste Link option button.

   The Paste Link option button creates a link between the original information in Excel, the source file, and the destination file in Word.

8 Click OK.

   The Excel information is inserted and linked to the Word document. Whenever the information changes in the Excel chart, the information in the Word document will be automatically updated.

Change the object format and size

In this exercise, you format the linked chart object to wrap the document text around it to the right, and then resize the object.

1   Be sure that the linked object is selected.

2   On the Format menu, click Object.

The Format Object dialog box appears.

3   Click the Wrapping tab, click Tight under Wrapping Style, and then click Right under Wrap To.

4   Click OK.

5   Drag the right center sizing handle on the linked object to the 5½-inch mark on the ruler.

Your screen should look similar to the following illustration.

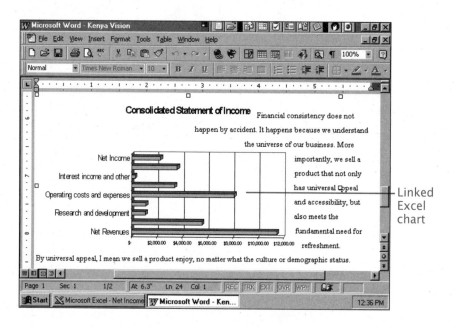

Update a linked object

In this exercise, you enter a change in the Consolidated Income worksheet. You then view how the change affects the chart in the Word document.

You can also double-click a linked object to open the source file.

1   On the taskbar, click the Microsoft Excel button, and then click the Consolidated Income worksheet tab.

2   Click cell B5, type **14521** and then press ENTER.

3   Click the Chart 1 worksheet tab.

The changes made in the Consolidated Income Statement worksheet are reflected in the chart.

4   On the Standard toolbar, click the Save button.

5   Close the Net Income workbook.

Save

6   On the taskbar, click the Microsoft Word button.

The chart is updated in the Word document.

TROUBLESHOOTING   If the linked object does not automatically update, click the linked object to select it, and then, on the Edit menu, choose Links. Click the "Update: Automatic" option button under Update, and then click Update Now. Click OK.

7   On the Standard toolbar, click the Save button.

8   On the Word window, click the Close button.

IMPORTANT   If the source filename or location changes, the link between the files will be broken. To reestablish the link, you must update the field code that creates the link to reflect the new filename or location. On the Edit menu, click Links, select the link that you need to reestablish, and then click Change Source. From this dialog box, you can select the new filename or location to reestablish the link.

Sharing a Workbook with Others

For a demonstration of how to create and modify a shared workbook, double-click the Camcorder Files On The Internet shortcut on your Desktop or connect to the Internet address listed on p. xxx.

Networks can provide a powerful medium for sharing and publishing information. You can share files from all the Office 97 programs over a network or distribute copies when a network is not available. For example, you created a workbook using information from other Office 97 files, and now you want your co-workers to review and verify the information. By making the workbook available to your co-workers over a network, you can ensure that everyone is using the most up-to-date information, that the edits can be made at the same time, and that everyone can see each other's changes.

Highlighting Changes in a Shared Worksheet

When several people are contributing to a workbook, it's important to be able to identify who originated each change. It can also be helpful to add *cell comments* to the workbook to explain how information is gathered or derived. By tracking changes and adding supplemental comments, you can monitor the development of a workbook and add explanations to workbook cells.

When you share a workbook with your co-workers, managing conflicting changes can be a challenge. Using Office 97, you can easily track the change history of a workbook to get information about past changes and conflicting changes that are accepted or rejected by other users.

You can also clarify information in a workbook by attaching a supplemental comment to a cell. For example, a cell might contain a reference to another worksheet or a formula that points to data in another location. To ensure that another user can identify the source of information, you can add a comment to the appropriate cell that explains the cell's contents.

IMPORTANT To edit a shared workbook created in Excel 97, you must use Excel 97. You cannot use earlier versions of Excel to edit shared files.

The necessary changes have been made to the Net Income workbook. You now need the Accounting department and other members of the annual report team to check the workbook for accuracy. By sharing the workbook, you can make sure everyone reviews the workbook, and then you can review all comments before making any changes to the workbook.

Create a shared workbook

In this exercise, you turn the Net Income workbook into a shared workbook.

WARNING When you use a shared workbook, you cannot delete worksheets, insert charts or objects, create a data table or PivotTable, create macros, or insert or delete blocks of cells. If you need to do any of these tasks, do so before you share the workbook. For additional limitations, refer to Online Help.

Open Office Document

1 On the Office Shortcut Bar, click the Open Office Document button.

The Open Office Document dialog box appears.

2 From your Office 97 SBS Practice\Lesson 5 folder, open the Assets worksheet.

This worksheet summarizes the assets of The Kenya Coffee Company.

3 Save the workbook as **Kenya Assets** in your Office 97 SBS Practice\Lesson 5 folder.

4 On the Tools menu, click Share Workbook.

The Share Workbook dialog box appears. The Editing tab is selected.

5 Select the Allow Changes By More Than One User At The Same Time check box.

By selecting this check box, you see information about past changes to a workbook and merged copies of a workbook.

Click here to allow editing by multiple users.

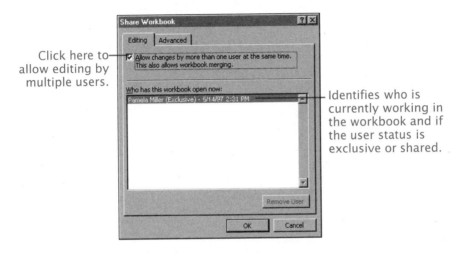

Identifies who is currently working in the workbook and if the user status is exclusive or shared.

6 Click OK.

A message appears, informing you that the workbook will now be saved.

7 Click OK.

Your screen should look similar to the following illustration.

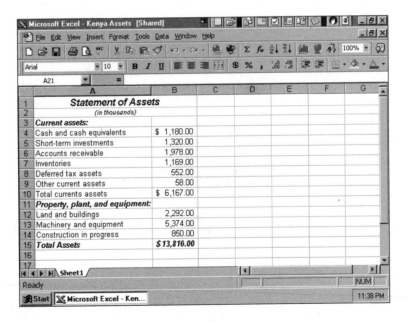

Modify the shared workbook

In this exercise, you modify the shared workbook, and then highlight the changes.

1 Click cell B7, and then type **2245**

2 Click cell B14, type **1250** and then press ENTER.

3 On the Tools menu, point to Track Changes, and then click Highlight Changes.

The Highlight Changes dialog box appears. You can use this dialog box to highlight changes by author, date, or location. You can also request a list of all the changes on a separate worksheet.

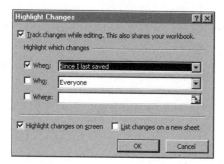

4 Be sure the following check boxes are selected: Track Changes While Editing, When: Since I Last Saved, and Highlight Changes On Screen. Click OK.

The changes you made earlier in this exercise are highlighted.

5 Position the pointer over cell B7.

A comment box appears. It contains the name of the user who made the change, when the change was made, and the original contents of the cell prior to the change. Your screen should look similar to the following illustration.

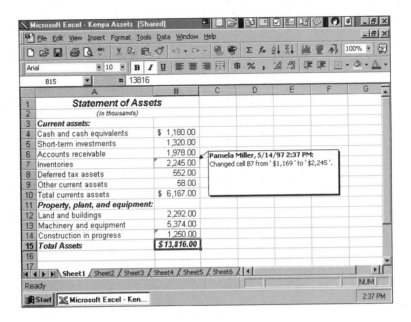

6   Position the pointer over cell B14.

The comment box displays the information regarding the change.

7   On the Standard toolbar, click the Save button.

Save

Add comments to a worksheet

In this exercise, you attach a supplemental comment to a cell to store additional information about the cell contents.

1   Click cell B12.

2   On the Insert menu, click Comment.

A comment box containing your name appears.

3   Type **According to the Facilities department, the correct figure is 2892.**

To display a cell comment at all times, use the right mouse button to click the cell containing the comment, and then click Show Comment.

4   Click outside the comment box.

The comment box closes, and the comment indicator (a red triangle in the upper-right corner of the cell) appears.

5   Position the pointer over cell B12.

The comment appears. Your screen should look similar to the following illustration.

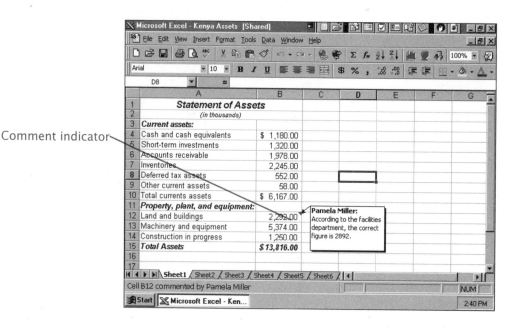

Comment indicator

Save

6 On the Standard toolbar, click the Save button.

 NOTE Comments are anchored to the contents of the cell, not the specific cell reference. For example, when you sort items in a worksheet, any comments attached to an item move with the item in the sorted rows or columns.

Reviewing Changes in a Workbook

When you review a workbook that has been edited by others, you want to know what changes have been made, who made the changes, and when the changes were made. With a shared workbook, you can review each change and either accept or reject them on a case-by-case basis.

Accept or reject changes to a workbook

In this exercise, you review each change made to the shared workbook and accept or reject the changes.

1 On the Tools menu, point to Track Changes, and then click Accept Or Reject Changes.

The Select Changes To Accept Or Reject dialog box appears. You can use this dialog box to view changes to a workbook by date, author, or cell range.

2 Be sure that the When Not Yet Reviewed check box is selected, and then click OK.

You can drag the dialog box to the lower-right corner of the document window.

The Accept Or Reject Changes dialog box appears, displaying the details of the first change. From this dialog box you can accept or reject any changes. Be sure that cell B7 is not hidden by the dialog box.

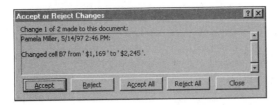

3 Click Accept.

The proposed change is accepted, and the highlight and comment are removed. The details about the next change appear in the Accept Or Reject Changes dialog box.

4 Click Reject.

The proposed change is discarded and the original information appears in the cell. The Accept Or Reject Changes dialog box closes.

5 On the Standard toolbar, click the Save button.

6 On the Excel window, click the Close button.

NOTE In addition to highlighting changes, you can also track changes using the change history. The change history enables you to see information from past editing sessions, including the author of the changes and the data that was entered and later replaced.

Creating Tasks

Whether you are working on a specific project or your daily activities, it can be important to keep track of what you have done and to keep a list of what you have to do. Using Outlook, you can create task lists and monitor your activities in files. You can keep a record of when a task was assigned to you, how long it took to complete, and when it was completed. You can monitor the time you spend on different projects as well as how often you have to access a specific file. You can also use Outlook to keep track of tasks you've assigned to others.

In Outlook, you can track many different elements of a task. You can enter the information before the task occurs to remind you to do it or after the task occurs as a record of what you did. The following is a list of some of the information you can track for a task.

- An estimate of how long it will take to complete the task.
- The task priority in relation to other tasks.
- Constraints, such as start date and end date.
- Actuals, such as date completed and number of work hours.

The Net Income workbook is ready for review by the Accounting department before you complete your final review and include it in the annual report. Before you send the workbook off for review, you create a task to track the time it takes the Accounting department to review the workbook, and for you to review it afterwards. You are also informed that you will be responsible for the final review of the workbook each month.

Create a task

In this exercise, you create a task to track the review of a workbook.

Tasks

New Task

1 Start Outlook using the Pamela Miller profile.

2 On the Outlook Bar, click the Tasks icon.

The contents of the Tasks folder appear in the Information viewer, including the sample task.

3 On the Standard toolbar, click the New Task button.

A blank task form appears, with the insertion point in the Subject box.

4 Type **Final review of the Kenya Assets workbook.**

5 Click in the notes area.

You can use the notes area to insert a file or type a brief explanation.

6 Type **Workbook being reviewed by Accounting department. Verify Accounting comments when returned.**

NOTE You can use the Status tab on the task form to record information about the completion of a task. For example, you can click in the Billing Information field and type any information related to billing, such as hours or the account to be billed.

Change settings for the task

Instead of typing a specific date, you can type a brief description, such as "next Wednesday" or "one week from today."

In this exercise, you set a start date and an end date for a task. You also change the priority of a task.

1 Click the Due down arrow, and then click the next business day on the calendar.

2 Click the Start down arrow, and then click Today.

The task is set to start on today's date and end the next business day.

If you don't set a reminder time, the default reminder time will appear on the task form.

3 Click the Priority down arrow, and then click High.

You can use the Priority to set the importance level of the task. By setting a priority level, you can sort your tasks based on their priority. You screen should look similar to the following illustration.

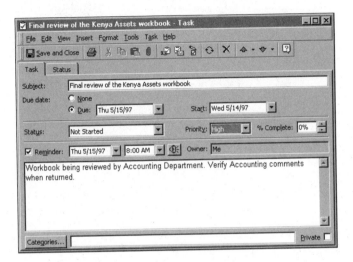

4 On the Standard toolbar, click the Save And Close button.

The changes to the task are saved, and the task appears in your task list with its due date.

Change the task to a recurring task

In this exercise, you change the Final Review task to a recurring task for the next 12 months.

1 Double-click the Final Review task in the Tasks window.

The task form opens.

Recurrence

2 On the Standard toolbar, click the Recurrence button.

The Task Recurrence dialog box appears. You use this dialog box to specify the interval at which this task repeats. Your screen should look similar to the following illustration.

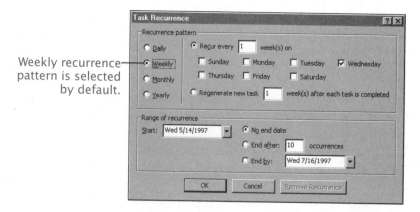

Weekly recurrence
pattern is selected
by default.

3   In the Task Recurrence dialog box, click the Monthly option button.

The frequency at which the task recurs is monthly. The dialog box displays options based on the time interval at which the task repeats.

4   Under Range Of Recurrence, click the End After option button.

5   Double-click the contents of the Occurrences box, type **12**, and then click OK.

The Task form appears.

6   On the Standard toolbar, click the Save And Close button.

The recurring task will end after 12 occurrences. In this case, the recurring task will end after 12 months. Your screen should look similar to the following illustration.

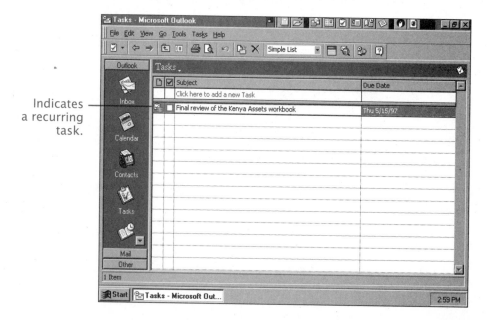

Indicates
a recurring
task.

7   On the Outlook window, click the Close button.

> ⚠ **NOTE**   If you'd like to build on the skills that you learned in this lesson, you can do the One Step Further. Otherwise, skip to "Finish the lesson."

One Step Further: Merging Different Workbook Versions

When working with a shared workbook, you might send separate copies of the workbook for review (for example, if you don't have a network, or if you want to keep separate copies of each person's comments). Once everyone has reviewed the shared workbook, you will want to compare the new versions to the original version. Suppose you forward copies of a shared workbook to each of your co-workers for review and comments. When the workbooks are returned, you could merge each version of the shared workbook together to view all the changes (shown as revision marks) at once. Merging copies of the same workbook lets you view all the changes, rather than opening or printing each file and comparing them one by one.

Merge different versions of a workbook

In this exercise, you compare different versions of the same shared workbook.

Open Office Document

You can only merge workbooks that are copies of the original shared workbook.

1   On the Office Shortcut Bar, click the Open Office Document button.

2   From your Office 97 SBS Practice\Lesson 5 folder, open the Shared Assets workbook.

3   On the Tools menu, click Merge Workbooks.

The Select Files To Merge Into Current Workbook dialog box appears.

4   From your Office 97 SBS Practice\Lesson 5 folder, click Asset Changes JS, hold SHIFT, click Asset Changes MD, and then click OK.

The two copies of the shared workbook, with changes, are merged with the Kenya Assets workbook.

5   Save the merged workbook as **Merged Asset Changes** in your Office 97 SBS Practice\Lesson 5 folder.

View changes in a merged workbook

1   On the Tools menu, point to Track Changes, and then click Highlight Changes.

The Highlight Changes dialog box appears.

2 Click the When down arrow, click Not Yet Reviewed, and then click OK.

All changes that have not been reviewed are highlighted. Because both reviewers made changes, different highlight colors appear. Your screen should look similar to the following illustration.

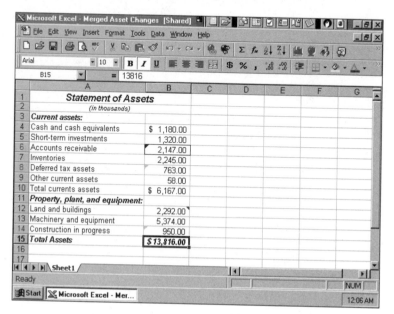

3 Place the pointer over cell B6.

The changes made by JS appear.

4 On the Standard toolbar, click the Save button.

5 On the Excel window, click the Close button.

Save

Finish the lesson

1 Delete the Final Review task in Outlook.

2 Close all open windows.

Lesson Summary

To	Do this	Button
Embed an object from an existing file	In the source file, select the information to embed, and then click the Copy button. In the destination file, position the insertion point where the information is to be embedded. On the Edit menu, click Paste Special, click the Paste option button, and then click OK.	
Edit and update an embedded object	Double-click the embedded object to open the object's source program. Edit the object. Click outside the object when you're finished.	
Link an object between two files	In the source file, select the information to be linked, and then click the Copy button. In the destination file, position the insertion point where the information is to be linked. On the Edit menu, click Paste Special, click the Paste Link option button, and then click OK.	
Edit and update a linked object	In the source file, edit the linked information. The object in the destination file is automatically updated.	
Create a shared workbook	Open the workbook to be shared. On the Tools menu, click Share Workbook. Select the Allow Editing By More Than One User At The Same Time check box, and then click OK.	
Highlight the changes in a shared workbook	Open the shared workbook. On the Tools menu, point to Track Changes, click Highlight Changes, and then click OK.	
Add comments to a workbook	Select the cell to which you want to attach a comment. On the Insert menu, click Comment. Type your comment, and then click outside the comment box.	

To	Do this	Button
Accept or reject changes in a shared workbook	Open the shared workbook. On the Tools menu, point to Track Changes, and then click Accept Or Reject Changes. Accept or reject the highlighted change by clicking the appropriate button.	
Create a task	Click the Tasks icon on the Outlook Bar. Click the New Task button. Enter the task information in the task form, and then click the Save And Close button.	
Change a task to a recurring task	Double-click the task you want to make recurring or create a new task. Click the Recurrence button. Select recurrence options, and then click OK.	

For online information about	On the Help menu, click Contents And Index, click the Index tab, and then type
Embedding an object	embedded objects
Linking an object	linked objects
Creating a shared workbook	*Excel*: sharing information
Adding comments to a workbook	*Excel*: comments
Creating a task	*Outlook*: tasks

Review & Practice

You will review and practice how to:

Estimated time
30 min.

- Create tasks to track your activities.
- Embed information between programs.
- Create a form letter.
- Share a workbook with others.
- Link information between programs.

Before you move on to Part 3, you can practice the skills you learned in Part 2 by working through the steps in this Review & Practice section. You will create tasks to remind you of things you need to do, embed information between programs, communicate with others using a form letter, collaborate with your co-workers using a shared workbook, and link information between programs.

Scenario

As manager of the Human Resources department at The Kenya Coffee Company, you are overseeing a project for the warehouse manager. You are responsible for tracking the project tasks, linking and embedding information, and creating a shared workbook.

Step 1: Create Project Tasks

Your first task is to assign employees to help the Facilities department inventory the surplus of coffee at the end of the year. You create a task list to summarize the tasks and their priorities.

1   Using Microsoft Outlook and the Pamela Miller profile, create the following tasks:

Determine the number of employees needed to inventory the coffee.

Review employee schedules to determine availability for inventory.

Assign the employees to the inventory.

2   Change the priority of all the tasks to High.

3   Set the start date for the tasks so that the first task starts on the business day after today, and each additional task starts one business day after the other with a duration of one day each.

4   Set the recurrence pattern to Yearly for each task with 5 occurrences.

5   Close Outlook.

For more information about	See
Creating tasks	Lesson 5

Step 2: Embed Workbook Data in a Document

The warehouse manager provided you with a workbook estimating the year-end coffee inventory. The estimates are fixed, so you won't need to make any content changes. You embed the workbook data in a letter that will be sent to the employees who will conduct the inventory.

1   From your Office 97 SBS Practice\Review & Practice 2 folder, open the Kenya Inventory document, and save it as **Year-End Inventory**

2   Create a blank line following the sentence, "The following table is an estimate of the coffee surplus."

3   Embed the Surplus Coffee workbook at the end of the letter. The Surplus Coffee file is located in your Office 97 SBS Practice\Review & Practice 2 folder. (Hint: Use the Object command on the Insert menu.)

4   Save the document.

For more information about	See
Integrating workbook data and document text	Lesson 5

Step 3: Communicate with Others Using a Form Letter

Now that you have created the Year-End Inventory letter, you want to send it to the employees who will conduct the inventory. Using the addresses in a workbook, you personalize a form letter by performing a mail merge between the two programs.

1   Start the mail merge process using the Year-End Inventory letter as the main document and the Regional Addresses database table in your Office 97 SBS Practice folder as the data source. (Hint: Use the Mail Merge command on the Tools menu in Microsoft Word.)

2   Insert merge fields to add the address and salutation at the beginning of the form letter. (Hint: Insert the merge fields <<FIRSTNAME>>, <<LASTNAME>>, <<ADDRESS>>, <<CITY>>, <<STATEORPROVINCE>>, and <<POSTALCODE>>.)

3   Merge the form letters with the data source to create a new document containing all the merged letters.

4   Save the merged documents as **Employee Memo** in your Office 97 SBS Practice\Review & Practice 2 folder, and then close the window.

5   Save the main document file as **Employee Memo Form** in your Office 97 SBS Practice\Review & Practice 2 folder, and then close the window.

For more information about	See
Starting a mail merge	Lesson 3
Merging a data source into a main document	Lesson 3

Step 4: Create a Shared Workbook

To ensure efficiency in the project, you create a shared workbook detailing the year-end coffee inventory data. That way, the employees conducting the inventory can enter information simultaneously and see the most up-to-date information.

1   From your Office 97 SBS Practice\Review & Practice 2 folder, open the Coffee Inventory workbook and save it as **Summary Inventory**

2   Allow editing by more than one user. (Hint: Use the Share Workbook command on the Tools menu.)

3   If you are prompted to save the file, save it under its existing name.

For more information about	See
Sharing a workbook with others	Lesson 5

Step 5: Link Workbook Data to a Document

After receiving the final inventory figures, you want to include the information in a report to the Accounting department. You're not expecting the information to change; however, if it does, you want the information in your report to be updated automatically. Link the information from the workbook to the report.

1. From your Office 97 SBS Practice\Review & Practice 2 folder, open the Final Inventory document, and save it as **Complete Inventory**

2. Position the insertion point on the blank line following the sentence that begins with "If you have questions or concerns regarding this data."

3. Switch to Microsoft Excel, and select cells A1 through B9 in the Summary Inventory worksheet.

4. Link the workbook data to the letter. (Hint: Use the Paste Special command on the Edit menu.)

5. Save and close letter.

For more information about	See
Integrating worksheet data in a document	Lesson 4

Finish the Review & Practice

1. On the Word window, click the Close button.
2. On the Excel window, click the Close button.
3. In Outlook, delete the three Coffee Inventory tasks.
4. Close all open windows.

Accomplishing Everyday Tasks in Record Time

Part **3**

Summarizing Complex Data

Estimated time
35 min.

In this lesson you will learn how to:

- Retrieve data from a database.
- Summarize data using a PivotTable.
- Create a chart based on data in a PivotTable.
- Send a workbook using e-mail.

If you are unfamiliar with using a database or find that the database design you are using does not suit your needs, it can be frustrating trying to make use of the information stored there. In either case, bringing that data into a workbook might make managing and summarizing your data easier and more efficient. For example, you might want to create a report on the sales figures for your larger clients. If you have a database containing detailed client information including sales figures, you would only need part of the information in the database. Creating a *query* to generate a report is one way to summarize the information, but it has its limitations. To reorganize the information, you might need to create another query or another report. If you want a chart depicting the sales figures, a database is of no use.

Using Microsoft Office 97, you can retrieve data from a variety of sources (such as Microsoft Access or dBASE) using MS Query, and put the data in a Microsoft Excel workbook. You can then easily summarize the retrieved data using PivotTable dynamic views. PivotTable dynamic views give you greater flexibility and ease of use over most methods of summarizing information. You can also easily create a chart from the PivotTable data.

In this lesson, you will help a co-worker retrieve data from an Access database containing sales figures for The Kenya Coffee Company. You will then place the data in an Excel workbook, create a PivotTable to summarize the data, and use the data to create a chart. You will complete the task by sending the workbook via e-mail to your co-worker for review.

Start the lesson

In this exercise, you open an Excel workbook that contains the worksheets that will hold the third quarter sales figures for The Kenya Coffee Company.

Open Office Document

1   On the Office Shortcut Bar, click the Open Office Document button.

The Open Office Document dialog box appears.

2   From your Office 97 SBS Practice\Lesson 6 folder, open the Sales workbook.

The Sales workbook opens in Excel. Cell A4 is selected on the Sales Data worksheet.

3   Save the file as **Third Quarter Sales** in your Office 97 SBS Practice\ Lesson 6 folder.

Analyzing Database Information

For a demonstration of how to run MS Query and how to define a query filter, double-click the Camcorder Files On The Internet shortcut on your Desktop or connect to the Internet address listed on p. xxx.

If you aren't experienced with databases, you may find it intimidating when you need to find certain information in a database. If you are an experienced database user, you may be looking for more efficient ways to query information and return it to other programs for further use. No matter what your experience level, you can use MS Query, an add-in program, to create queries and retrieve data.

MS query is an easy-to-use yet powerful tool that retrieves and organizes database information from several popular database formats, including Access, dBASE, FoxPro, and Paradox, as well as SQL Servers and Text Drivers. With MS Query you can add and edit data, perform calculations, format data, sort data, and transfer data to other programs.

NOTE   For further information on using MS Query with data sources other than Access and returning MS Query results to non–Office 97 programs, see online Help.

A co-worker at The Kenya Coffee Company has asked for your help in summarizing sales data for the third quarter. The sales data is stored in an Access database file that contains all the sales figures for the year. You would like to retrieve just the data for the third quarter, create a summary of the data, and then create a chart to display the data graphically.

> **IMPORTANT** Microsoft Query is not installed as part of a typical installation of Microsoft Office 97. To install Microsoft Query, refer to Appendix B, "Adding Microsoft Office 97 Components," before continuing the lesson.

Run MS Query

In this exercise, you start MS Query and create a new data source to identify the file location of the data and the program it was created in.

1   On the Data menu, point to Get External Data, and then click Create New Query.

    MS Query starts, and the Choose Data Source dialog box appears. The text "<New Data Source>" is highlighted on the Databases tab.

2   Click OK.

    The Create New Data Source dialog box appears.

3   Type **96 Sales** in the What Name Do You Want To Give Your Data Source box.

    This is the name of the new data source reference you are creating. By naming the data source, you can use it at a later date by simply selecting the data source name in the Choose Data Source dialog box.

4   Click the Select A Driver For The Type Of Database You Want To Access down arrow, and then click Microsoft Access Driver (*.mdb).

    Access is the program that your database file was created in. Your dialog box look similar to the following illustration.

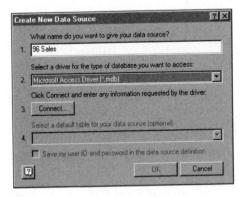

5   Click Connect.

    The ODBC Microsoft Access 97 Setup dialog box appears.

6   Click Select.

    The Select Database dialog box appears.

7 From your Office 97 SBS Practice folder, click Kenya Coffee Company, and then click OK.

The location of your database file and the program in which it was created are identified.

8 Click OK three more times.

The Query Wizard-Choose Columns dialog box appears. Your screen should look similar to the following illustration.

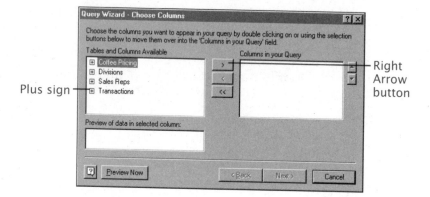

Define the query fields

In this exercise, you use the Query wizard to identify the database table that contains the divisional sales figures. You also define the specific *fields* within the table to be used in the divisional sales query.

1 Click the plus sign (+) next to Transactions in the Tables And Columns Available box to expand the list.

All of the fields available in the Transactions table appear.

2 Click Date, and then click the Right Arrow button.

The Date field is moved to the Columns In Your Query box.

3 Click Coffee Type, and then click the Right Arrow button.

The Coffee Type field is moved to the Columns In Your Query box.

4 Click Total Sale Price, and then click the Right Arrow button.

The Total Sale Price field is moved to the Columns In Your Query box.

5 Click Division, and then click the Right Arrow button.

The Division field is moved to the Columns In Your Query box.

6 Click Next.

The Query Wizard-Filter Data dialog box appears.

Define a query filter

Once you have determined what table and fields of information you will query for, you can further define the query using a *filter*. A filter allows you to retrieve a specific portion of your data, such as a date range. In this exercise, you create a filter to obtain the third quarter sales data only.

1   Click Date in the Column To Filter box.

The first drop-down box becomes active under Only Include Rows Where.

2   Click the first Date down arrow, and then click "is greater than or equal to."

3   In the second box, type **7/1/96**

4   Click the And option button.

The next criteria row becomes active.

5   Click the second Date down arrow, and then click "is less than or equal to."

6   In the second box, type **9/30/96**

The fields of data will be filtered to display only those transactions in the third quarter of 1996. Your dialog box should look similar to the following illustration.

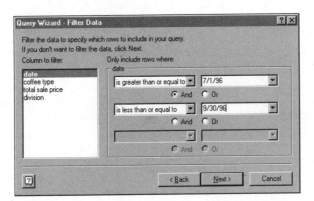

7   Click Next.

The Query Wizard-Sort Order dialog box appears.

8   Click Next.

The Query Wizard-Finish dialog box appears.

Return query data to Excel

Now that you have successfully retrieved the sales data for the third quarter, you want to summarize the data in a workbook. In this exercise, you save the query and then return the results of your query to a Excel workbook.

1 Click Save Query.

The Save As dialog box appears.

2 Save the query as **Third Quarter Query** in your Office 97 SBS Practice\Lesson 6 folder.

3 Be sure that the Return Data To Microsoft Excel option button is selected, and then click Finish.

The Returning External Data To Excel dialog box appears. The cell reference =$A$4 appears in the Existing Worksheet box. This is the starting position where the query data being returned to Excel will be placed.

Save

4 Click OK.

The third quarter sales data you queried appears in the Third Quarter Sales workbook. The External Data toolbar is displayed.

5 On the Standard toolbar, click the Save button.

Summarizing Data Using PivotTable Dynamic Views

Now that you have retrieved the necessary information from the sales database, you are faced with columns and rows of individual pieces of data. To create a report, you need to combine all this data into a cohesive summary that provides the necessary information at a glance.

With Excel, you can create *PivotTable* dynamic views to summarize your data. Each column, which will represent a field within the PivotTable, can be moved around to display different relationships. This is what makes a Pivot-Table a dynamic view. The arrangement of each field in the PivotTable can be quickly changed to display different orientations, which lets you focus on the data in a different way. For example, if you have sales figures based on the salesperson, department, and division, you might organize the PivotTable to show the division totals by department. Or, if you need to know how each salesperson is doing, you can reorganize the PivotTable to show the sales figures for each salesperson by division.

You can also update the PivotTable easily. The summarized data in a Pivot-Table is linked to the query list that the PivotTable is created from. If you change the data list, the PivotTable will reflect the changes when you execute the Refresh Data command.

Creating a PivotTable from Database Information

Creating a PivotTable is easy when you use the PivotTable wizard. All you need to do is select a cell within the data list you are using and then start the

PivotTable wizard. The PivotTable wizard presents each column of data as a field that can be placed in one of four areas within the PivotTable. The four areas of a PivotTable are Page, Column, Row, and Data. Each data field can be placed in any of the PivotTable areas. You can also change the location of each field as many times as it takes to develop a PivotTable that meets your needs.

Create a PivotTable

In this exercise, you create a PivotTable using the retrieved data from the sales database.

1 Be sure that at least one cell in the query list, or the entire query list that now appears in Excel, is selected.

2 On the Data menu, click PivotTable Report.

The PivotTable Wizard-Step 1 Of 4 dialog box appears.

3 Be sure that the Microsoft Excel List Or Database option button is selected in the Where Is The Data That You Want To Analyze area, and then click Next.

The PivotTable Wizard-Step 2 Of 4 dialog box appears. The Range field should display $A$4:$D$24.

4 Click Next.

The PivotTable Wizard-Step 3 Of 4 dialog box appears. Your screen should look similar to the following illustration.

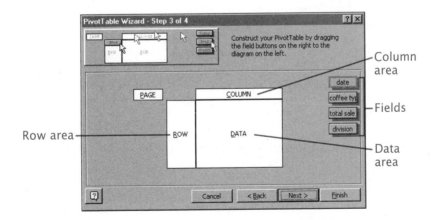

5 Drag the Division field to the Row area.

The division will appear as rows in the PivotTable.

6 Drag the Coffee Type field to the Column area.

7 Drag the Total Sale Price field to the Data area.

Your dialog box should look like the following illustration.

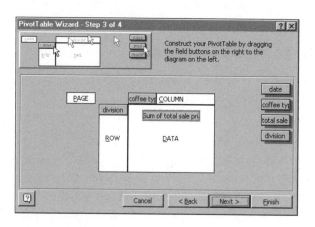

You can create more than one PivotTable from the same data list by indicating a different location on either an existing worksheet or a new worksheet.

8 Click Next.

The PivotTable Wizard-Step 4 Of 4 dialog box appears.

9 Click the Existing Worksheet option button.

If the PivotTable Wizard dialog box is covering cell A2, you can drag the dialog box to the right.

The PivotTable will be placed on an existing worksheet within the Third Quarter Sales workbook.

10 Click the Sales Summary worksheet tab, and then click cell A2.

The text 'Sales Summary'!$A$2 appears in the Existing Worksheet box.

11 Click Finish.

The PivotTable is created on the Sales Summary worksheet beginning at cell A2. The PivotTable toolbar appears. Your screen should look similar to the following illustration.

PivotTable—

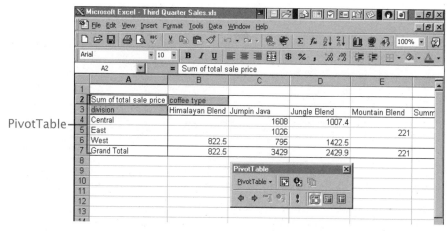

Save

12 On the Standard toolbar, click the Save button.

Change the layout of the PivotTable

In this exercise, you rearrange the PivotTable to summarize your data with a different layout and demonstrate how easy it is to manage a PivotTable.

PivotTable Wizard

1   Be sure that a cell within the PivotTable is selected.

2   On the PivotTable toolbar, click the PivotTable Wizard button.

The PivotTable Wizard-Step 3 Of 4 dialog box appears.

3   Drag the Coffee Type field to the Row area.

You can drag either the field button on the right side of the dialog box or the field button in one of the areas of the PivotTable layout.

4   Drag the Division field to the Column area, and then click Next.

The PivotTable Wizard-Step 4 Of 4 dialog box appears.

5   Be sure that =A2 appears in the Existing Worksheet box, and then click Finish.

The reorganized PivotTable replaces the previous PivotTable.

Save

6   On the Standard toolbar, click the Save button.

Creating Charts Using PivotTable Data

Now that you have created a summary of the third quarter sales data by creating a PivotTable, you need to provide a chart of the data for the annual report. In Excel, the Chart wizard can create a chart based on the PivotTable. Just like the link created between the data list and the PivotTable, a link will be created between the PivotTable and the chart. This way, the chart is always up to date.

Create a chart

In this exercise, you use the Chart wizard to create a chart of the third quarter sales figures from the PivotTable you just created.

1   On the PivotTable toolbar, click PivotTable.

A drop-down list appears.

If you cannot make the selection, repeat steps 1 and 2, and then try selecting the cells again.

2   Point to Select, and then click Enable Selection.

This will allow you to select any portion of the PivotTable.

3   Drag to select the range A3:D9, starting at cell D9.

If you try to drag from cell A3, you will change the PivotTable layout because this is a layout field. For the chart you are creating, it is not necessary to select the Grand Totals or the top row of the PivotTable.

Chart Wizard

4   On the Standard toolbar, click the Chart Wizard button.

The Chart Wizard-Step 1 Of 4-Chart Type dialog box appears.

5 Be sure that the Column chart type is selected and the first chart sub-type, Clustered Column, is selected.

6 Click Next.

The Chart Wizard-Step 2 Of 4-Chart Source Data dialog box appears. The Data Range field should display ='Sales Summary'!$A$3:$D$9.

7 Under Series In, click the Rows option button, and then click Next.

The Chart Wizard-Step 3 Of 4-Chart Options dialog box appears.

8 On the Titles tab, click in the Chart Title box, and then type **Third Quarter Coffee Sales**

9 Click Next.

The Chart Wizard-Step 4 Of 4-Chart Location dialog box appears.

10 Click the As Object In down arrow, click Sales Chart, and then click Finish.

The Third Quarter Coffee Sales chart appears on the Sales Chart worksheet. The Chart toolbar is displayed. Your screen should look similar to the following illustration.

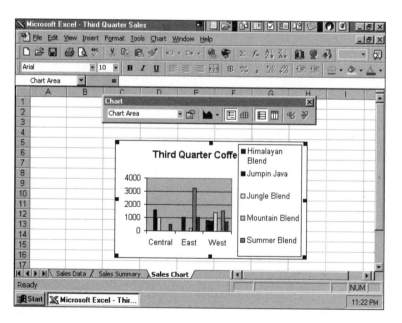

Resize a chart

In this exercise, you resize the chart to display the data.

1 Point to the top-middle sizing handle.

The pointer changes to a two-headed arrow.

You can also make the chart wider by dragging a middle sizing handle on either the right or left side.

2 Drag the sizing handle up to the top of the worksheet.

The chart is resized so that the data can be viewed more easily.

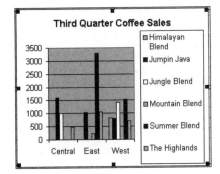

Save

3 On the Standard toolbar, click the Save button.

Sending Files in Messages

Suppose you need to send a workbook to your co-workers so they can review it or add information. You can mail files directly from any Office 97 program by inserting your file directly into your message. Sending files as attachments directly from a program (such as Excel) can save time. There is no need to open your mail program or sift through folders to find a file location.

When you send an attached file, your recipients can easily open the file by double-clicking the file icon. They can then copy the file to their own computer, and they can edit the file if they have the same program.

IMPORTANT Because you will be exploring the use of e-mail, you will need to have a mail program available to you and someone to whom you can send mail.

Send mail from Excel

In this exercise, while working in Excel, you mail a workbook to a co-worker for review.

1 On the File menu, point to Send To, and then click Mail Recipient. Use the Pamela Miller profile.

The Third Quarter Sales.XLS-Message window appears.

2 Click the To button.

Your address book appears in the Select Names dialog box.

3   Scroll to locate the mail recipient's name, click the name, and then click the To button.

4   Click OK.

The message window reappears with the name of the recipient in the To box. The Subject box contains the Excel workbook name, and the attachment icon appears in the message pane. Your screen should look like the following illustration.

Attachment for Excel workbook

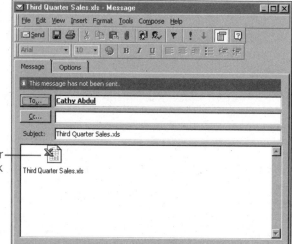

5   Click in the message area.

An insertion point appears below the attachment icon.

6   Type **For your review, as requested.**

7   On the Standard toolbar, click the Send button.

The Third Quarter Sales workbook is sent. After opening the message, the recipient can double-click the attachment icon to display the workbook.

 NOTE   If you'd like to build on the skills that you learned in this lesson, you can do the One Step Further. Otherwise, skip to "Finish the lesson."

One Step Further: Changing the Format of a PivotTable

When data is retrieved from a database using MS Query, any formatting is lost. For example, if your data is formatted as currency in the database file, the data returned to Excel by MS Query will show the general number format. If you want to enhance the appearance of a PivotTable, you can reformat the data in several number formats.

Format the data in a PivotTable

In this exercise, you format the total sales data as currency.

1 Click the Sales Summary tab, and then click any cell in the data area of the PivotTable.

2 On the PivotTable toolbar, click the PivotTable button, point to Select, and then click Enable Selection.

3 On the PivotTable toolbar, click the PivotTable Field button.

The PivotTable Field dialog box appears.

PivotTable Field

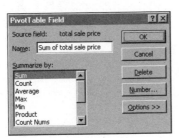

4 Click Number.

The Format Cells dialog box appears.

5 Click Currency in the Category list.

A sample of the selected format appears. You can also select how negative numbers are displayed in the selected format.

6 Click OK twice.

The data in the PivotTable is now formatted as currency. Your screen should look similar to the following illustration.

131

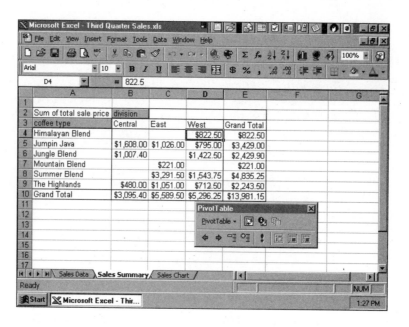

Save

7   On the Standard toolbar, click the Save button.

8   On the Excel window, click the Close button.

Finish the lesson

   Close all open windows.

Lesson Summary

To	Do this
Run MS Query	On the Data menu, point to Get External Data, and then click Create New Query.
Select a new data source	In the Choose Data Source dialog box, click New Data Source, and then click OK. Name the new data source and then select the driver type. Click Connect, and then click Select. Select the database file in the Select Database dialog box, and then click OK until the Query Wizard-Choose Columns dialog box appears.

To	Do this	Button
Add table fields to a query	In the Query Wizard-Choose Columns dialog box, click the plus sign next to the table that contains the fields to be queried. Click a field, and then click the Right Arrow button. Repeat for each field that will be part of the query. Click Next.	
Define query criteria	In the Query Wizard-Filter Data dialog box, click the field to be used in the filter. Click the first criteria down arrow, and select an operator. In the second criteria box, type the test value. Continue adding criteria as necessary. Click Next.	
Return query data to Excel	In the Query Wizard-Finish dialog box Click Save Query. Type a name for the query and the location the file is to be stored in, and then click Save. Be sure that the Return Data To Microsoft Excel option is selected, and then click Finish. In the Returning External Data To Excel dialog box, enter the cell reference where the returned data is to be placed.	
Create a PivotTable	Be sure that at least one cell in the query data is selected. On the Data menu, click PivotTable Report, and then follow the instructions in each PivotTable Wizard dialog box.	
Create a chart using PivotTable data	On the PivotTable toolbar, click PivotTable, point to Select, and then click Enable Selection. Drag to select the cells in the PivotTable to be included in the chart. On the Standard toolbar, click the Chart Wizard button, and then follow the instructions in each Chart Wizard dialog box.	

To	Do this	Button
Send e-mail from Excel	Open the file that is to be sent. On the File menu, point to Send To, and then click Mail Recipient. Address and add any message text, and then click the Send button.	Send

For online information about	On the Help menu, click Contents And Index, click the Index tab, and then type
Retrieving data using MS Query	*Excel*: **Microsoft Query**
Creating a PivotTable	*Excel*: **PivotTable wizard**
Creating a chart using PivotTable data	*Excel*: **Chart wizard**

Consolidating Data in a Database

Estimated time
40 min.

In this lesson you will learn how to:

- Import a text file to a new database table.
- Import a document table to an existing database table.
- Link text to a database form.

Data and information can come to you in many forms, and sometimes not in a form that is suited to your needs. For example, if you receive a word-processing document that lists new vendors, you don't want to retype the information to add it to your new vendor database. The text can easily be brought into a database by converting the information into a format that the database can interpret. You can also link text from a word processing document to a database form.

With Microsoft Office 97, you can import text from a word processing document, such as Microsoft Word, into a database file using Microsoft Access. Word converts the text into a format that a database can interpret, and then the Import Text wizard in Access takes you through the steps to bring the data into a database table. Integrating data this way helps eliminate possible duplication errors and saves you time and effort.

In this lesson, you will assist a co-worker in importing data that was received in an inter-office memo. You will incorporate some of the text from the Word memo into an existing Access database table, create a new database table for other text in the memo, and link document text in a database form.

In the following exercises, you open an Access database file containing several corporate database tables and an entry form. You will also open a Word document that contains new product and new employee data.

Start the lesson

Open Office Document

1 On the Office Shortcut Bar, click the Open Office Document button.

The Open Office Document dialog box appears.

2 From your Office 97 SBS Practice folder, open the Kenya Coffee Company database file.

The Kenya Coffee Company database file opens. It contains the Coffee Products table and the Employee Roster table.

3 In the Database window, click the Employee Roster table on the Tables tab.

Copy

4 On the Database toolbar, click the Copy button.

By making another copy of the Employee Roster table, you can work with a new copy while leaving the original intact.

Paste

5 On the Database toolbar, click the Paste button.

The Paste Table As dialog box appears. The copy of the Employee Roster table must be given a new name. You cannot have two tables with the same name in a single database file.

6 In the Table Name box, be sure the Structure And Data option is selected, type **97 Employee Roster** and then click OK.

7 Click the Forms tab, and click the Employee Entry form.

8 On the Database toolbar, click the Copy button.

9 On the Database toolbar, click the Paste button.

The Paste As dialog box appears. The copy of the Employee Entry form must be given a new name. You cannot have two forms with the same name in a single database file.

10 In the Form Name box, type **New Employee Form** and then click OK.

Open a Word document

1 On the Office Shortcut Bar, click the Open Office Document button.

The Open Office Document dialog box appears.

2 From your Office 97 SBS Practice\Lesson 7 folder, open the Inter-office Memo document.

The Inter-office Memo document opens in Word. The document contains new product and new employee data.

3 Save the file as **New Data Memo** in your Office 97 SBS Practice\ Lesson 7 folder.

Integrating Document Text into a Database

The ability to integrate text from a word-processing document into a database file lets you make the data a permanent part of your database, saving you time. When integrating Word text into an Access database file, the data must be in a file format that Access can interpret. The converted data can then be imported or copied and pasted into an Access database.

When you have a Word document that contains text you would like to place in an Access database, the file not only must be in a file format that Access can interpret, but the text must also be *delimited*. Delimited text is text that is separated by tabs, paragraph marks, commas, semicolons, or any other character. Tabs and paragraph marks are common delimiter separators. A table in a Word document is not delimited, and must be converted to a delimited format before being imported to Access. A table in a Word document becomes delimited when the columns and rows separating the text are removed and replaced with a delimiter, such as tabs.

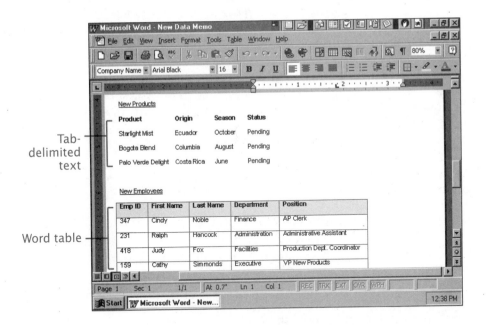

Once the text is delimited and in an appropriate file format, you can determine whether the data will be placed in an existing database table or a new database table. If you are placing the data in a new table, you can import the data without the concern of continuity between the existing table and the new data. When you are *appending* data to the end of an existing database table, you must make sure the data will flow into the database table's fields by preparing the data to meet the following conditions:

■ Each field must have the same data type (for example, numbers, dates, or text) as the corresponding field in the destination table in Access.

Field names can be different from field captions. Review the table in Design view to be sure you are using the correct field names.

■ If you are not using the first row of data as the field names, each field must be in the same order as the fields in the destination table in Access.

■ If you are using the first row of data as the field names, the field names must match exactly. The matching field names ensure that the data will flow into the correct fields in the table, even if they are in a different order.

Importing Delimited Text into a Database

To review integration methods in each Office 97 program, see Appendix C, "Integration Techniques."

Documents produced in a word processor, such as Word, may already be delimited if the text is separated by tabs or by one of the other delimited characters. However, the database may not be able to interpret the file type. Before you import the file, you should determine whether the document contains additional text that you do not want to import. If you need only a portion of text in a document, you can place a copy of that text in a separate file. You can then save the new file as a text-only file. This ensures that only the data you want to import, and not the surrounding data, is imported in the correct file format.

Suppose a co-worker has come to you with an inter-office memo created in Word that contains data that also needs to be in an Access database file. You first determine that you want the new product data to be placed in a new table within the Kenya Coffee Company database.

Copy text to a separate file

In this exercise, you copy and paste tab-delimited text into a new file before importing it into Access.

1 Be sure that the New Data Memo is the active window, and then drag to select the text from "Product" through the last "Pending."

You should have four lines of tab-delimited text selected in the memo.

Copy

2 On the Standard toolbar, click the Copy button.

3 On the Standard toolbar, click the New button.

A new blank document appears.

New

4 On the Standard toolbar, click the Paste button.

The copied text is pasted into the new document.

Paste

Convert the file format

In this exercise, you convert the new file into a file format that can be imported into Access.

1   On the File menu, click Save As.

The Save As dialog box appears.

2   Be sure that Lesson 7 appears in the Save In box, and then type **New Products** in the File Name box.

3   Click the Save As Type down arrow, and then click Text Only With Line Breaks.

The Text Only With Line Breaks file format saves the text without formatting, except for line breaks.

4   Click Save, and then click Yes.

The New Products file is saved as a text file and is now ready for importing into Access.

You must close the file before you can import it into Access.

5   On the File menu, click Close.

The New Data Memo document appears.

Import a text file into a new database table

In this exercise, you switch to Access and import the tab-delimited text file into a new table in an existing database file.

1   On the taskbar, click the Microsoft Access button. Be sure that the Kenya Coffee Company database window is active.

2   On the File menu, point to Get External Data, and then click Import.

The Import dialog box appears.

3   Click the Files Of Type down arrow, and then click Text Files.

4   From your Office 97 SBS Practice\Lesson 7 folder, click New Products and then click Import.

The first dialog box of the Import Text wizard appears.

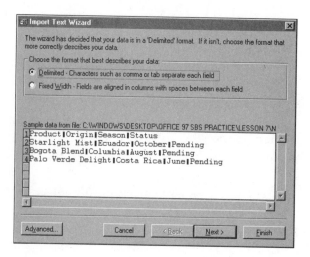

5 Be sure that the Delimited option button is selected, and then click Next.

The second dialog box for the Import Text wizard appears.

If the text fields in the file to be imported are each enclosed in quotes or apostrophes, select that as the text qualifier.

6 Be sure that the Tab option button is selected, select the First Row Contains Field Names check box, and then click Next.

The third dialog box for the Import Text wizard appears.

7 Be sure that the In A New Table option button is selected, and then click Next.

The New Product data will be placed in a new table within the database file. The fourth dialog box for the Import Text wizard appears.

8 Click Next.

The fifth dialog box for the Import Text wizard appears. This dialog box is used to change information about the fields—their names, the type of data they hold, etc.

9 Be sure that the Let Access Add Primary Key option button is selected, and then click Next.

The sixth dialog box for the Import Text wizard appears.

10 Click Finish.

Access imports the Word file and creates a new database table from the information. A message appears confirming that the import was successful.

11 Click OK.

The message box closes and the database window, with the Tables tab selected, appears. Your screen should look like the following illustration.

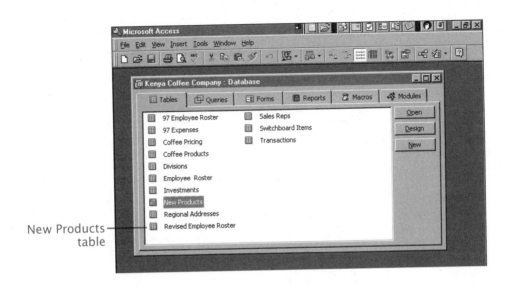

New Products table

Open the new database table

In this exercise, you open the table you created when you imported text from Word.

1   Be sure the New Products table is selected, and then click Open.

The New Products table opens, displaying the data you imported. Your screen should look like the following illustration.

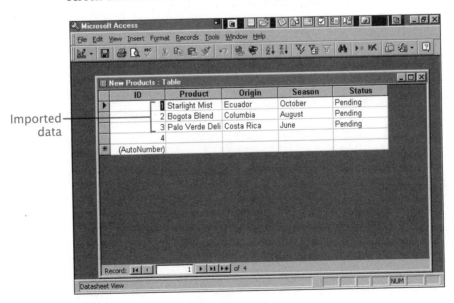

Imported data

2   Close the New Products table window.

Importing Text from a Document Table into an Existing Database Table

Unlike text that is already delimited, a formatted document table in Word needs to be converted to delimited text prior to importing. Word makes this process easy by replacing the column divisions with a separator such as a tab, and replacing the row divisions with paragraph marks. After you have converted the document table to delimited text, you can import it to a new database table or an existing database table.

If you are importing a document table to an existing database table (also called *appending*), you need to first compare the column headings of the document table with the field names of the database table. This can sometimes be easier prior to converting the document table to delimited text. You need to make sure that the first row of your document table contains column headings that match the database table field names, and that those headings are in the same order as the database table field names. To accomplish this, you may have to reorganize your document table. If the database table you are importing to contains field names that are not similar to any information in your document table, you can insert columns with only the column header as placeholders. If a column is a placeholder, it does not necessarily have to contain text.

If the field names in the database and the column headings in the document table are different, modify the headings in the document table before importing.

Now that you and your co-worker have imported delimited document text into a new Access database table, you're ready to try importing a Word table into an existing database table. You willtake the New Employee table from the New Data Memo, convert the table to tab-delimited text, match up the column headings and field names, and then append it to the 97 Employee Roster table that already exists in the Kenya Coffee Company database.

Review field names and column headings

In this exercise, you review the field name structure of the 97 Employee Roster database table, and then copy the New Employee table in Word to a new file for importing.

When importing text from Word to Access, the entire file is imported. If you want to import only part of a file's text, copy the text to a separate file before importing.

1   Be sure that the Kenya Coffee Company database window is active, click the 97 Employee Roster table, and then click Open.

   The 97 Employee Roster table opens.

2   Review the field names and compare them with the Word table.

3   Close the 97 Employee Roster table window.

4   On the taskbar, click the Microsoft Word button.

5   Click anywhere within the New Employees table, and then on the Table menu, click Select Table.

   The entire table is selected. Notice that the column headings for the table are the same as the 97 Employee Roster table, and are in the same order. Your screen should look like the following illustration.

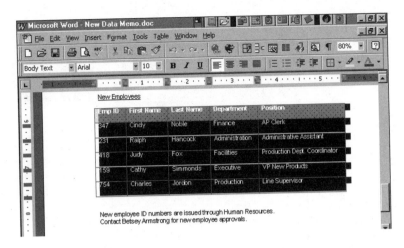

Copy

New

Paste

6 On the Standard toolbar, click the Copy button.

7 On the Standard toolbar, click the New button.

A new blank document appears.

8 On the Standard toolbar, click the Paste button.

The New Employees table is copied to the new document.

Convert a document table to delimited text

In this exercise, you convert the document table to delimited text and then save the file in a format that can be imported into Access.

1 Click anywhere within the New Employees table you just created, and then on the Table menu, click Select Table.

2 On the Table menu, click Convert Table To Text.

The Convert Table To Text dialog box appears.

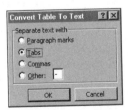

3 Be sure that the Tabs option button is selected, and then click OK.

The table is converted to text with tab delimiters. Your screen should look like the following illustration.

143

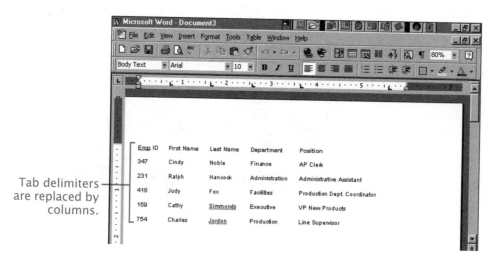

Tab delimiters are replaced by columns.

4 On the File menu, click Save As.

The Save As dialog box appears.

5 Be sure that Lesson 7 appears in the Save In box, and then type **New Employees** in the File Name box.

6 Click the Save As Type down arrow, and then click Text Only With Line Breaks.

7 Click Save, and then click Yes.

The New Employee file is saved as a text file and is now ready for importing into Access.

8 Close the New Employee window.

The New Employee document closes and the New Data Memo document appears.

Import a Word file into an existing database table

In this exercise, you import and append the document table that you converted to delimited text into an existing database table.

1 On the taskbar, click the Microsoft Access button.

The Kenya Coffee Company database window appears.

2 On the File menu, point to Get External Data, and then click Import.

The Import dialog box appears.

3 Click the Files Of Type down arrow, and then click Text Files.

4 Be sure that New Employees is selected, and then click Import.

The first dialog box for the Import Text wizard appears.

5 Be sure that the Delimited option button is selected, and then click Next.

The second dialog box for the Import Text wizard appears.

6 Be sure that the Tab option button is selected, select the First Row Contains Field Names check box, and then click Next.

The third dialog box for the Import Text wizard appears.

7 Click the In An Existing Table down arrow, click 97 Employee Roster, and then click Next.

The fourth dialog box for the Import Text wizard appears.

8 Click Finish.

Access imports the Word file and appends the data to the existing database table. A message appears confirming that the import was successful.

9 Click OK.

Open the database table

In this exercise, you open the appended database table to review the contents.

1 Be sure that the 97 Employee Roster table is selected, and then click Open.

The 97 Employee Roster table opens, displaying the existing data and the data you imported. Your screen should look similar to the following illustration.

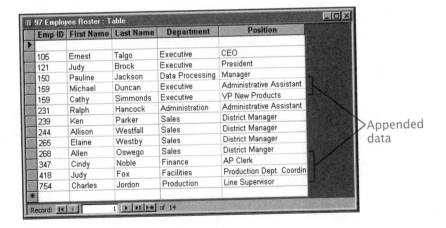

2 Close the 97 Employee Roster table window.

Linking Document Text to a Database Form

Document text can also be used in a database form to meet several needs. You can paste text into a database form, eliminating the need to type the text again. Or you can link text from another document to a database form so that the text in the form is updated any time the text in the document changes. Linking text is useful when you have text in a form that is subject to change. Linking ensures that the text in the *destination* form will always be the same as the text in the *source* document. For example, if you have a document that lists the resource contacts in your company and a database form for requesting supplies, you could link the resource contact text in the document to the database form. By linking the text to the form, anyone entering a supply request who has a question will know who is the current contact for supply information.

You have already taken text from the inter-office memo and created a new database table and appended an existing database table within the Kenya Coffee Company database. At the bottom of the inter-office memo, some text refers to procedure and a department contact—useful information for anyone filling out the Employee Entry form. This information is updated regularly. You link the text to the form used to enter new employee information to keep it up to date.

Link text to a form

In this exercise, you locate the source text and link it to the destination form.

1 On the taskbar, click the Microsoft Word button.

2 Drag to select the last two lines of text at the bottom of the New Data Memo.

The selected text will be linked to the New Employee Entry form. The memo is the source document.

3 On the Standard toolbar, click the Copy button.

4 On the taskbar, click the Microsoft Access button.

5 In The Kenya Coffee Company database window, click the Forms tab.

6 Be sure that New Employee Form is selected, and then click Design.

The New Employee Form opens in Design view. The form is the destination document.

7 On the Edit menu, click Paste Special.

8 Click the Paste Link option button, and then click OK.

9 Drag the sizing box down below the Position label on the form.

10 On the Standard toolbar, click the Form View button.

The linked text appears in the form. Your screen should look like the following illustration.

Copy

To link the text in Word to the Access form, you must use Paste Special. Using the Paste button pastes only a copy of the text.

Form View

146

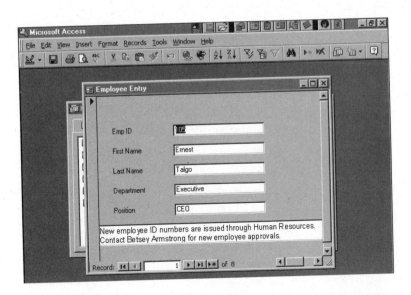

TIP You can also embed existing Word text in an Access form. Start by selecting and copying the text. In Access, open the form in Design view, and then paste the text. After the information is embedded, you can move and size the text box and edit the text by double-clicking the text block. Text that will not change or that has formatting options not available in Access is ideal for embedding. Text that is embedded is not linked to the source document.

Edit the linked text

In this exercise, you change the contact name in the New Data Memo to reflect the change in department staff. You then view the change to the form.

1   On the Standard toolbar, click the Design View button.
2   On the taskbar, click the Microsoft Word button.
3   Drag to select the text, Betsy Armstrong, at the bottom of the memo.
4   Type **Neil Strong**
5   On the Standard toolbar, click the Save button.
6   On the Word window, click the Close button.

    The New Data Memo closes, and you exit Word.

7   On the Standard toolbar, click the Form View button.

    The text Neil Strong has replaced the text Betsy Armstrong in the form because of the link between the text in the memo and the form.

Save

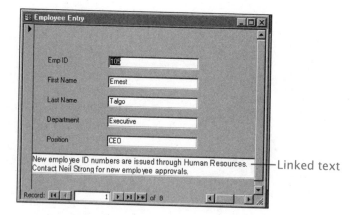

Linked text

Save

8 On the Form Design toolbar, click the Save button.

> **NOTE** If you'd like to build on the skills that you learned in this lesson, you can do the One Step Further. Otherwise, skip to "Finish the lesson."

One Step Further: Formatting a Database Form

Database forms can be formatted to enhance the form's appearance and direct the user's attention to specific information. If the form's background does not meet your needs, you can change the color of the background as well as select from several predefined background formats. You can also format the text color, font, and font size.

You can easily change the format of a form by using the *AutoFormat* feature. AutoFormat is a collection of predefined formats that determine the appearance of a form or report. AutoFormat can change the background of a form and determine whether the font, color, and border of the predefined format will be applied. If you do not like any of the formats in AutoFormat, you can also change the format of a form using the Formatting toolbar.

Change the form format

In this exercise, you change the background of the form using AutoFormat.

Design View

1 Be sure that the Employee Entry form is open in Form view, and then click the Design View button.

The Employee Entry form appears in Design view.

Form Selector

AutoFormat

2 Click the Form Selector in the upper-left corner of the form in Design view.

3 On the Form Design toolbar, click the AutoFormat button.

The AutoFormat dialog box appears.

4 In the Form AutoFormats box, click Stone.

A preview of the Stone format appears in the preview window.

5 Click OK.

The background and the text of the form change to the Stone format.

Change the text color for the linked text

In this exercise, you will change the background color of the linked text box so that the text is easier to read.

1 In the form, scroll to locate the linked text, and click the text to select the text box.

2 On the Formatting toolbar, click the Fill/Back Color down arrow.

A grid of color choices for the background of the text box appears.

Fill/Back Color

3 Click the color light gray.

The background color for the linked text box changes to light gray.

4 On the Form Design toolbar, click the Form View button.

5 On the Form Design toolbar, click the Save button.

Form View

6 Close the Employee Entry form.

7 On the Access window, click the Close button.

Finish the lesson

➤ Close all open windows.

Lesson Summary

To	Do this	Button
Copy document text to a separate file prior to importing to a database table	Select the text to be copied. On the Standard toolbar, click the Copy button, and then click the New button. Be sure that the new document is visible. Click the Paste button.	
Convert document text to a delimited file format	On the File menu, click Save As. Type a new filename. Click the Save As Type down arrow, and click Text Only With Line Breaks.	

149

To	Do this
Import delimited text file to a new database table	On the File menu in Access, point to Get External Data, and then click Import. Click the Files Of Type down arrow, and then click Text Files. Select the file, click Import, and then follow the instructions in each dialog box.
Convert a document table to delimited text	Click in the table, and on the Table menu, click Select Table. On the Table menu, click Convert Table To Text. Select the Tab option button, and then click OK.
Import delimited text into an existing database file	On the File menu in Access, point to Get External Data, and then click Import. Click the Files Of Type down arrow, and then click Text Files. Select the file, click Import, and then follow the instructions in each dialog box.
Link document text to a database form	Select the text to be linked from the document. On the Standard toolbar, click the Copy button. In Access, click the Forms tab. Select the form the text is to be linked to, and then click Design. On the Edit menu, click Paste Special. Click the Paste Special option button, and then click OK. Drag the linked text box to the location.
Edit linked text	In the document, make necessary changes to the linked text. The changes are automatically made to the linked text on the form.

For online information about	On the Help menu, click Contents And Index, click the Index tab, and then type
Preparing text for importing into Access	*Access*: importing data
Importing text in Access	*Access*: importing data
Preparing a Word table to import into Access	*Word*: converting table data
Linking text	*Access*: linked objects

Using Workbook Data in a Database

Estimated time
35 min.

In this lesson you will learn how to:

■ Import worksheet data to new and existing database tables.

■ Link worksheet data to a database table.

■ Embed a workbook in a database table field.

■ Schedule a meeting.

In the previous lesson, you appended data to an existing database table and created a new database table using text from a word processing document. As with text in a word processing document, you may receive data in a spreadsheet that you want to incorporate into a database. The data in a spreadsheet can easily be appended to an existing database table or used to create a new database table. Although spreadsheets are often used to store lists of information, a database will make more efficient use of the information. In a database, you can perform advanced queries, create data forms, and generate reports—things you cannot do in a spreadsheet. For example, if you keep a list of office supply vendors on a spreadsheet, it may become too large to efficiently view and manage. By moving the spreadsheet data into a database, you can continue to add more vendors, edit existing vendors, perform searches, and even link the vendor information to a form to quickly enter supply orders and create invoices.

With Microsoft Office 97, you can append, import, embed, and link spreadsheet data from Microsoft Excel to database tables in Microsoft Access. Integrating data is made easy by copying and pasting and by using the Import Spreadsheet wizard and the Link Spreadsheet wizard.

In this lesson, you are given an Excel workbook to keep track of several Human Resource items for new employees. You need to incorporate the workbook data into the Kenya Coffee Company database. You will do this by appending a database table, creating a new database table, linking a workbook to a database table, and embedding an object in a table field. You will also use Microsoft Outlook to schedule a meeting to present the new data format to Human Resources.

In the next exercises, you will open an Excel workbook containing several worksheets with new employee information. You will also open an Access database containing the current employee data.

Start the lesson

*Open Office
Document*

1   On the Office Shortcut Bar, click the Open Office Document button.

The Open Office Document dialog box appears.

2   From your Office 97 SBS Practice\Lesson 8 folder, open the Employee Data workbook.

The Employee Data workbook opens. The workbook contains four worksheets of data.

3   Save the file as **New Employee Data** in your Office 97 SBS Practice\Lesson 8 folder.

Be sure that the Excel window is maximized.

Open a database file

1   On the Office Shortcut Bar, click the Open Office Document button.

The Open Office Document dialog box appears.

2   From your Office 97 SBS Practice folder, open the Kenya Coffee Company database file.

The Kenya Coffee Company database file opens. Be sure that the Access window is maximized.

3   In the Database window, click the Revised Employee Roster table on the Tables tab.

Copy

4   On the Standard toolbar, click the Copy button.

By making another copy of the Revised Employee Roster table, you can work with a new copy while leaving the original intact.

Paste

5   On the Standard toolbar, click the Paste button.

The Paste Table As dialog box appears. You cannot have two tables with the same name in a single database file, so you must give the new table a different name.

6   In the Table Name box, type **Corporate Roster**, be sure that the Structure And Data option button is selected, and then click OK.

7   Click the Investments table.

8   On the Standard toolbar, click the Copy button.

9   On the Standard toolbar, click the Paste button.

10   In the Table Name box, type **Corporate Investments**, be sure that the Structure And Data option button is selected, and then click OK.

Integrating Workbook Data into an Existing Database

Although putting a list together in a spreadsheet may seem easier than creating a database file, it is better to store large amounts of data in a database because a database gives you more ways to work with information. For example, in a database you can create advanced queries, create forms for quick data entry, and generate reports to use your data more efficiently.

Because worksheets within an Excel workbook look similar to Access database tables (both contain rows and columns), it's easy to bring worksheet data into a database table. You can do this in several ways.

- Append the worksheet data to an existing database table.

- Import worksheet data to a new database table.

- Link worksheet data to a database table.

- Embed a workbook in a field with a database table.

NOTE   To review integration methods in each Office 97 program, see Appendix C, "Integration Techniques."

Appending Worksheet Data into an Existing Database Table

When you have an Excel worksheet that contains data similar to an existing Access database table, you can append the worksheet data to the existing database table so all the data is in one location. When appending data, the data in both the worksheet and the database table should be arranged and formatted in the same way so that when they are brought together, the data matches up. You do this by making sure the columns of data are in the same position (for example, the first column in each is the date column). You also make sure that the format for each column is the same (numbers are formatted as numbers, dates as dates, text as text, and currency as currency). If you are using the first row of the worksheet as field names, the column names in the worksheet must match the field names in the database table. If your worksheet contains more columns of data than the database table, you can either add the additional fields to the database table and then append, or not use the additional worksheet columns when you append.

Before you append worksheet data to an existing database table, you should first delete any blank rows in your worksheet. Although blank rows can be used as separators between headings and data in a worksheet to improve readability, the blank rows will become blank *records* in a database. Blank records are a waste of space and will give you an inaccurate record count in a database table. However, you may need to add blank columns in a worksheet before appending it to a database table. Blank columns work as placeholders for columns of data that appear in the database table but not in the worksheet.

You are currently working with the Kenya Coffee Company database and the New Employee Data workbook. You see that the list of new employees in March should be added to the employee database table to update the database. You will first compare and modify the worksheet, and then append the worksheet data to an existing database table.

Compare a worksheet and a database table in a single window

In this exercise, you tile the two open files on your screen so that you can first compare the fields and columns of data, and check for blank rows, before bringing them together.

1 Be sure that the only open programs are Access and Excel.

It is easier to view multiple windows when only those programs you wish to view are open.

2 Click the Corporate Roster table, and then click Open.

The Corporate Roster table opens.

3 Use the right mouse button to click a blank area on the taskbar, and then click Tile Horizontally.

The Access and Excel windows are tiled so that they are both visible on your screen. Your screen should look similar to the following illustration.

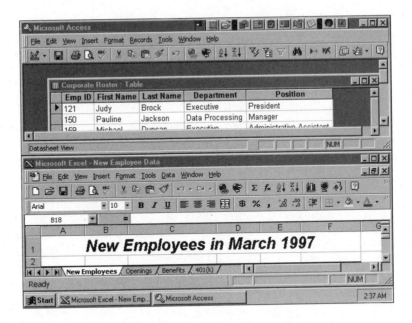

4 Review the database table fields and the worksheet column headings.

The worksheet has more column headings than the database table has fields. There are three columns and fields that have similar data.

Modify the worksheet to match the database table

Now that you have identified the differences in the worksheet and the database table, you are ready to modify the worksheet so you can append it to the database table. In this exercise, you add two blank columns to the New Employee worksheet. One column will be a placeholder for the employee ID number and the other will be for the employee position name. The employee ID and position data will be added later by Human Resources.

1 On the Corporate Roster table window, click the Close button.

The table closes but the database window remains open.

2 Maximize the Excel window.

3 Use the right mouse button to click the column A header.

The entire column is selected and a shortcut menu appears.

It is not necessary to name the column headings if they are just acting as placeholders for the append.

4 On the shortcut menu, click Insert.

A new blank column appears to the left of the First Name column.

5 Use the right mouse button to click the column E header, and then click Insert on the shortcut menu.

A new blank column is inserted between the Department Name and Date Hired columns. The worksheet columns are now in the same order as the database table fields.

Save

6 On the Standard toolbar, click the Save button.

Append worksheet data to an existing database table

You have modified the worksheet so it has the same number of columns as the database table has fields. You have also made sure that the columns are in the same position and that the data format is the same. In this exercise, you append the New Employee worksheet data to the Corporate Roster database table.

1 Drag to select cells A5 through E10.

These records will be appended to the Corporate Roster table.

Copy

2 On the Standard toolbar, click the Copy button.

3 On the File menu, click Close.

The New Employee Data workbook closes. Excel remains open.

4 On the taskbar, click the Microsoft Access button.

5 Maximize the Access window.

6 Double-click the Corporate Roster table.

You can click the last record indicator or any field in the blank record to append the data.

7 Click the blank record at the end of the table to select it.

8 On the Edit menu, click Paste Append.

A message appears, asking whether you're sure you want to paste six records.

9 Click Yes.

The records are copied to the end of the Corporate Roster table. The table should look like the following illustration.

Appended records

10 On the Corporate Roster table window, click the Close button.

Importing Worksheet Data into a New Database Table

When you have data in a worksheet that does not relate to data in any existing database table, you can import the worksheet data and create a new database table. Importing creates a new database table from an entire worksheet or a named range within a worksheet.

The Import Spreadsheet wizard steps you through the process of importing data from an Excel worksheet into an Access database table. Because you are creating a new database table, you do not have to worry about matching column headings or data types. However, you should remove any blank rows or columns before importing data.

You have identified a benefits worksheet that does not relate to any of the existing database tables. Human Resources informs you that they will continue to track employee benefits and costs for new employees and, by the end of the year, expand the database to include all employees.

Start the Import Spreadsheet wizard

In this exercise, you identify the workbook containing the benefits data and start the Import Spreadsheet wizard.

*Before import-
ing, you must
close the Excel
workbook con-
taining the
worksheet you
are importing.*

1 On the File menu, point to Get External Data, and then click Import.

The Import dialog box appears.

2 Be sure that the Office 97 SBS Practice\Lesson 8 folder appears in the Look In box.

3 Click the Files Of Type down arrow, and then click Microsoft Excel.

A list of the Excel files in the Office 97 SBS Practice\Lesson 8 folder appears.

4 Click New Employee Data, and then click Import.

The first dialog box for the Import Spreadsheet wizard appears. Your dialog box should look like the following illustration.

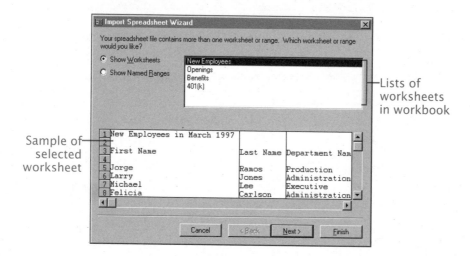

Lists of
worksheets
in workbook

Sample of
selected
worksheet

Import an entire worksheet into a new database table

In this exercise, you use the Import Spreadsheet wizard to outline how the Benefits worksheet is to be imported.

1 Be sure the Show Worksheets option button is selected.

2 Click Benefits, and then click Next.

The second dialog box for the Import Spreadsheet wizard appears.

*The fourth dialog
box for the Im-
port Spreadsheet
wizard lets you
change field op-
tions. You can
also choose not
to import a spe-
cific column.*

3 Select the First Row Contains Column Headings check box, and then click Next.

The first row of data in the worksheet will become the column headings in the database table. The third dialog box for the Import Spreadsheet wizard appears.

4 Click Next, and then click Next again.

The fifth dialog box for the Import Spreadsheet wizard appears.

5 Be sure that the Let Access Add Primary Key option button is selected, and then click Next.

The sixth dialog box for the Import Spreadsheet wizard appears.

6 Be sure that Benefits appears in the Import To Table box, and then click Finish.

A message appears confirming that the spreadsheet has been imported to the database file.

7 Click OK.

The Benefits table appears in the Kenya Coffee Company database window on the Tables tab.

Open the new database table

In this exercise, you open the new Benefits database table to see how the data appears after being imported from Excel to Access.

1 Be sure that the Benefits table is selected, and then click Open.

The Benefits table opens. Only the Benefits worksheet was imported, not the entire New Employee Data workbook. Your screen should look like the following illustration.

ID	First Name	Last name	Start Date	Dept	Benefits
1	Susan	Foelzer	1/2/97	Production	
2	Clark	Pelesky	1/3/97	Administration	
3	Sharilyn	Nomura	1/4/97	Executive	
4	Henry	Haarmann	1/5/97	Finance	
5	Cynthia	Harrison	1/8/97	Marketing	
6	Linda	Johnson	1/16/97	Marketing	
7	Leticia	Ames	1/29/97	Production	
8	Mark	Hunt	1/22/97	Production	
9	Jorge	Ramos	1/30/97	Production	
10	Larry	Jones	2/2/97	Administration	
11	Michael	Lee	2/6/97	Executive	
12	Felicia	Carlson	2/6/97	Administration	
13	Beth	Jansen	2/15/97	Finance	
14	Richard	Warner	2/27/97	Finance	
15					

Record: I◀ ◀ 1 ▶ ▶I ▶* of 16

2 On the Benefits table window, click the Close button.

The Benefits table closes.

 TIP You can also import an Excel worksheet into Access by selecting the data in Excel and then, on the Excel Data menu, clicking Convert To Access. The Import Spreadsheet wizard appears. Follow the wizard steps to import the worksheet to a new Access database table.

Linking Worksheet Data to a Database Table

Linking worksheet data to a database table maintains the same data in both places at all times. For example, if you have a pricing list on an Excel worksheet where the prices are updated frequently, and you need to have the same data in an Access database table, you could link the two together. By linking the worksheet to the database table, whenever you change the prices in the worksheet, the database table will automatically be updated. This eliminates both the need to enter the data in two places and the possibility of typing errors when entering the data a second time.

The New Employee Data workbook contains a list of personnel openings that is frequently updated by each department. To reduce access to the employee database, you will link the Openings worksheet to a new database table within the Kenya Coffee Company database file. By linking the worksheet to the database table, each department can make changes to the worksheet and the database table will be updated at the same time.

Prepare a worksheet for linking to a database table

In this exercise, you delete any unnecessary text and blank rows from the Openings worksheet to prepare it to be linked to a new database table.

When you link a worksheet to a database table, the entire worksheet is linked. Any rows not containing necessary data should be deleted.

1   On the taskbar, click the Microsoft Excel button.

2   From your Office 97 SBS Practice\Lesson 8 folder, open the New Employee Data workbook.

    The New Employee Data workbook appears.

3   Click the Openings worksheet tab to make it active.

4   Select rows 1 and 2 by dragging across the row headers.

    Row 1 is a title for the worksheet and row 2 is blank.

5   Use the right mouse button to click a selected row header, and then click Delete.

    Rows 1 and 2 are deleted. The remaining data moves up in the worksheet.

6   On the Standard toolbar, click the Save button.

7   On the File menu, click Close.

8   On the taskbar, click the Microsoft Access button.

    The Kenya Coffee Company database window appears, and the Tables tab is selected.

Save

The Excel workbook containing the worksheet you are linking must be closed before establishing the link.

Link a worksheet to a database table

In this exercise, you create a new Employee Openings database table and use the Link Spreadsheet wizard to create a link to the Openings worksheet.

You can also link a worksheet to a database table by using the Get External Data: Link Tables command in Access.

1   On the Tables tab in the Kenya Coffee Company database window, click New.

The New Table dialog box appears.

2   Click Link Table, and then click OK.

The Link dialog box appears.

3   Click the Files Of Type down arrow, and then click Microsoft Excel.

A list of the Excel files in the Office 97 SBS Practice\Lesson 8 folder appears.

4   Click New Employee Data, and then click Link.

The first dialog box for the Link Spreadsheet wizard appears.

5   Be sure that the Show Worksheets option button is selected, click Openings, and then click Next.

The second dialog box for the Link Spreadsheet wizard appears.

6   Select the First Row Contains Column Headings check box, and then click Next.

7   Type **Employee Openings** in the Linked Table Name box, and then click Finish.

A message appears confirming that the worksheet has been linked to the database file.

8   Click OK.

The Employee Openings table is added to the Tables tab with a linked icon next to it. Your database window should look like the following illustration.

Link icon —

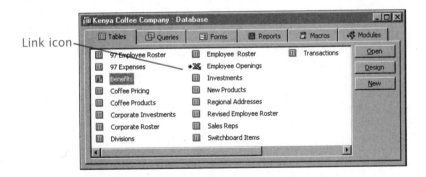

Edit the linked spreadsheet

In this exercise, you edit the Openings worksheet and verify that the changes are made to the linked Employee Openings database table:

1 Double-click the Employee Openings table to open it.

The data appears as it did in the Excel worksheet.

Before you edit the worksheet, you must close the Access database table that is linked to the worksheet.

2 On the Employee Openings table window, click the Close button.

3 On the taskbar, click the Microsoft Excel button.

4 From your Office 97 SBS Practice\Lesson 8 folder, open the New Employee Data workbook.

5 In cell A5, change Executive to **Production**

6 In cell B5, change Executive Assistant to **Stocker**, and then press ENTER.

7 On the Standard toolbar, click the Save button.

Save

8 On the File menu, click Close.

9 On the taskbar, click the Microsoft Access button.

10 Double-click the Employee Openings table.

The Employee Openings table appears. The changes made on the linked Excel worksheet are reflected in the Openings table.

11 On the Employee Openings table window, click the Close button.

Using a Workbook in a Database Table Field

For a demonstration on how to create an OLE object field, and embed a workbook in a database table, double-click the Camcorder Files On The Internet shortcut in your Desktop or connect to the Internet address listed on p. xxx.

Worksheet data can be embedded into a database table field to provide detailed information as part of a database record. When you embed a worksheet into a field within an Access database table, the entire workbook is embedded and you have access to all Excel commands and tools. You can embed an entirely new workbook or an existing workbook as an object in a database field. For example, a worksheet that calculates the amount of vacation time an employee is entitled to can be embedded as an object into the database table for vacation time. By embedding the workbook, you can double-click the workbook object, and Excel and a copy of the worksheet will open for you. Unlike linked objects, the changes you make to the embedded worksheet are saved with the object and do not affect the original worksheet.

The field in the database table that the workbook object is embedded into must be set up to accept *OLE* objects. OLE is a *protocol* used to link or embed data between different programs.

You have integrated all but one worksheet into the Kenya Coffee Company database. The last worksheet is the 401(k) investment distribution graph. This graph will change depending on the individual employee's investment elections. In order to have a separate graph for each employee, you embed the graph into an OLE object field for each employee in the Investments database table.

Open the workbook and database table

In this exercise, you make the 401(k) worksheet active so that when the embedded object is opened, it will be the first worksheet you see. You will also open the Investments database table.

1 On the taskbar, click the Microsoft Excel button.

2 From your Office 97 SBS Practice\Lesson 8 folder, open the New Employee Data workbook.

3 Click the 401(k) worksheet tab.

All worksheets in the workbook are available when you embed. The 401(k) worksheet will be the active worksheet when you open the embedded workbook.

4 On the taskbar, click the Microsoft Access button.

5 Double-click the Corporate Investments table to open it.

Add an OLE object field to the database table

The Investments database table currently contains three fields: First Name, Last Name, and Department. Before you can embed a worksheet, you must create a field that can accept an embedded object. In this exercise, you add an OLE object field to the Corporate Investments table.

View

1 On the Table Datasheet toolbar, click the View button.

The Corporate Investments table is now in Design view.

2 Click in the first blank Field Name field after Department, and type **401(k)**

This is the name for the OLE Object field.

3 Click in the Data Type field next to 401(k), click the Data Type down arrow, and then click OLE Object.

This indicates that the new field will contain an OLE Object, which is either embedded or linked.

4 On the General tab under Field Properties, click in the Caption field, and then type **Investment Choices**

5 On the Table Design toolbar, click the View button.

A message appears asking you to save changes.

6 Click Yes.

The table is saved and you are now in Datasheet view.

7 Place the mouse pointer at the right edge of the Investment Choices field column header, and double-click.

The column is widened so that all the text is visible. Your screen should look similar to the following illustration.

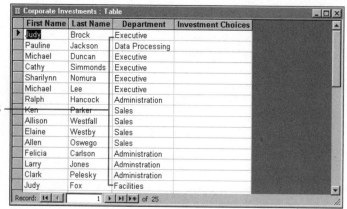

OLE object fields ──

Embed a workbook in a database table

In this exercise, you embed the New Employee Data workbook with the 401(k) worksheet in the Investment Choices field you have created.

Because embedding a worksheet inserts the entire workbook file, the size of your database file can be significantly increased.

> **TIP** You can also embed a new workbook object. In the Insert Object dialog box, click the Create New option, click Microsoft Excel Worksheet, and then click OK.

1 Click the Investment Choices field for Record 1.

2 On the Insert menu, click Object.

   The Insert Object dialog box appears.

3 Click the Create From File option button, and then click Browse.

   The Browse dialog box appears.

4 Be sure that the Office 97 SBS Practice\Lesson 8 folder appears in the Directories box, click New Employee Data.xls in the File Name box, and then click Open.

5 Click OK.

   The workbook has been embedded in the OLE Object field for Record 1.

Copy

6 On the Table Datasheet toolbar, click the Copy button.

7 Click the Investment Choices field for Record 2.

Paste

8 On the Table Datasheet toolbar, click the Paste button.

   The workbook is embedded into Record 2. Your screen should look similar to the following illustration.

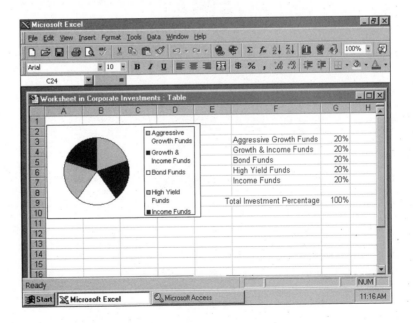

Embedded Excel workbook

For the purposes of this exercise, you will only embed the object for two records. Normally you would repeat this process for each record that requires the embedded object.

Edit the embedded workbook object

In this exercise, you edit the embedded object for Record 1 to show that employee's investment choices. You then open the embedded object for Record 2 to see that it has not changed.

1 Double-click the embedded workbook object in Record 1.

The embedded workbook opens in an Excel window. You screen should look similar to the following illustration.

2 In column G, make the following cell changes.

Cell	Change to
G3	35%
G4	25%
G5	15%
G6	15%
G7	10%

Save

3 On the Standard toolbar, click the Save button.

The changes to the embedded workbook for Record 1 are saved.

4 On the Worksheet In Corporate Investments table window, click the Close button.

The embedded workbook closes and the Corporate Investments table appears.

5 Double-click the embedded object in Record 2.

The embedded workbook for Record 2 opens with the data from the original file. Embedded objects are copies of the source file and are not linked to one another. Instead, they are separate and independent files within each record.

6 On the Worksheet In Corporate Investments table window, click the Close button.

7 On the Corporate Investments table window, click the Close button, and then click Yes.

8 Close Microsoft Access and Microsoft Excel.

TIP Another way to embed worksheet data is to select any portion of a Microsoft Excel workbook and click the Copy button. In Microsoft Access, click the OLE Object field where you want to embed the object, and then click the Paste button. The entire workbook is embedded in the object field.

Scheduling a Meeting

Meetings can be difficult to plan because of busy schedules. Before finding a date and time that is convenient for everyone, you might have to call or e-mail each attendee several times. With the Calendar folder in Outlook, you can use the Meeting Planner feature to view your schedule and the schedules of your co-workers. The AutoPick feature will search the schedules of each attendee for the first available time that meets your requirements.

When a meeting time is determined, the Meeting Planner will send out meeting notices and track the responses. If a response indicates that someone's schedule has changed, you can reschedule the meeting in your Calendar.

Now that you have integrated the New Employee Data workbook into the Kenya Coffee Company database in Access, you need to schedule a meeting with Human Resources to present the new data format. The meeting should be held as soon as possible and should last about two hours. You will use Outlook to schedule a meeting based on each person's schedule.

IMPORTANT Because this exercise explores the interactive aspects of the Calendar folder in Outlook, you need to recruit some help from one or two other people on your network to complete the exercises. Each person must be using Outlook with Microsoft Exchange Server. If you do not have access permission to their schedules, you will only be able to see their free/busy times, not their schedule details.

Open the Calendar folder in Outlook

In this exercise, you start Outlook and view your schedule in Calendar.

1 Start Outlook using the Pamela Miller profile.

2 On the Outlook Bar, click the Calendar icon.

The contents of your Calendar folder appear in the Information viewer; your schedule for the current date appears.

TIP Suppose you need to plan a meeting with a group of individuals, each of whom has a very tight schedule. You could use AutoPick, but what if the next available date it can find is three months away? In situations like this, it is often easier to organize a meeting by selecting a specific time in the Meeting Planner and then asking co-workers to reschedule items if your meeting takes precedence.

Plan a group meeting

In this exercise, you select attendees for the employee database training and use the AutoPick feature to schedule a meeting date and time.

Plan A Meeting

1 On the Standard toolbar, click the Plan A Meeting button.

The Plan A Meeting dialog box appears. The current date appears in the Meeting Planner grid. The time periods during which you have an appointment or a meeting scheduled are marked with a solid colored line.

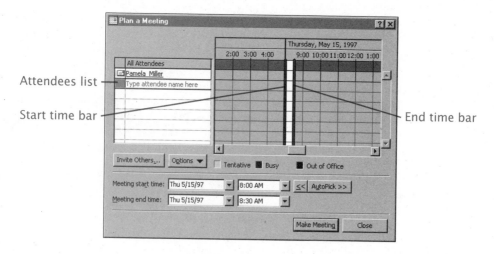

Attendees list —

Start time bar —

End time bar

2   In the Plan A Meeting dialog box, click Invite Others.

The Select Attendees And Resources dialog box appears. Names from your company's global address list are shown, in addition to your own name.

You can also make attendance optional for those co-workers whose attendance is not required.

3   Select the names of the people working with you on this exercise, and then click Required.

The names appear in the list of required attendees.

4   Click OK.

The names of your co-workers appear in the All Attendees list, and their busy times are marked in the Meeting Planner grid. Busy times appear in blue, tentative appointments in light blue, and out-of-office appointments in purple. Your dialog box should look similar to the following illustration.

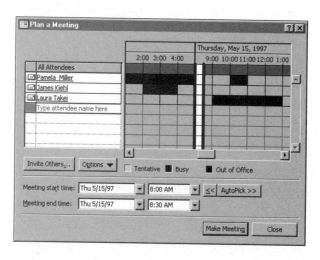

You can also drag the meeting selection handles to change the meeting duration.

5 Click the first Meeting Start Time down arrow.

A calendar appears with the current date selected.

6 Click the next business day on the calendar.

The next business day's date appears in the start and end date boxes.

7 Click the second Meeting End Time down arrow.

A list of times and durations appears.

8 Select the time that corresponds to a two-hour duration.

The time you choose will vary, depending on the current time on your computer. In the Meeting Planner grid, the meeting selection bars move to enclose a two-hour time period.

9 Click AutoPick.

The meeting selection bars appear around the first two-hour time period available for all attendees.

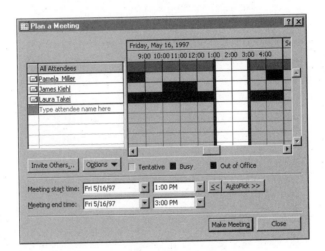

Send meeting requests

In this exercise, you send a meeting request to all attendees of the database training. You also schedule a meeting reminder.

1 Click Make Meeting.

A blank meeting request form appears. The names of your co-workers appear in the To box, and a note appears on the Information Bar at the top of the form, informing you that invitations to this meeting have not been sent. Your window should look like the following illustration.

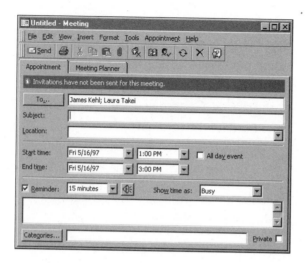

You may have to enlarge the window if the notes area at the bottom of the Meeting Request form is not visible.

2 In the Subject box, type **Employee database training**

3 In the note area at the bottom of the form, type **The employee database has been revised to handle employee data more efficiently.**

4 Make sure the Reminder check box is selected.

You want each attendee to receive a reminder for the meeting when it comes up in their schedule.

5 On the Standard toolbar, click the Send button.

The meeting request is sent, and the meeting is added to your schedule. Your screen should look like the following illustration.

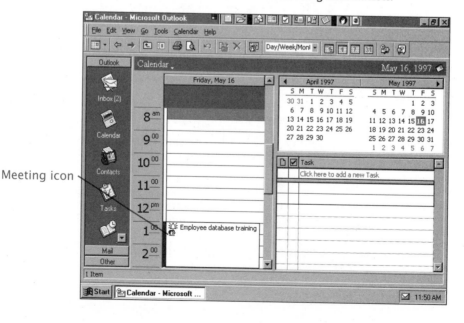

Meeting icon

NOTE If you'd like to build on the skills that you learned in this lesson, you can do the One Step Further. Otherwise, skip to "Finish the lesson."

One Step Further: Creating a Database Form

If you are using an Access form to enter data into a database table that also holds an embedded object, you can display the embedded object on the form just like a data field. The embedded object can be opened and edited as if you were working directly from the object field.

Because the embedded object in each field is independent of the others, Access displays a different object for each individual record. Each embedded object is tied, or bound, to the specific field and record in the database table on which the form is based. Therefore, these embedded objects are called *bound objects*.

Forms can simplify the task of entering data into a database table. The Kenya Coffee Company database already has an employee entry form, but it needs a form that makes it easier to enter the employee 401(k) investment choices. Human Resources has asked you to create a form that will help them change employee investment options and enter new employees into the 401(k) program.

Create a form with an embedded workbook

In this exercise, you create a form based on the Corporate Investments database table.

Open Office Document

1 On the Office Shortcut Bar, click the Open Office Document button.

2 From your Office 97 SBS Practice folder, open the Kenya Coffee Company database file.

3 Double-click the Corporate Investments table.

The Corporate Investments table opens.

New Object

4 On the Table Datasheet toolbar, click the New Object button down arrow, and then click AutoForm.

Access creates and opens a new form based on the Corporate Investments database table. All fields, including the embedded 401(k) object, are on the form.

171

5 Double-click the Investment Choices field for Record 1.

An Excel object editing window opens on the form. The Excel toolbars also appear. Your screen should look similar to the following illustration.

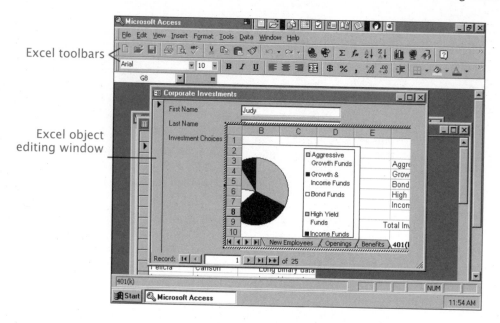

Excel toolbars

Excel object editing window

Edit the embedded object within the form

1 Use the arrow keys on your keyboard to scroll through the data on the right side of the pie chart.

2 Change cell G3 to **25%**

3 Change cell G5 to **25%**

4 Press HOME to bring the chart back into view.

5 Click outside the object editing window.

The object editing window closes. The chart is still visible.

6 Click the Next Record arrow to view Record 2.

Because the embedded object window has not been used before, the object does not appear in the window.

7 Double-click the Investment Choices field for Record 2.

8 Scroll through the object editing window.

The charts for Records 1 and 2 are different because the data in Record 2 has not been changed. The object windows for Records 3 through 25 are blank because objects have not been embedded in them yet.

9 Click anywhere outside the object editing window.

Save the new form

In this exercise, you save the form you created from a database table.

1 On the Corporate Investments form window, click the Close button.

A message appears asking to save changes to the new form.

2 Click Yes.

The Save As dialog box appears.

3 Be sure that the text Corporate Investments appears in the Form Name box, and then click OK.

The form is named and saved. The form appears on the Forms tab.

4 On the Corporate Investments table window, click the Close button.

5 On the Access window, click the Close button.

 TIP Objects can be embedded into OLE Object fields from Table view as well as Form view. To embed an object in an OLE Object field on a form, click the object frame to make it active. On the Insert menu, click Object, and then click Create From File. Enter the path to the workbook file, or click the Browse button, and then click OK. On the Form View toolbar, click the Save button to save the changes to the form.

Finish the lesson

Delete

1 In the Outlook Calendar folder, click the Employee Database Training meeting, and then click the Delete button. Send a cancellation.

2 Close all open windows.

Lesson Summary

To	Do this	Button
Append a worksheet to an existing database table	Be sure that the field order in the database table and the worksheet column names match. In Excel, select the cells to be appended, and then click the Copy button. In Access, select the last record in the database table you are appending to. On the Edit menu, click Paste Append, and then click OK.	
Import a worksheet to a new database table	In Access, on the File menu, point to Get External Data, and then click Import. Click the Files Of Type down arrow, and then click Microsoft Excel. Click the name of the workbook that contains the worksheet you want to import, and then click Import. Follow the instructions in each Import Spreadsheet Wizard dialog box.	
Link a worksheet to a database table	In Access, on the Tables tab, click New. Click Link Table, and then click OK. Click the Files Of Type down arrow, and then click Microsoft Excel. Click the name of the workbook that contains the worksheet you want to link, and then click Link. Follow the instructions in each Link Spreadsheet Wizard dialog box.	

To	Do this	Button
Embed a workbook as an OLE object in a database table field	Open the database table that will contain the embedded workbook. Click the View button so you are in Design view. Click in the first blank Field Name field and type a new field name. Click in the Data Type field for the new field, click the Data Type down arrow, and then click OLE Object. Click the View button, and then click Yes. Click in the new field for Record 1. On the Insert menu, click Object. Click the Create From File option button, and then click Browse. Click the name of the workbook that contains the data you want to embed, and then click OK.	
Schedule a meeting	Start Outlook and view the Calendar folder. On the Standard toolbar, click the Plan A Meeting button. Click Invite Others, and then select names from the address list. Set the meeting date and duration, and then click AutoPick. Click Make Meeting, type a subject and any other information, and then click the Send button.	

For online information about	On the Help menu, click Contents And Index, click the Index tab, and then type
Appending worksheet data	*Access*: **appending data from other programs**
Importing worksheet data	*Access*: **importing data** *or* **appending data from other programs**
Linking worksheet data	*Access*: **importing data** *or* **appending data from other programs**
Embedding worksheet data	*Access*: **embedded objects**
Scheduling meetings	*Outlook*: **meeting requests**

Review & Practice

You will review and practice how to:

Estimated time
35 min.

- Retrieve data from a database.
- Summarize data using a PivotTable.
- Import a document table to an existing database.
- Import worksheet data to a new database table.
- Embed a workbook in a database table field.
- Schedule a meeting.

Before you move on to Part 4, you can practice the skills you learned in Part 3 by working through this Review & Practice section. In this Review & Practice, you will retrieve data from a database file and create a PivotTable summarizing the data, import a document table and worksheet data to a database table, embed a workbook in a database table field, and schedule a meeting.

Scenario

As the newest member of the Information Systems department at The Kenya Coffee Company, your assignment is to summarize the corporate expense data. You will start by summarizing the first quarter expenses and incorporating several documents into the Kenya Coffee Company database. When you finish, you will then schedule a meeting with your co-workers to demonstrate how to use the revised Kenya Coffee Company database.

Step 1: Retrieve External Data and Create a PivotTable

You have been asked to summarize the expense data in the Kenya Coffee Company database for each department. Your job is to develop the easiest method of summarizing the first quarter data. You use MS Query to retrieve the data, and then you create a PivotTable to summarize the data.

1 Using Microsoft Excel, start MS Query using the Get External Data command, and connect to the Microsoft Access Kenya Coffee Company database in your Office 97 SBS Practice folder. Name your new data source **First Quarter Expenses**

2 Create a query to extract the Date Expense Type, Amount, and Department in the first quarter of 1997 from the 97 Expenses table.

3 Run the query and return the data to Excel. Save the query as **First Quarter 97 Expenses** in your Office 97 SBS Practice\Review & Practice 3 folder.

4 Using the PivotTable wizard, create a PivotTable with the data from the First Quarter 97 Expenses query. (Hint: The PivotTable should be arranged so that the Department is in columns, the Expense Type is in rows, and the Amount is the data.)

5 Place the PivotTable on a separate worksheet. Save the PivotTable workbook as **Quarterly Expense Summary** in your Office 97 SBS Practice\Review & Practice 3 folder. Close the workbook.

For more information about	See
Using MS Query	Lesson 6
Creating a PivotTable	Lesson 6

Step 2: Import a Document Table to an Existing Database

Your next task is to import text from an interoffice memo to the Kenya Coffee Company database. You will convert a document table within a memo and import and append it to an existing database table.

1 Open the Company Picnic Summary memo in your Office 97 SBS Practice\Review & Practice 3 folder.

2 Copy the picnic expense table to a new document file and convert the table to text. (Hint: Use tabs as the delimiter.)

3 Save the new file as **Picnic Expenses** in your Office 97 SBS Practice\Review & Practice 3 folder, with the Text Only With Line Breaks file format. Close the Picnic Expenses memo.

4 Open the Kenya Coffee Company database in your Office 97 SBS Practice folder. Make a copy of the 97 Expenses table, and then name it **General Expenses**

5 Import the Picnic Expenses memo into the General Expenses table using the Text Import wizard.

6 Open the General Expenses table to view the imported data at the end of the database table. Close the General Expenses table.

For more information about	See
Converting a Word table to text	Lesson 7
Importing text to an existing database table	Lesson 7

Step 3: Import Worksheet Data to a New Database Table

In addition to the expense information in the memo, you have also identified expense information being tracked in an Excel workbook. You review the workbook to prepare it for importing, and then use the Import Spreadsheet wizard to create a new database table from the data in one of the worksheets.

1 Open the Satellite workbook in your Office 97 SBS Practice\Review & Practice 3 folder, and save it as **Branch Data**

2 In the Branch Expenses worksheet, delete any unnecessary information, such as worksheet titles, totals, blank rows, or columns. Save and close the workbook.

3 Using Access, begin the import process using the Get External Data command and the Branch Data workbook.

4 Import the Branch Expenses worksheet, including column headings, to a new database table named **Branches** in the Kenya Coffee Company database.

5 Open the Branches table to view the imported data, and then close the table.

For more information about	See
Importing a worksheet to a new database table	Lesson 8

Step 4: Embed Worksheet Data in a Database Table

To ensure that expenses are not entered into the Kenya Coffee Company database without the proper authorization level, you embed the Corporate Signoff worksheet in the General Expenses table. You then edit the embedded object to reflect a temporary authorization change for an expense item.

1 From the Kenya Coffee Company database, open the General Expenses table in Design view.

2 Create a new field below the existing Comment fields as an OLE object field. Name the new field **Verification**

3 Embed the Corporate Signoff workbook as an object in the Verification field for the first two records in the table. (Hint: Use the Object command on the Insert menu.)

4 For Record 2, edit the authorization level for Pauline Jackson to $30,000.00.

5 Close the General Expenses table window.

6 Close Access.

For more information about	See
Embedding a workbook in a database table	Lesson 8

Step 5: Schedule a Meeting

Now that you have completed the incorporation and revision of the Kenya Coffee Company database, you need to hold a meeting to demonstrate how to use the revised database. You have recently learned to schedule meetings using Microsoft Outlook. You use your new skills to schedule a meeting with all department heads at the earliest possible time. To complete this exercise, you'll need to recruit some co-workers on your network who use Outlook.

1 Using Outlook and the Pamela Miller profile, view your Calendar.

2 Use the Meeting Planner to schedule a two-hour meeting as soon as possible with several co-workers. (Hint: Use AutoPick to find the soonest available meeting time.)

3 Send meeting requests with the subject, **Database training**, and the message, **The Expense database has been revised. This training will update you on it use.**

4 Include a reminder to the attendees when it comes up in their schedules.

5 Close Outlook.

For more information about	See
Scheduling a meeting	Lesson 8

Finish the Review & Practice

1 Delete the Database Training meeting in your Outlook Calendar.

2 Close all open windows.

Creating Effective Presentations with Shared Information

Integrating Documents for an Informative Presentation

Estimated time
40 min.

In this lesson you will learn how to:

■ Create a presentation from a word processing document.

■ Embed and link text in a presentation.

■ View a presentation within a word processing document.

■ Route a presentation to others for input.

When you create a presentation, the information you use often comes from existing resources such as outlines, document text, and tables. Recreating this information can be time-consuming. To make the process more efficient, you can quickly integrate items from a word processing document into a new presentation. For example, suppose you produce a report and then need to create a presentation for a meeting. You can use the outline of the report to create the foundation of the presentation.

Using Microsoft Office 97, you can easily import a Microsoft Word document or outline structure into a new or existing Microsoft PowerPoint presentation. From the Word outline, PowerPoint slides are created containing titles, subtitles, and bullets. You can save even more time by embedding and linking Word text and tables in a slide so you don't have to keep separate data sources up to date. In addition, a PowerPoint presentation can be embedded and viewed within a Word document.

In this lesson, you will create a presentation for The Kenya Coffee Company shareholders' meeting. To simplify the task, you will import a Word document into PowerPoint and then apply a design template to create a consistent look in the presentation. From the foundation provided by the document, you will add more text and a table to the document to clarify specific topics. You will also embed the final presentation in a Word document for online viewing, create audience handouts, and route the presentation for review.

Start the lesson

Open Office Document

1 On the Office Shortcut Bar, click the Open Office Document button.

The Open Office Document dialog box appears.

2 From your Office 97 SBS Practice\Lesson 9 folder, open the Preliminary Report document.

The Preliminary Report document opens in Word. The document contains text with heading styles.

When you import a document to create a new presentation, the document cannot be open.

3 Save the file as **Shareholders' Report** in your Office 97 SBS Practice\Lesson 9 folder.

4 On the File menu, click Close.

The Shareholders' Report file closes.

Creating a Presentation from a Document

Using an existing document to create the foundation of a presentation is a great time-saver, if the document is similar to the presentation you're creating. You can import either an outline or a text document, and when the text is imported, PowerPoint uses the built-in heading *styles* in the Word document to produce the presentation. If there are no heading styles in the document, paragraph indentations (such as tabs) define the outline structure. You can also insert an outline into an existing presentation to create additional slides. Small documents are great time-savers for creating bulleted slides.

Heading 1, Heading 2, and Heading 3 are all examples of heading styles in Word.

 NOTE You can create your own heading styles, use the default heading styles from the Normal template, or use the AutoFormat feature to apply heading styles. As long as you use a built-in heading style name, such as Heading 1, the heading text in Word will import into PowerPoint.

Importing a Document into a Presentation

When importing a Word document or outline, PowerPoint looks for heading styles in the document to create the slides for the presentation. Heading 1 text becomes a slide title, and text in Headings 2 through 5 becomes either slide subtitles or bulleted text, depending on the slide layout. The number of slides created will depend on the number of Heading 1 styles. After you import the document, you can add, delete, and edit slides as needed.

You've been given the preliminary version of The Kenya Coffee Company Shareholders' report. The shareholders' meeting coordinator has asked you to use this report to create a presentation for the meeting.

Create a presentation from a document

You can also start PowerPoint by clicking the Microsoft PowerPoint button on the Programs Shortcut Bar.

1 Click Start, point to Programs, and then click Microsoft PowerPoint.

PowerPoint opens and the PowerPoint dialog box appears.

2 Select the Open An Existing Presentation option button, and then click OK.

The Open dialog box appears.

3 Click the Files Of Type down arrow, and then click All Outlines.

4 From your Office 97 SBS Practice\Lesson 9 folder, click Shareholders' Report, and then click Open.

A new presentation is created and appears in Outline view. Your screen should look similar to the following illustration.

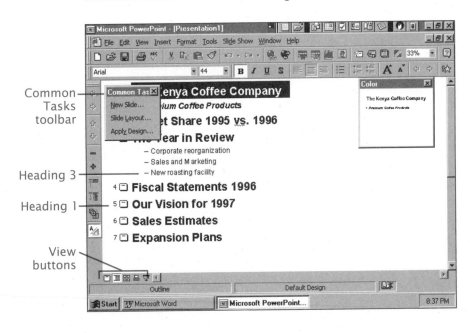

185

Save

5 On the Standard toolbar, click the Save button.

The Save dialog box appears.

6 Save the new presentation as **Shareholders' Presentation** in your Office 97 SBS Practice\Lesson 9 folder.

Files saved as Word documents are identified by PowerPoint as outlines.

TIP In Word, you can also use the Send To Microsoft PowerPoint command on the File menu to quickly create a presentation from a Word document. This command imports the active Word document into a new presentation. Whether you use the Send To command in Word or you import the Word document from within PowerPoint, the result is the same. The method you use depends on what program you're using at the time.

Maintaining Consistency with a Design Template

If the Common Tasks toolbar prevents you from viewing or working on a slide, you can reposition the toolbar by dragging it to a new location.

When a document or outline is imported into PowerPoint, it has no *design template* applied to it. A design template gives a presentation a professional look by coordinating the colors, formats, and fonts used on each slide. If you've ever seen a presentation where each slide has different fonts, color schemes, or backgrounds, you know how distracting inconsistency can be. Inconsistency in appearance takes away from the presentation's message. A design template helps you create a polished presentation that draws attention to the information rather than the design flaws.

Apply a design template

In this exercise, you apply a design template to a presentation to give it a consistent, professional look.

Slide View

1 Click the Slide View button located just above the status bar.

The first slide in the presentation appears in Slide view.

Apply Design

2 On the Standard toolbar, click the Apply Design button.

The Apply Design dialog box appears. Predefined design templates are listed in the Look In Presentation Designs box. A preview of the selected design template appears to the right.

3 Click on several design templates to preview the various templates available.

4 Click Contemporary Portrait, and then click Apply.

The Contemporary Portrait design template is applied to each slide in the Shareholders' Presentation.

5 On the Standard toolbar, click the Save button.

Integrating Document Text in a Presentation

For additional information on integrating information in a PowerPoint presentation, see Lesson 10, "Integrating Workbook Data in a Presentation."

Importing a Word outline is just one step in polishing your presentation. If you have a table or phrases you'd like to use, you can link or embed them onto any slide. Using information from other documents saves you time, maintains consistency, and streamlines the task of gathering data.

The following table is a guide to help you determine which method of integrating information—linking or embedding—best suits your task.

If your task meets these criteria	Use this method
You do not want changes to the source object to be reflected in the destination object.	Embed
or	
You want to make changes to the destination object, but you don't have access to the source object.	
You want any changes to the sources object to be reflected in the destination object.	Link

You've already created the foundation for the Shareholders' Presentation by importing a Word document into PowerPoint. The document also contains a company motto and a table of sales estimates that can be integrated by linking and embedding the information into the presentation.

 NOTE To review integration methods in each Office 97 program, see Appendix C, "Integration Techniques."

Embedding Document Text in a Presentation

When using document text on a presentation slide, you should limit the amount of text you use. Text in a presentation should be brief and to the point, and should supplement the spoken presentation. This type of text can be easily embedded in a presentation. Embedding the text, instead of copying and pasting, gives you editing capabilities that can be very useful when fine-tuning the presentation.

Change the slide layout

In this exercise, you change the page layout of a slide from Bulleted List to Title Only.

1   Drag the vertical scroll box to Page 5 of 7: Our Vision for 1997.

2   On the Common Tasks toolbar, click the Slide Layout button.

    The Slide Layout dialog box appears.

Although the Bulleted List layout will not interfere with an object you embed, you'll find it easier to work with the slide if you change the layout to Title Only before embedding the object.

3 Click the third diagram in the third row of the Slide Layout box.

The Title Only slide layout is selected. Your screen should look similar to the following illustration.

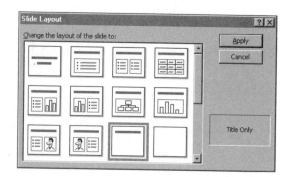

4 Click Apply.

The layout of the fifth slide changes from a Bulleted List to Title Only. Now when you embed the company motto, you can position it anywhere on the slide.

Embed text on a slide

If you want a static copy instead of embedded text, use the Paste Special command on the Edit menu and click the Paste Picture option.

In this exercise, you embed text from a document on a presentation slide.

1 On the taskbar, click the Microsoft Word button.

2 From your Office 97 SBS Practice\Lesson 9 folder, open the Shareholders' Report document.

3 At the bottom of the first page, select the text "A coffee blend for every occasion," including the quotation marks.

4 On the Standard toolbar, click the Copy button.

5 On the taskbar, click the Microsoft PowerPoint button.

6 On the Standard toolbar, click the Paste button.

The text is embedded on the slide.

Copy

Paste

Edit the embedded text

In this exercise, you edit the embedded text to improve its readability.

1 Double-click the embedded text block.

The toolbars change to Word tools.

2 Drag the bottom center sizing handle down so you can see all the text.

3 Drag to select the text.

Font Size

Font Color

Center

4 On the Formatting toolbar, click the Font Size down arrow, and then click 36.

The size of the text font changes to 36.

5 On the Formatting toolbar, click the Font Color down arrow.

A palette of font colors appears.

6 Click the color Dark Red.

The font color changes to dark red.

7 On the Formatting toolbar, click the Center button.

The text is centered.

8 Drag the right center sizing handle to the right until all the text is on one line. If necessary, drag the sizing handles until you can see all the text, and center the text block on the slide.

9 Click outside the text block.

The embedded text appears on the slide. Your screen should look similar to the following illustration.

Embedded text object —

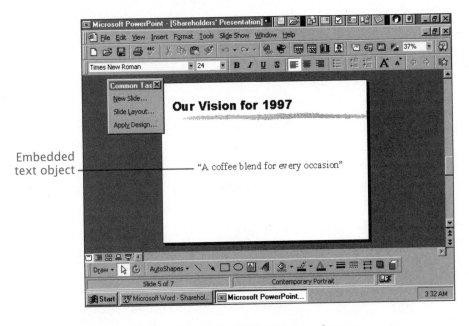

Save

10 On the Standard toolbar, click the Save button.

Linking a Word Table to a Presentation

Although you can create tables within PowerPoint, you may find that the information you want to place on a slide is already organized in a Word table. If you have such a table, you can link it from the document to a slide in

PowerPoint. There are several advantages to linking a table to a slide: You save time because you don't have to re-create the table and because the information on the slide is updated whenever changes are made to the document table.

Change the slide layout

In this exercise, you change the slide layout before linking a document table to it.

Next Slide

1   Click the Next Slide button.

Page 6 of 7: Sales Estimates appears.

2   On the Common Tasks toolbar, click the Slide Layout button.

The Slide Layout dialog box appears.

3   Click the third diagram in the third row of the Slide Layout box, and then click Apply.

The slide is changed from a Bulleted List layout to a Title Only layout.

As with embedding objects, it can be easier visually to work with a slide if you change the slide layout before you link an object.

Link a document table to a slide

In this exercise, you copy a document table and then link it to a slide.

1   On the taskbar, click the Microsoft Word button.

2   Scroll down to the top of the second page, and then click in the sales estimates table.

3   On the Table menu, click Select Table.

The entire table is selected.

Copy

4   On the Standard toolbar, click the Copy button.

5   On the taskbar, click the Microsoft PowerPoint button.

6   On the Edit menu, click Paste Special.

The Paste Special dialog box appears.

To link objects, use the Paste Special command. The Paste button only allows you to embed objects.

7   Click the Paste Link option button.

8   Under As, be sure that Microsoft Word Document Object is selected, and then click OK.

The linked table appears on the slide.

9   On the Standard toolbar, click the Save button.

Save

Format the linked object

In this exercise, you change the size of the linked object in PowerPoint to improve its readability.

1   Be sure that the linked object is selected.

2   On the Format menu, click Object.

You can also drag the sizing handles to adjust the height and width of the linked object. By changing the height scale, the width scale is proportionally adjusted for you.

The Format Object dialog box appears.

3   Click the Size tab.

4   Under Scale, select the text in the Height box, type **180** and click OK.

The right sizing handles will appear off the slide. This will have no effect on the slide show.

Edit the source table

In this exercise, you edit the source table and view the changes in the linked object.

1   On the taskbar, click the Microsoft Word button.

2   Select the Quarter 3 sales estimates for the South region, and then type **300,000**

3   On the Standard toolbar, click the Save button.

4   On the taskbar, click the Microsoft PowerPoint button.

The changes in the Quarter 3 sales estimate for the South region have not been updated.

5   Use the right mouse button to click the linked object, and then click Update Link.

The changes you made in the Word table are now reflected in the linked object. Your screen should look like the following illustration.

Linked object

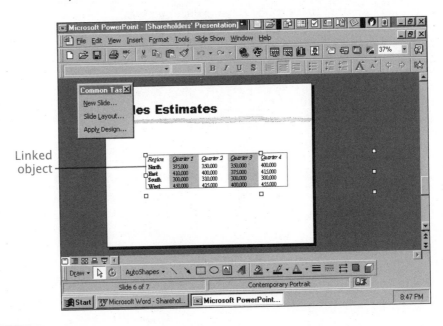

6   On the Standard toolbar, click the Save button.

TIP You can create a presentation or use an existing presentation on the Web or company intranet by saving the presentation as HTML text. To do this, open the presentation. On the File menu, click Save As HTML, and then follow the steps in the Internet Assistant to create a folder or file that can be moved to your Internet or intranet Web server. To make sure your presentation colors are appropriate for online viewing, use one of the Internet presentation templates available in PowerPoint.

Viewing a Presentation in a Document

When a presentation is in final form, you may want others to review it before its debut. If the presentation was originally created from a document, you may find that embedding the presentation in the document saves time because all the pieces are together in one location. You can embed single slides, a group of slides, or an entire presentation. A presentation can also be linked in a document.

To view an embedded presentation, you double-click the object representing the presentation. PowerPoint starts, and the presentation appears as a *slide show*. Changes made to an embedded presentation do not affect the source presentation.

An embedded presentation can be represented in a document as an icon or as a picture of the first slide in the presentation. The icon takes up only a small amount of space in your document, and the presentation filename appears under the icon. If you use a slide to represent the presentation, the filename does not appear, but you can resize the presentation object so it takes up as little or as much space in the document as you want.

Embed a presentation in a document

In this exercise, you embed a presentation in the originating document so that others can preview both at the same time.

1 On the taskbar, click the Microsoft Word button.
2 Press CTRL+END to go to the end of the Shareholders' Report document.
3 On the Insert menu, click Object.

   The Object dialog box appears.
4 Click the Create From File tab.
5 Click Browse.

   The Browse dialog box appears.

After you clear the Float Over Text check box, the icon behaves like regular text. If the Float Over Text check box is selected, the icon can be placed in front or behind text and other objects.

6 From your Office 97 SBS Practice\Lesson 9 folder, click Shareholders' Presentation, and then click OK.

7 Clear the Float Over Text check box, select the Display As Icon check box, and then click OK.

The presentation is embedded into the document as an icon. Your screen should look similar to the following illustration.

Shareholders' Presentation icon

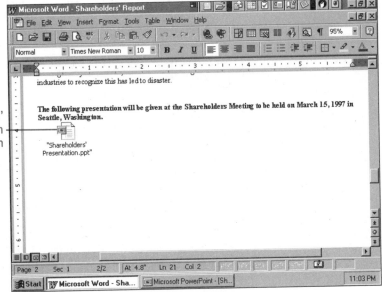

8 On the Standard toolbar, click the Save button.

Save

View an embedded presentation

In this exercise, you view the presentation from within the document.

1 Double-click the Shareholders' Presentation.ppt icon.

The presentation slide show begins.

2 Click the mouse button to advance from slide to slide.

When the presentation is completed, you return to the Shareholders' Report document.

 TIP If you need to create a document based on a presentation, you can use the Send To Microsoft Word command on the File menu in PowerPoint to create a Word outline from the presentation.

Routing a Presentation on a Network

Before you finalize a presentation, you may want others to review it. In the past, you may have hand-delivered or e-mailed a copy to each person who would review it. Then you might have compiled their comments into a single document—or continually shuffled through them while making changes. If you *route* your presentation, you can eliminate this problem. When you route a presentation, you send a copy online to each recipient, one after another. Each recipient can view the previous recipient's comments, and when the last recipient is done, the presentation will automatically be returned to you in a compiled form.

When routing a presentation, you can protect certain parts of the document from change. You can also track the progress of your presentation from recipient to recipient.

Now that you have integrated the preliminary Shareholders' Report into a presentation, you want several of your co-workers to review it. You will route the Shareholders' Report document to them so that they can view each other's comments and so that all comments are compiled when it's returned to you.

 IMPORTANT Because you will be exploring the use of e-mail routing, you will need to have Microsoft Exchange or another 32-bit mail system that is compatible with MAPI available to you, and at least one person you can send e-mail to. The following exercises illustrate how to route files using Exchange.

Route a document containing an embedded presentation

If necessary, log on to your mail system.

In this exercise, you route the Shareholders' Report with the embedded Shareholders' Presentation to others in the company for comments.

1 On the File menu in Word, point to Send To, and then click Routing Recipient.

   The Routing Slip dialog box appears. The document title from the Properties dialog box is automatically inserted in the Subject box.

2 Click Address.

   The Address Book dialog box appears.

To change the order of the recipient list, select a name in the To list, and then click one of the Move arrows.

3 Select the name of a co-worker, and then click To.

4 Repeat step 3 for each recipient, and then click OK.

5 Click in the message text area, and then type **Please review the Shareholders' Report and Presentation. The presentation is embedded for viewing.**

6 Be sure that the One After Another option button is selected and that the Return When Done and Track Status check boxes are selected. Tracked Changes should appear in the Protect For box.

Your screen should look similar to the following illustration.

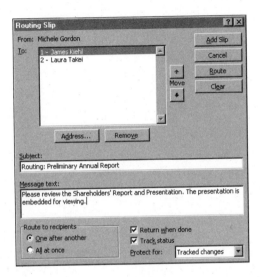

7 Click Route.

The report with the presentation is routed to the first recipient.

8 On the Standard toolbar, click the Save button.

Save

 NOTE If you are a recipient of a routed file and wish to send it to the next routing recipient, open the file. On the File menu, point to Send To, and then click Next Routing Recipient. Be sure the Route Document To *recipient name* option button is selected in the Send dialog box, and then click OK. The last recipient will route the document back to the originator.

Creating Presentation Handouts

Before you deliver a presentation, you can print handouts that help the audience follow your presentation. Handouts can be created with two, three, or six slides on a page. Each image on the page is a copy of a slide in the presentation. When printing either two or six slides per page, the slide images take up the entire page. With three slides per page, the slide images are on the left side of the page, leaving the right side for audience notes.

Print handouts

In this exercise, you print audience handouts with three slides on each page.

1 On the taskbar, click the Microsoft PowerPoint button.

2 On the File menu, click Print.

The Print dialog box appears.

3 Click the Print What down arrow, and click Handouts (3 Slides Per Page).

4 Be sure that the Frame Slides check box is selected.

When printed, a frame will appear around each slide.

5 Click OK.

The handouts are printed.

 NOTE If you'd like to build on the skills that you learned in this lesson, you can do the One Step Further. Otherwise, skip to "Finish the lesson."

One Step Further: Working with the Slide Master

Placing graphics in a presentation can enhance the message of a single slide, develop a theme throughout the presentation, or identify the origins of a presentation. For example, if you are giving a presentation where audience members come and go, you want to make sure they can identify what company you're from at all times. You can accomplish this by placing the company name or logo on each slide. Going to each slide and typing the company name or inserting the company logo can be time-consuming, and you run the risk of inconsistencies in the slides. You can use the *slide master* to make sure your company name and/or logo appears in the same place, with the same font, and in the same size on every slide. You can also enter headers, footers, and any other common slide elements on the slide master.

At the shareholders' meeting, people will be entering the room at different times. To make sure everyone knows that the presentation is about The Kenya Coffee Company, a co-worker suggests that the company logo appear on each slide.

Add a graphic to the slide master

In this exercise, you add The Kenya Coffee Company logo to the slide master so it appears on every slide in your presentation.

1   On the View menu, point to Master, and then click Slide Master.

The screen changes to the slide master for the Shareholders' Presentation. The Master toolbar appears.

2   On the Insert menu, point to Picture, and then click From File.

The Insert Picture dialog box appears.

3   From your Office 97 SBS Practice\Lesson 9 folder, click KCCLOGO, and then click Insert.

The picture is inserted onto the slide master. The Picture toolbar appears.

4   Drag the image to the lower-right corner of the Object Area For AutoLayouts on the slide master.

Your screen should look similar to the following illustration.

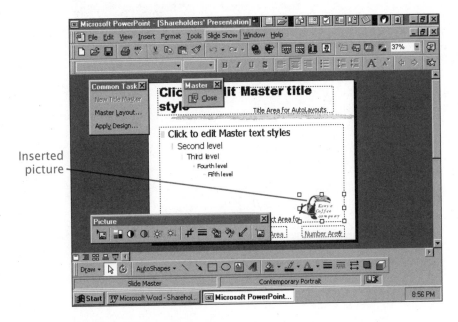

Inserted picture

5   On the Master toolbar, click the Close button.

The screen changes back to Slide view. The Kenya logo appears on the slide. Your screen should look similar to the following illustration.

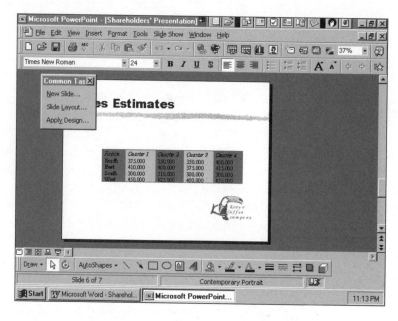

Previous Slide

6 Click the Previous Slide button.

The previous slide in the presentation appears with the Kenya logo in the same location.

7 On the Standard toolbar, click the Save button.

Save

8 On the PowerPoint window, click the Close button.

Finish the lesson

1 On the Word window, click the Close button.

2 Close all open windows.

Lesson Summary

To	Do this
Import a Word document into a presentation	In the PowerPoint Open dialog box, click the Files Of Type down arrow, and then click All Outlines. Select the document you want to import, and then click Open.

To	Do this	Button
Apply a design template	On the Standard toolbar, click the Apply Design button. Click a design template from the Presentation Designs folder, and then click Apply.	
Change the slide layout	Select the slide on which you want to change the layout. On the Common Tasks toolbar, click Slide Layout. Click a layout, and then click Apply.	
Embed text	In the source document, select the text to be embedded. On the Standard toolbar, click the Copy button. Switch to PowerPoint. Select the slide to which you want to embed. Click the Paste button.	
Link a document table	In the source document, select the table to be linked. On the Standard toolbar, click the Copy button. Switch to PowerPoint. Select the slide to which you want to link. On the Edit menu, click Paste Special. Click the Paste Link option. Under As, be sure that the Microsoft Word Document Object is selected, and then click OK.	
Embed a presentation in a document as an icon	In the document, click where you want to embed the presentation. On the Insert menu, click Object. Click the Create From File tab. Click Browse. Click the file you want to embed, and then click OK. Clear the Float Over Text check box, select the Display As Icon check box, and then click OK.	
Print handouts	From the presentation, on the File menu, click Print. Click the Print What down arrow, and click the handout type you want. Be sure the Frames Slides check box is selected, and then click OK.	

To	Do this
Route a presentation	In the document, on the File menu, point to Send To, and then click Routing Recipient. (You may need to log on to your mail system.) Click Address, click the name of each recipient, and then click To. Click OK. Type a message in the message text area. Be sure that the One After Another option button is selected, and that the Return When Done and Track Status check boxes are selected. Tracked Changes should appear in the Protect For box. Click Route.

For online information about	On the Help menu, click Contents And Index, click the Index tab, and then type
Creating a presentation from a document	*PowerPoint*: importing data
Embedding text in a presentation	*PowerPoint*: embedded objects
Linking a table in a presentation	*PowerPoint*: linked objects
Viewing a presentation in a document	*Word*: embedded objects
Routing a presentation	*Word*: routing documents

Integrating Workbook Data in a Presentation

Estimated time
35 min.

In this lesson you will learn how to:

- Embed a chart in a presentation.
- Link a chart to a presentation.
- Embed a workbook in a presentation.
- View a workbook during a presentation.
- Embed a presentation in a workbook.

As you learned in the previous lesson, it's easy to integrate word processing documents with presentations. The same is true for spreadsheets. Complex information in a spreadsheet, such as a chart, can be useful in a presentation. You can report on summary cost figures or use a chart to show sales trends. If you keep your financial information in a spreadsheet and create charts to graphically represent the data, you shouldn't have to recreate the chart just to use it in a presentation. Instead, you can embed or link the spreadsheet chart to a presentation.

With Microsoft Office 97, you can quickly link and embed Microsoft Excel workbook data and charts to create an effective Microsoft PowerPoint presentation. If you link a chart to a slide, when you update the chart in Excel, the linked information in PowerPoint is updated automatically. With embedding, you can edit data and charts in a presentation using all the features of Excel without changing the original data or chart. You can also embed a presentation in an Excel workbook for online viewing.

In this lesson, you will continue to create a presentation for The Kenya Coffee Company shareholders' meeting. The Financial workbook contains two charts that are to be either linked or embedded in the presentation. The Product Information workbook is to be embedded as a reference tool for the presenter. You will also embed the presentation in the source workbook for online viewing and verification by the Accounting department.

Start the lesson

Open Office Document

1   On the Office Shortcut Bar, click the Open Office Document button.

    The Open Office Document dialog box appears.

2   From your Office 97 SBS Practice\Lesson 10 folder, open the Finalize Shareholders' presentation.

    The Finalize Shareholders' presentation opens.

3   Save the file as **Shareholders' Meeting** in your Office 97 SBS Practice\Lesson 10 folder.

4   On the Office Shortcut Bar, click the Open Office Document button.

    The Open Office Document dialog box appears.

5   From your Office 97 SBS Practice\Lesson 10 folder, open the Financial workbook.

    The Financial workbook for The Kenya Coffee Company opens. It contains two data worksheets, two chart sheets, and a presentation worksheet.

6   Save the file as **Market and Income Data** in your Office 97 SBS Practice\Lesson 10 folder.

Using Workbook Data in a Presentation

Using Excel workbooks in presentations can be valuable to both the presenter and the audience. The data and charts in a workbook are often more detailed than the simple tables or charts you can create in other programs. For example, a table created in a word processor cannot perform the complex calculations that your data may require. Integrating workbook information can save time and allow you to include vital information in the presentation. By embedding and linking workbook information, you can add clarity and professionalism to your presentation.

You now have the data you need to complete the Shareholders' Meeting presentation for The Kenya Coffee Company. You will embed a chart that may need some formatting changes later, and you will link a chart that hasn't been finalized yet. The presenter has indicated that it would be nice to have the Product Information workbook available if details are needed during the presentation. You will embed the workbook as an icon so it can be activated during the presentation.

> **NOTE** To review integration methods in each Office 97 program, see Appendix C, "Integration Techniques."

Embedding a Worksheet Chart in a Presentation

When you embed information from a workbook in a presentation, all the tools and capabilities of Excel are available to the embedded object. If you change the data in the embedded workbook, the source data remains unchanged, and if you change the source data, the embedded or destination data remains unchanged. The source and destination objects are independent when you embed, unlike linking, where the destination data is dependent on the source data.

Embedding is a useful tool when you need the editing capabilities of Excel within the presentation, but you don't need an ongoing relationship with the source data. For example, if you have a workbook chart for sales goals that needs to be updated as the goals change, you can embed the chart in reports or presentations. By embedding the chart, you do not have to worry about changes to the source data affecting the embedded chart, and you'll have full access to the editing capabilities of Excel without maintaining a separate file.

You can embed both new and existing Excel workbooks in a presentation slide. When you embed workbook information in a presentation, the entire workbook file is embedded. The selected worksheet or cell range is the only visible element when the object is inactive. Once you activate the embedded object, all the workbook data is available. You can then change the data, display a different worksheet, and add new worksheets and data to the embedded workbook.

Embed a chart in a slide

In this exercise, you copy a workbook and then embed it in a presentation slide so you can modify it later without changing the source workbook.

1 Click the Market Share Chart worksheet tab.

A chart created from the Market Share data appears.

2 On the Standard toolbar, click the Copy button.

3 On the taskbar, click the Microsoft PowerPoint button.

Slide 1 of 8: The Kenya Coffee Company appears.

4 Click the Next Slide button.

Slide 2 of 8: Market Share 1995 vs. 1996 appears.

5 On the Standard toolbar, click the Paste button.

The entire Market and Income Data workbook is embedded in the slide. Only the Market Share chart is visible, because it was the active worksheet tab when the workbook was embedded.

Copy

Next Slide

Paste

When you copy a workbook, the active worksheet tab is the image that's visible when it is embedded. When you edit the embedded object, you can change the active worksheet tab to show a different worksheet image.

NOTE In PowerPoint, pasting a chart on a slide embeds it as an Excel chart object. You can also embed an Excel chart by clicking Paste Special on the Edit menu, clicking the Paste option button, and then clicking Microsoft Excel Chart Object in the As box.

Format the slide

In this exercise, you resize the chart and omit the slide master background from the slide because the Kenya logo will be partially obscured by the chart.

1   At the bottom of the slide, drag the middle sizing handle down below the Kenya logo to enlarge the object.

2   On the Format menu, click Background.

   The Background dialog box appears.

3   Select the Omit Background Graphics From Master check box, and then click Apply.

   The Kenya Coffee Company logo and the yellow line are removed from the current slide. Your screen should look similar to the following illustration.

If you click Apply To All, the Slide Master background graphics will be omitted from all slides in the presentation.

The embedded
workbook
object with
the active
chart
worksheet
visible

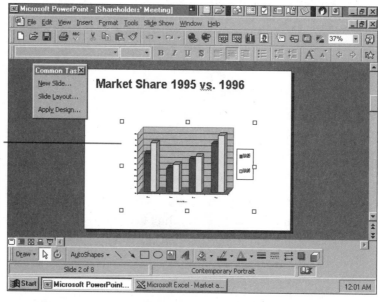

Save

4   On the Standard toolbar, click the Save button.

Linking a Worksheet Chart to a Presentation

Linking and embedding differ in where the data is stored and how changes to the source data affect the object that's linked or embedded. When you link workbook information, an image of the selected information is stored in the destination slide, but the actual data is still stored in the source file. If any changes are made in the source file, the destination file is automatically updated. You cannot make changes to the object from the destination file. For example, if your company gives a monthly presentation for new employees that contains benefits and salary information that changes periodically, you could link the information in the presentation to the source file so that it's always current.

Unlike embedding, when you create a link to workbook information, the entire workbook is not available to you. Linking is a good choice when file size is a consideration or you want changes in the source information to be reflected. A linked object takes up less file space than an embedded object.

Link a chart to a slide

In this exercise, you copy a chart and then link it to a presentation slide.

Copy

1   On the taskbar, click the Microsoft Excel button.
2   Click the 97 Projections Chart worksheet tab.

    A chart created from the 97 Income Projections data appears.
3   On the Standard toolbar, click the Copy button.

    The entire chart is copied.
4   On the taskbar, click the Microsoft PowerPoint button.
5   Drag the vertical scroll box to Slide 8 of 8: 1997 Income Projections.
6   On the Edit menu, click Paste Special.

    The Paste Special dialog box appears.
7   Click the Paste Link option button, and then click OK.

    The chart is linked to the slide.

Format the slide

In this exercise, you resize the chart and omit the slide master background from the slide.

1   At the bottom of the slide, drag the middle sizing handle down below the Kenya logo to enlarge the object.
2   On the Format menu, click Background.

    The Background dialog box appears.

3 Select the Omit Background Graphics From Master check box, and then click Apply.

Edit the source data

When an Excel chart is created from existing data, the data and the chart are linked. Therefore, the linked chart in PowerPoint is indirectly linked to the data.

In this exercise, you edit the source data for the linked chart, and then view the changes in the presentation slide.

1 On the taskbar, click the Microsoft Excel button.

2 Click the 97 Income Projections worksheet tab.

The data used to create the 97 Projections chart appears on the worksheet.

3 Click cell B11, type **75000** and then press ENTER.

4 On the Standard toolbar, click the Save button.

Save

5 On the taskbar, click the Microsoft PowerPoint button.

The changes to the linked chart are updated on the slide. Your screen should look similar to the following illustration.

The change made to the interest income on the worksheet is reflected in the linked object.

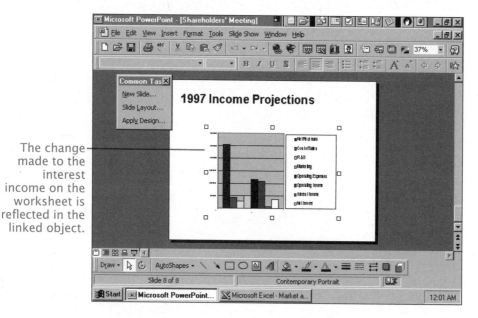

6 On the Standard toolbar, click the Save button.

IMPORTANT A link is dependent on the source file location. If you move the source file to a different drive, or if it is deleted, the link in the destination file cannot be updated. You can reestablish a link by updating the source location. With the linked object selected, on the Edit menu, click Links. With the original link source selected in the Source File box, click Change Source. Select the source file in its new location, and then click Open. Click Update Now to refresh the view, and then click Close.

Embedding a Workbook for Viewing During a Presentation

Workbook information can provide valuable backup data during a presentation. But when you are viewing a presentation as a screen show, the other parts of an embedded workbook are not available, because only the image of the active worksheet is visible. If you need to view an entire workbook during a screen show, you can change the settings for the embedded object so you can view it and return to the presentation where you left off. For example, you can embed a workbook as an actionable object, and then click on the actionable object during the presentation—and the workbook will open, displaying the information you need.

An embedded object can be represented as an icon or an image of the object. If you embed a workbook as an icon, not only can you locate it anywhere on a slide, but you can place it on an existing slide. For example, if you have a slide listing your company products, and you would also like to show product descriptions, costs, and availability, you can embed the workbook containing this information as an icon on the slide. When you click the icon, the workbook opens. In some cases the information may not be needed, but it's good to have it on hand without taking up valuable space on a slide.

Embed a workbook as an icon

1   Drag the vertical scroll box to Slide 5 of 8: Our Vision for 1997.

2   Click any blank area on Slide 5 of 8: Our Vision for 1997.

3   On the Insert menu, click Object.

    The Insert Object dialog box appears.

4   Click the Create From File option button, and then click Browse.

    The Browse dialog box appears.

5   From your Office 97 SBS Practice\Lesson 10 folder, click Product Information, and then click OK.

    The Insert Object dialog box appears.

6 Select the Display As Icon check box, and then click OK.

The Product Information workbook is embedded in the slide as an icon.

You can resize the Excel icon by dragging the sizing handles.

7 Drag the Excel icon to the lower-left corner of the slide.

Your screen should look similar to the following illustration.

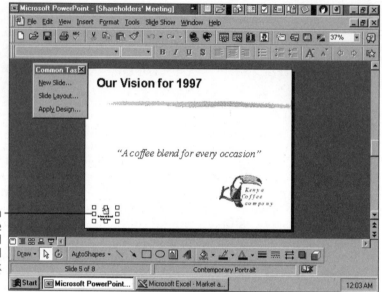

Icon represents the embedded Excel workbook

8 On the Standard toolbar, click the Save button.

Save

Change object action settings

In this exercise, you change the settings for the embedded workbook to open when you click the Excel icon during a slide show.

1 Be sure that the Excel icon is selected.

2 On the Slide Show menu, click Action Settings.

The Action Settings dialog box appears. The Mouse Click tab is selected.

3 Click the Object Action option button.

4 Click the Object Action down arrow, and then click Open.

When you click the Excel icon during a presentation, the embedded workbook will open.

5 Click OK.

6 On the Standard toolbar, click the Save button.

View the presentation and embedded workbook

In this exercise, you view the slide show and open the embedded workbook.

You can also use the Slide Show button if you want to view the slide show starting with the current slide.

1 On the Slide Show menu, click View Show.

The slide show begins. The first slide in the presentation appears.

2 Click the mouse button to advance to the next slide in the presentation.

3 Click the mouse button three more times until you reach the Our Vision for 1997 slide.

The slide appears with the embedded workbook icon.

You may have to maximize the Excel window to view the entire workbook.

4 Move the mouse to make the mouse pointer visible.

5 Click the embedded workbook icon.

After a few moments, the embedded Product Information workbook opens.

You can move from worksheet to worksheet within the workbook and edit the data as with any embedded object.

6 On the File menu, click Close & Return To PowerPoint Slide Show–[Shareholders' Meeting].

The embedded workbook closes and the slide show reappears.

7 Click the mouse button four times.

The slide show concludes and you return to the PowerPoint window.

8 On the PowerPoint window, click the Close button.

A message appears asking if you want to save changes.

9 Click Yes.

PowerPoint closes, and the Market and Income Data workbook appears.

 TIP You can run a PowerPoint slide show on a computer that doesn't have PowerPoint installed by using the PowerPoint Viewer. The PowerPoint Viewer is located in the ValuPack folder on the Office 97 CD-ROM, or you can download it from the World Wide Web.

Embedding a Presentation in a Workbook

Not only can you embed workbook data in a presentation, you can also embed a presentation in a workbook. If you have a presentation that contains information from a workbook, you can embed the presentation in the workbook as part of the workbook history. You can also embed the presentation as part of a reviewing process in which you send the workbook to others. That way, the workbook information and the presentation can be reviewed at the same time, in one file.

You have now completed the Shareholders' Meeting presentation. The Accounting department wants to see how their figures are used in the presentation. You embed the presentation in the workbook so it can be viewed by others without changing the source presentation.

Embed a presentation in a workbook

In this exercise, you embed a presentation on a worksheet within a workbook.

1 Click the Maximize button on the Market and Income Data window.

2 Click the Last Worksheet button, and then click the Presentation worksheet tab.

Last Worksheet

A worksheet prepared for the presentation appears.

3 Click cell A4.

4 On the Insert menu, click Object.

The Object dialog box appears.

5 Click the Create From File tab, and then click Browse.

The Browse dialog box appears.

You can also embed the presentation as an icon by selecting the Display As Icon check box in the Object dialog box.

6 From your Office 97 SBS Practice\Lesson 10 folder, click Shareholders' Meeting, and then click Insert.

The Object dialog box reappears.

7 Click OK.

An image of the first slide in the presentation appears on the worksheet.

The embedded presentation appears as an image of the first slide in the presentation.

Save

8 On the Standard toolbar, click the Save button.

9 On the Excel window, click the Close button.

> **NOTE** If you'd like to build on the skills that you learned in this lesson, you can do the One Step Further. Otherwise, skip to "Finish the lesson."

One Step Further: Adding a Presentation File to a Binder

For more information on Microsoft Office Binder, see Lesson 2, "Organizing Related Files."

Binders can be used to store related files, such as files for a report or client information. If you create a binder for a report, you might add placeholders as reminders for specific items you have yet to complete. Then, at a later time, you can replace the placeholder with the document, workbook, or presentation that the placeholder was made for.

The Summary binder, which contains information for the Annual Report, has a placeholder for the shareholders' presentation. You add the shareholders' presentation and delete the placeholder to complete the binder file.

Open a binder file

In this exercise, you open an existing binder file.

Open Office Document

A file being added to a binder can be open or closed when you add it because it is a copy of the file that's being added to the binder.

1 On the Office Shortcut Bar, click the Open Office Document button.

The Open Office Document dialog box appears.

2 From your Office 97 SBS Practice\Lesson 10 folder, open the Summary binder.

The Summary binder containing related Annual Report files opens.

3 Save the file as **Annual Report** in your Office 97 SBS Practice\Lesson 10 folder.

Replace a placeholder with a file

In this lesson, you replace a presentation placeholder in a binder with the actual presentation file.

1 In the left pane of the binder, click the Section 1 icon.

The menu, toolbars, and other screen controls for PowerPoint appear.

2 On the Section menu, click Add From File.

The Add From File dialog box appears.

3 From your Office 97 SBS Practice\Lesson 10 folder, click Shareholders' Meeting, and then click Add.

The Shareholders' Meeting presentation is added to the Annual Report binder file. An icon appears in the left pane of the binder below the Section 1 icon.

4 Be sure that the Section 1 icon is selected in the left pane of the binder.

5 On the Section menu, click Delete.

A message appears asking if you want to delete the section from the binder.

6 Click OK.

The presentation placeholder is deleted. A message appears asking if you want to update the links in the Annual Report binder.

7 Click OK.

The Shareholders' Meeting presentation icon is selected. Your screen should look similar to the following illustration.

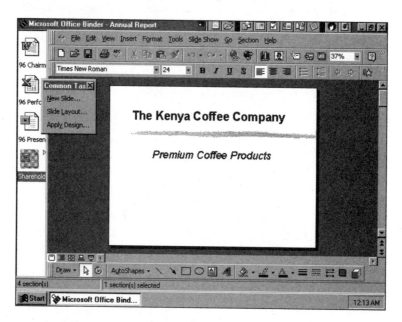

Clicking the Save button on the Standard toolbar saves only the document that is currently selected.

8 On the File menu, click Save Binder.

9 On the Binder window, click Close.

Office Binder closes.

Finish the lesson

➤ Close all open windows.

Lesson Summary

To	Do this	Button
Copy a chart	Click the chart to select it. On the Standard toolbar, click the Copy button.	
Embed a chart in a slide	Switch to the slide the chart will be embedded in. Click the Paste button. *or* On the Edit menu, click Paste Special. Be sure the Paste option button is selected. In the As box, click Microsoft Excel Chart Object, and then click OK.	
Link a chart to a slide	Copy the chart to be linked. Switch to the slide the chart will be linked to. On the Edit menu, click Paste Special. Click the Paste Link option button, and then click OK.	
Omit background graphics on a single slide	On the Format menu, click Background. Select the Omit Background Graphics From Master check box, and then click Apply.	
Embed a workbook as an icon in a slide	Switch to the slide the chart will be embedded in and click the slide to make it active. On the Insert menu, click Object. Click the Create From File option button, and then click Browse. Select the workbook file to embed, and then click OK. Select the Display As Icon check box, and then click OK.	
Change icon action settings to open when clicked	Be sure the object is selected. On the Slide Show menu, click Action Settings. On the Mouse Click tab, click the Object Action button. Click the Object Action down arrow, click Open, and then click OK.	

213

To	Do this
View an embedded workbook during a presentation	On the Slide Show menu, click View Show. Click to advance to the next slide. When you reach the slide with the Excel icon, double-click the Excel icon. When you are finished viewing the workbook, on the File menu, click Close & Return To PowerPoint Slide Show. Continue viewing the remainder of the slide show by clicking.
Embed a presentation in a workbook	On the Insert menu, click Object. Click the Create From File tab, and then click Browse. Select the presentation file to embed, click Insert, and then click OK. A picture of the first slide in the presentation appears on the worksheet. *or* Before clicking OK, select the Display As Icon check box. The presentation is displayed as an icon on the worksheet.

For online information about	On the Help menu, click Contents And Index, click the Index tab, and then type
Embedding a chart in a presentation	*PowerPoint*: embedded objects
Linking a chart to a presentation	*PowerPoint*: linked objects
Embedding a presentation in a workbook	*Excel*: embedded objects

Review & Practice

Estimated time

25 min.

You will review and practice how to:

- Import an existing word-processing document to create a presentation.
- Embed text in a presentation slide.
- Link a worksheet chart to a presentation slide.
- View a presentation within a word-processing document.

Before you move on to Part 5, you can practice the skills you learned in Part 4 by working through this Review & Practice section. You will create a presentation from an existing document, embed document text on a slide, link a chart to a slide, and view a presentation from within a document.

Scenario

With your new Microsoft Office 97 integration skills, you are helping Human Resources create a presentation for new employee orientations at The Kenya Coffee Company. You will import an existing orientation document with heading styles into Microsoft PowerPoint to create the presentation slides. You will embed the company motto from the orientation document on a slide, and link a coffee product chart to a slide. You will also embed the presentation as an icon in the orientation document for historical reference.

Step 1: Create a Presentation From an Existing Document

You have been provided with a document that was previously given to new employees during orientation. The information in the document will make up the slide titles and bullets for the new employee orientation presentation. You import the document into PowerPoint, and then apply a design template for consistency throughout the presentation.

1 Using the Office Shortcut Bar, open the Orientation document from your Office 97 SBS Practice\Review & Practice 4 folder.

2 Save the Orientation document as **Orientation Outline** in your Office 97 SBS Practice\Review & Practice 4 folder. Close the file.

3 Start PowerPoint, and open the Orientation Outline from your Office 97 SBS Practice\Review & Practice 4 folder. (Hint: Use the All Outlines file type to find the document.)

4 Apply the Portrait Notebook presentation design template.

5 Save the new presentation as **New Employee Orientation** in your Office 97 SBS Practice\Review & Practice 4 folder.

For more information about	See
Importing a document into a presentation	Lesson 9
Maintaining consistency with a design template	Lesson 9

Step 2: Embed Document Text in a Presentation

The company motto did not import over to the presentation because it does not have one of the heading styles applied to it. You use copy and paste to embed the company motto onto a slide.

1 Embed the text under the company name on slide 4: Employee Benefits.

2 Change the font of the embedded text to 26 and the color to Dark Red. Resize the text block as necessary.

For more information about	See
Embedding document text in a presentation	Lesson 9

Step 3: *Link a Chart to a Presentation*

The slide on coffee products should contain a chart that shows the current popularity of the company's coffee products. Since this information changes monthly, you link the chart to the presentation so that the information is always up to date.

1 Switch to slide 3: Coffee Products, and change the slide layout to Title Only.

2 Use the Office Shortcut Bar to open the Coffee Popularity workbook from your Office 97 SBS Practice\Review & Practice 4 folder.

3 Save the Coffee Popularity workbook as **Product Chart** in your Office 97 SBS Practice\Review & Practice 4 folder.

4 Link the chart on the Popularity worksheet tab to slide 3: Coffee Products.

For more information about	See
Linking a worksheet chart to a presentation	Lesson 10

Step 4: *View a Presentation Within a Document*

To retain the old orientation document for future reference, you embed a copy of it in the new orientation document.

1 Embed a copy of the New Employee Orientation presentation as an icon at the end of the Orientation Outline. (Hint: Insert it as an object from a file.)

2 View the presentation from the Orientation Outline document.

3 Save the outline, and then exit Word.

For more information about	See
Viewing a presentation in a document	Lesson 9

Finish the Review & Practice

➤ Close all open windows.

Going Online with Office Programs

Establishing Hyperlinks to Documents and Internet Sites

Estimated time
30 min.

In this lesson you will learn how to:

■ Create and use hyperlinks within and between files.

■ Use hyperlinks to access the Internet.

■ Send e-mail using a hyperlink.

As you learned in previous lessons, you can integrate information between all Microsoft Office 97 programs by importing, exporting, embedding, and linking. This type of integration is useful, but at times it's not necessary to maintain information in its original source form or within another document.

With so many organizations and individuals using computers, viewing information online is becoming commonplace. Viewing documents online lets us obtain information and respond to it faster than ever before. It also provides us with documentation opportunities, such as providing backup or reference information instantaneously about specific subjects in a document. For example, if you've created a report about relocating your company's headquarters, instead of including detailed plans and cost figures, you could reference that information so that the reader can choose whether or not to read it.

Hyperlinks are sometimes referred to as links or hot spots. The World Wide Web is also known simply as the Web.

Using Office 97, you can create *hyperlinks* to give readers quick access to referenced information. A hyperlink jumps to related information located elsewhere—it's similar to a cross-reference or a footnote, but the computer finds the information for you. When you click a hyperlink, it acts as a shortcut that jumps you to another location—within your current file, to other files on your hard drive, to your organization's intranet, or to a document on the Internet or World Wide Web. Using hyperlinks, you can introduce more information without being limited by things like page count, file size, or reader attention. Hyperlinks allow the online reader the option of pursuing related topics or detailed information based on their specific needs.

In this lesson, you are given a document that will be placed on The Kenya Coffee Company's intranet. The document is a combination of a memo to all employees, a letter to shareholders, and the 1996 Annual Report. You will create hyperlinks that jump the reader from within the online document to related topics, to other documents that give the reader detailed information, and to related sites on the Internet and World Wide Web. You will also create a hyperlink that lets the reader send e-mail to a specific address from within the intranet document.

Start the lesson

Open Office Document

1   On the Office Shortcut Bar, click the Open Office Document button.

The Open Office Document dialog box appears.

2   From your Office 97 SBS Practice\Lesson 11 folder, open the 96 Financials workbook.

3   Save the file as **Financial Statements 96** in your Office 97 SBS Practice\Lesson 11 folder.

4   On the Excel window, click the Close button.

5   On the Office Shortcut Bar, click the Open Office Document button.

The Open Office Document dialog box appears.

6   From your Office 97 SBS Practice\Lesson 11 folder, open the Kenya Intranet document.

7   Save the file as **Year in Review 96** in your Office 97 SBS Practice\ Lesson 11 folder.

Moving Within and Between Documents

Although the default appearance of hyperlinks is blue and underlined in most browsers and programs, most allow you to customize the color.

If you've ever been on the Internet, you will recognize hyperlinks as the blue underlined text that, when clicked, takes you to other pages on the same *Web site* or on another Web site. Just as you create hyperlinks on the Web, you can create hyperlinks in your Office 97 files that can take you to other locations within the current file, to other files on your hard drive, to your company's intranet, and to the Internet and World Wide Web. Hyperlinks are used to enrich Web pages and documents that are designed to be read online.

There are several ways to create hyperlinks in your Office 97 files. You can use automatic formatting by typing an Internet address or *URL*, or by using the Insert Hyperlink button. In addition, you can drag and drop hyperlinks in Word. The following table lists the various methods of creating a hyperlink in each of the Office 97 programs.

Program	Hyperlink methods
Access	Add HyperlinkAddress properties Insert Hyperlink button
Excel	Insert Hyperlink button
Outlook	Automatic formatting
PowerPoint	Insert Hyperlink button Using Action Settings
Word	Automatic formatting Drag-and-drop Insert Hyperlink button

Hyperlinks can be displayed in two forms: as the actual address or location, or as text or an object that's connected to an address or location. In Office 97, hyperlinks typically appear as blue underlined text. When you return to a hyperlink that you've used, the hyperlink text color changes to purple by default.

Hyperlinks are meant to be used when a document will be read online. The hyperlink jumps the reader directly to the information that's referenced by the hyperlink text. If a document containing hyperlinks is printed, the hyperlinks are much less effective because the reader can see only the address or location of a document or the object to which the link is connected.

The Kenya Coffee Company employees are just beginning to explore the capabilities of their new intranet. To introduce them to it, a document is being placed on the intranet containing the 1996 Annual Report, the Shareholders letter, and a memo from the CEO. You'll create hyperlinks in the document to move the reader to related topics and supporting documents.

Creating Hyperlinks to Move Within a Document

For a demonstration of how to create hyperlinks, double-click the Camcorder Files On The Internet shortcut on your Desktop or connect to the Internet address listed on p. xxx.

When working with long documents or files, you may spend a lot of time trying to locate specific information. By creating hyperlinks to jump you to related information in the document, you can save time and provide a helpful tool to others who read the document. For example, you could place hyperlinks in the cover letter for a report. The hyperlinks in the cover letter can take the reader to the part of the report that deals with the topics outlined in the cover letter.

To create a hyperlink, you must have a named location for the hyperlink to follow. Specifying a named location is easy in each Office 97 program—Word uses bookmarks, Microsoft Excel uses a cell or range name, Microsoft Access uses a database object, and Microsoft PowerPoint uses a slide number. If you want the hyperlink to jump to a different file, you use the file location in addition to a named location within the file.

The document you're preparing for The Kenya Coffee Company intranet is really three documents combined into one. To allow readers to follow a specific topic throughout the document, you add several hyperlinks.

Add bookmarks

1 On page 3 of the Year in Review 96 document, select the heading text "Market Share 1995 Vs. 1996."

2 On the Insert menu, click Bookmark.

The Bookmark dialog box appears.

Bookmark names cannot contain spaces.

3 Type **MarketShare** and then click Add.

A bookmark is placed at the selected text.

4 On page 4 of the Year in Review 96 document, select the heading text "Sales Estimates."

5 On the Insert menu, click Bookmark.

6 Type **SalesEstimates** and then click Add.

7 On the Standard toolbar, click the Save button.

Save

The Year in Review 96 document is saved with the inserted bookmarks.

Create a hyperlink to a named location

In this exercise, you create hyperlinks to move the reader within a document.

1 On page 2 of the Year in Review 96 document, click after the sentence in the second line of the second paragraph, which ends with "publicly stated long-term goals," and then press the SPACEBAR.

2 On the Standard toolbar, click the Insert Hyperlink button.

Insert Hyperlink

The Insert Hyperlink dialog box appears.

File path or Internet address —

Named location —

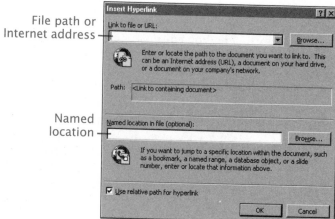

3 Click Browse next to the Named Location In File (Optional) box.

The Bookmark dialog box appears.

4 In the Bookmark Name box, click MarketShare, and then click OK.

The Insert Hyperlink dialog box appears. The named location, MarketShare, appears in the Named Location In File box.

If text is not selected when you insert the hyperlink, the hyperlink address will be inserted.

5 Click OK.

The text "MarketShare" is inserted into the document and appears as blue underlined text. Your screen should look similar to the following illustration.

MarketShare hyperlink →

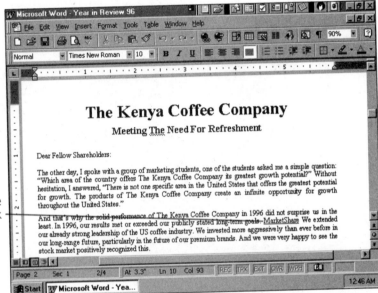

6 On page 2 of the Year in Review 96 document, click at the end of the fifth paragraph, which ends with "fundamental need for refreshment," press the SPACEBAR, and then type **Click here for sales estimates.**

7 Select the sentence you just typed.

8 On the Standard toolbar, click the Insert Hyperlink button.

The Insert Hyperlink dialog box appears.

9 Click Browse next to the Named Location In File (Optional) box, click SalesEstimates, and then click OK.

The Insert Hyperlink dialog box appears.

10 Click OK.

The text "Click here for sales estimates" appears as blue underlined text.

11 On the Standard toolbar, click the Save button.

> **WARNING** If you alter the name of a bookmark in the Named Location In File (Optional) box in the Insert Hyperlink dialog box, the hyperlink may not work properly.

Use a hyperlink

When you place the pointer over a hyperlink, the pointer changes to a hand and a ToolTip appears displaying the hyperlink address.

In this exercise, you use one of the hyperlinks you created to move within a document.

1 Click the Click Here For Sales Estimates hyperlink.

The hyperlink jumps you to the Sales Estimates heading and table. The Web toolbar is displayed. Your screen should look similar to the following illustration.

Web toolbar

Address window with address of hyperlink just used

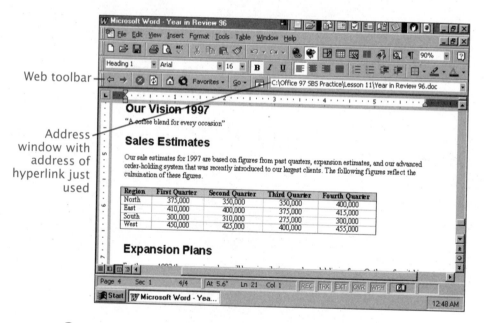

2 On the Web toolbar, click the Back button.

You return to your original location on page 2 prior to clicking the Sales Estimates hyperlink. The text of the hyperlink changes to purple, indicating that you have used the hyperlink.

3 On the Standard toolbar, click the Save button.

Back

Save

Using Hyperlinks to Move Between Documents

When you create a document, it is sometimes difficult to plan how much information to include. If you are creating a document for online viewing, you can use hyperlinks to give readers the option of viewing as little or as much information as they like. For example, suppose you are producing a document for the intranet that addresses a study about how many cups of coffee people drink each day. You could include a hyperlink that leads to a summary of the study results, and then create another hyperlink that goes to the study's details. This way, a reader who only needs a summary of the study doesn't have to wade through lots of data, yet the details are easily accessible for those who require them.

Create hyperlinks to other files

As part of preparing the Year in Review 96 document for the intranet, you also want to reference the complete financial data workbook. In this exercise, you create hyperlinks that jump the reader between files.

Insert Hyperlink

1   On page 4 of the Year in Review 96 document, click after the text "For complete details, see"

2   On the Standard toolbar, click the Insert Hyperlink button.

    The Insert Hyperlinks dialog box appears.

3   Click Browse next to the Link To File Or URL box.

    The Link To File dialog box appears.

4   Be sure that your Office 97 SBS Practice\Lesson 11 folder is selected, click Financial Statements 96, and then click OK.

    The path of the Financial Statements 96 workbook file appears in the Insert Hyperlinks dialog box.

5   Click OK.

    The text "Financial Statements 96.xls" appears at the end of the sentence.

6   Place the pointer over the hyperlink.

    A ToolTip appears with the complete path of the Financial Statements 96 workbook. Your screen should look similar to the following illustration.

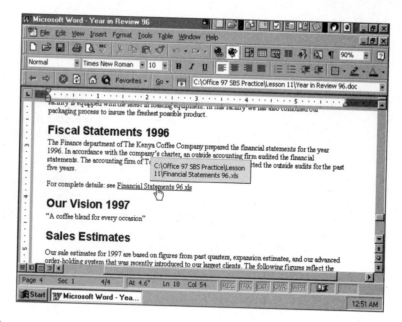

Save

7 On the Standard toolbar, click the Save button.

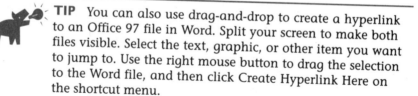

TIP You can also use drag-and-drop to create a hyperlink to an Office 97 file in Word. Split your screen to make both files visible. Select the text, graphic, or other item you want to jump to. Use the right mouse button to drag the selection to the Word file, and then click Create Hyperlink Here on the shortcut menu.

Use a hyperlink to access a file

In this exercise, you use the hyperlink you created to jump to the workbook containing the financial statements.

1 Click the Financial Statements 96.xls hyperlink.

The hyperlink jumps you to the Financial Statements 96 workbook in Excel.

2 On the Web toolbar, click the Back button.

Back

You return to your original location in the Year in Review 96 document. Excel and the Financial Statements 96 workbook remain open. The hyperlink changes color to indicate that it has been used.

IMPORTANT By default, hyperlinks are set to use a relative path and not an absolute path when you use the Insert Hyperlink button. By using the default relative path, such as "Financials," you can change the location of the file containing the hyperlink and the destination of the hyperlink without breaking the hyperlink. If you type in an absolute path, such as "C:\Work\Financials," or clear the Use Relative Path For Hyperlink check box in the Insert Hyperlink dialog box, and then move the files, the hyperlink will be broken. This is similar to linking information between files.

Automating Access to the Internet

With the growing popularity and usefulness of the Internet and the World Wide Web, more and more information is available to us instantly. When you watch television or read a magazine, you can't help but notice the number of companies and organizations with Internet addresses. In addition to using hyperlinks to access information we have control over, we can also use them to inform others of handy Internet addresses we've found.

Using Office 97, you can easily incorporate ways to access the Internet into your daily work. For example, when you type an Internet address in Word, the address is automatically displayed as a hyperlink. In all Office 97 programs, you can quickly create a hyperlink to the Internet using the Insert Hyperlink command.

IMPORTANT To complete the following exercises, you must have access to the Internet through an Internet service provider (ISP) or your company network and a Web browser, such as Microsoft Internet Explorer.

Create a hyperlink to the Internet

In this exercise, you create hyperlinks that can be used to access Web pages on the Internet.

1   On page 1 of the Year in Review 96 document, click after the text "Microsoft Web site at:" in the third paragraph.

2   Type **www.microsoft.com** and then press ENTER.

The Web address is automatically formatted as a hyperlink. Your screen should look similar to the following illustration.

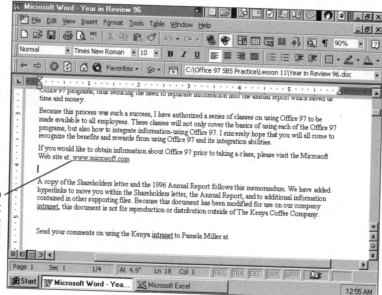

Hyperlink to
the Microsoft
Web page
on the World
Wide Web

3 On the taskbar, click the Microsoft Excel button.

4 Click cell A15.

Cell A15 contains the text that will become a hyperlink to the Internet.

Insert Hyperlink

5 On the Standard toolbar, click the Insert Hyperlink button.

The Insert Hyperlink dialog box appears.

6 In the Link To File Or URL box, type **www.microsoft.com/msexcel/**

7 Click OK.

The text in cell A15 changes to a hyperlink.

Save

8 On the Standard toolbar, click the Save button.

TROUBLESHOOTING If automatic formatting of hyperlinks is not working or you want to disable the feature, you can change the settings. On the Tools menu, click AutoCorrect. Click the AutoFormat As You Type tab. Under Replace As You Type, select the Internet And Network Paths With Hyperlinks check box to enable the feature, or clear the check box to disable the feature.

Use a hyperlink to the Internet

Depending on how your system is set up to access the Internet, you may need to log on.

In this exercise, you use a hyperlink you created to access the Internet.

1 Click the For Excel Information, Click Here hyperlink.

   The Microsoft Excel Web page is displayed in your browser window.

2 On the Microsoft Excel Home Page window, click the Close button.

3 On the Excel window, click the Close button. Click Yes to save any changes.

4 If necessary, on the taskbar, click the Microsoft Word button to restore the Word window.

Connecting Hyperlinks to E-mail

If you have information that you'll be making available on the Internet or an intranet, you may want to provide a means for readers to respond to you or to the *Webmaster* who maintains the Web site. Using Office 97, you can make it easy for others to send you e-mail about what they're reading. For example, on an intranet you've posted a document that outlines a proposal. By adding a hyperlink to your e-mail address, a reader who wants to comment on the proposal can quickly send e-mail. Individuals are more likely to respond if it's easy to do so.

At The Kenya Coffee Company, the CEO would like employees to comment on the posting of company documents online and the general use of the company intranet. You've been asked to add an e-mail hyperlink to the document you've been working on to encourage employees to submit their comments.

 IMPORTANT Because you will be exploring the use of e-mail, you will need to have either a company or an Internet mail program available to you, and you'll need at least one person to whom you can send e-mail. For the purposes of this exercise, Outlook is used as the e-mail program.

Create and use an e-mail hyperlink

You can also use the Insert Hyperlink button to use the existing text as the hyperlink base.

1 On page 1 of the Year in Review 96 document, click at the end of the sentence "Send your comments on using the Kenya intranet to Pamela Miller at," and then press the SPACEBAR.

2 Type the e-mail address of the person helping you with this exercise, and then press ENTER.

   The address of the e-mail recipient appears as a hyperlink.

3 Click the e-mail hyperlink.

Be sure to type the full e-mail address, including the @ symbol.

4 Use the Pamela Miller profile.

A message window appears with the correct e-mail address already in the To: line. Your screen should look similar to the following illustration.

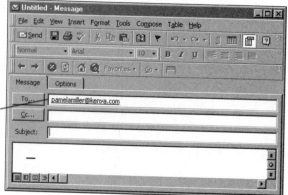

E-mail address from hyperlink

5 In the Subject box, type **Kenya intranet** and then press TAB.

The insertion point moves to the message box.

6 Type **It has already increased my productivity.**

7 On the Standard toolbar, click the Send button.

The message is sent to the addressee.

8 On the Standard toolbar in Word, click the Save button.

Save

NOTE If you'd like to build on the skills that you learned in this lesson, you can do the One Step Further. Otherwise, skip to Finish the Lesson.

One Step Further: Changing the Appearance of Hyperlinks

By default, unused hyperlinks appear as blue underlined text in Office 97 files, and hyperlinks you have used appear as purple text. The appearance of hyperlinks, including font characteristics like color and underlining, can be modified in individual documents or as part of a template in Word. When you modify the appearance of a hyperlink, all hyperlinks in the documents using the template will be changed. You cannot modify the appearance of a single hyperlink, although you can modify the text or image of a hyperlink.

Modify hyperlink appearance

In this exercise, you modify the appearance of used hyperlinks.

1   Be sure that the Year in Review 96 document is active.

2   On the Format menu, click Style.

The Style dialog box appears.

3   In the Styles box, click FollowedHyperlink, and then click Modify.

The Modify Style dialog box appears.

4   Click Format, and then click Font.

The Font dialog box appears. The Font tab is selected.

5   Click the Color down arrow, and then click Bright Green.

6   Click the Underline down arrow, and then click Thick.

A preview of the new format appears in the Preview box.

7   Click OK twice, and then click Apply.

The modifications made to the FollowedHyperlink style appear. Your screen should look similar to the following illustration.

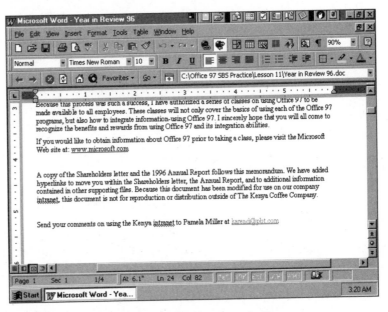

Save

9   On the Standard toolbar, click the Save button.

10   On the Word window, click the Close button.

Finish the lesson

➤   Close all open windows.

Lesson Summary

To	Do this	Button
Creating a hyperlink within a document	Name the location you wish to jump to. Click where you want the hyperlink or select the text that will become the hyperlink. Click the Insert Hyperlink button. Click Browse next to the Named Location In File (Optional) box. Click the named location, and then click OK twice.	
Create a hyperlink to another file	Click where you want the hyperlink or select the text or image that will become the hyperlink. Click the Insert Hyperlink button. Type the filename or URL in the Link To File Or URL box, and click OK. *or* Click Browse next to the Link To File Or URL box. Click the filename or URL, and click OK twice.	
Create a hyperlink to the Internet and World Wide Web	Click where you want the hyperlink, and type the Internet address. Press the SPACEBAR, or press ENTER. *or* Select the text or image that will become the hyperlink. Click the Insert Hyperlink button. Type the URL in the Link To File Or URL box, or click Browse next to the Link To File Or URL box. Click the URL, and click OK twice.	
Create a hyperlink to automatically send an e-mail response	Click where you want the e-mail hyperlink, and type the e-mail address. Press the SPACEBAR, or press ENTER. *or* Select the text or image that will become the hyperlink. Click the Insert Hyperlink button. Type the e-mail address.	

For online information about	On the Help menu, click Contents And Index, click the Index tab, and then type
Creating hyperlinks	*Word*: **hyperlinks** *Excel*: **hyperlinks** *Access*: **hyperlinks** *PowerPoint*: **hyperlinks**

234

Publishing Office Documents on the World Wide Web

Estimated time
55 min.

In this lesson you will learn how to:

- Create a Web site using a wizard.
- Integrate existing files into a Web site.
- Create hyperlinks.
- Format Web pages.

The Internet has become a valuable tool that can help you communicate with people in your own city and around the world. By placing information on the Internet, you potentially gain an international audience of millions. More and more companies are creating sites on the World Wide Web to provide information about their company and their products to this vast audience. In the past, creating a Web site required specific programming knowledge, but the advent of Web publishing software has made creating a Web site quicker and easier than ever. Web publishing software lets users of all skill levels create Web sites.

With Microsoft FrontPage, you can create your own professional-looking Web site in no time. FrontPage is a Web authoring and management tool that requires no programming knowledge, but is powerful enough to satisfy even an experienced Web developer. Because FrontPage is part of the Microsoft family, you can easily integrate information from Microsoft Office 97 programs into a FrontPage Web (in FrontPage, the term "Web" means Web site). If you are creating a Web site for the first time, FrontPage comes with wizards and templates that walk you through the process. You can also use an empty Web to create a Web site from scratch if you want total control over the process. However you use it, FrontPage will make creating a Web site faster and easier than ever before.

In this lesson, The Kenya Coffee Company has decided to create a corporate Web site. By creating a Web site with information on the company's recent successes and their line of products, they hope to expand consumer recognition, which may open up new markets. As the company's most experienced Internet user, you have been asked to create a Web site using the annual report, supporting financial information, and a recent press release. You will provide links to guide the viewer through the Web site, and you'll establish a polished format to make the site visually appealing.

NOTE You can download the latest version of Microsoft FrontPage from www.microsoft.com/frontpage/

Creating a Web Site

Creating a successful Web site requires planning and ingenuity. Two vital elements are knowing who you want your information to reach and how you want it to be received. If you start to create a Web site without a focus, you could end up with an unorganized, unfocused mess that deserves little attention.

Many Web sites are created by professional Web site designers who know what works and what doesn't. If you don't want to hire a professional, if you've worked on Web sites before, or if you'd rather do it yourself, a Web publishing program like FrontPage is just what you're looking for. FrontPage can give you as little or as much help as you need. It provides the bells and whistles that the experienced Web designer wants, and it offers the wizards and templates that help the new designer create a solid foundation for a site.

Understanding and Planning a Web Site

Before you create a site on the Web, it's important to have a basic understanding of both the Web and the purpose for your site. The Web is one of several Internet services. What makes the Web unique is that it combines standard text with pictures, sounds, and animation. This allows you to present information in a more dynamic format: multimedia. As most people would probably admit, multimedia is more likely to attract and hold an audience's attention than plain text. Information in Web pages is created and formatted using *HTML* (Hypertext Markup Language). A Web *browser* reads the HTML text and translates it into a formatted Web page. When you view a Web page using a Web browser, you do not see the HTML formatting codes—you just see the text, graphics, and animation.

A Web site is made up of a series of pages that are grouped together, although when you view it, you can't tell where one page ends and another page (or site) begins. You move between Web pages and Web sites using *hyperlinks*. By clicking a hyperlink, you jump to the location referenced by the hyperlink.

With a basic understanding of the Web, you now need to focus on planning your Web site. Planning the site is important because without a solid plan, your site could be a failure. When you plan your site, some fundamental issues must be addressed.

- Why are you creating the site? Is it for personal use or corporate use? What is the objective or goal? Always keep this in mind while building your site.

- Who is your audience? How will you attract them? Are there any common denominators in your audience?

- What type of information do you want to provide? Will you include historical, current, and future information?

- What are your cost considerations? How much time do you want to spend creating the site, and how much money can you spend on it?

Once you have established a plan for your site, you need to determine how the Web site will be structured. All Web sites have a home page that welcomes the viewer and provides a starting point and fallback point for the Web site. You will also need to decide how many pages to include, how to link them, and how to use colors, fonts, and graphics in the site's format.

 TIP   For ideas on how to design your Web site, look at other sites on the Web. You can get expert help on Web page creation at http://www.microsoft.com/workshop.

Using a Wizard to Create a Web Site

FrontPage is basically three programs in one. It is a Web server that holds the information to be viewed on your Web site, the FrontPage Explorer that you use to view and manage your site, and the FrontPage Editor that you use to create and edit your Web pages. All three of these programs come together so you can create and manage a site without needing to know HTML. FrontPage also allows you to create a site directly on your computer's hard drive, without a Web server. (When you are ready to publish your Web site, you will need access to a Web server.)

To create your Web site, you can use one of the 30 built-in templates and wizards in FrontPage. A wizard is an interactive tool that helps you create the foundation of your Web site, using your answers to questions about your company and the kind of information you want to present. With wizards like Corporate Presence, Personal Web, and Discussion Web, you can build your own home page, create a feedback form for viewer response, create a presentation style, and establish other elements of your Web site structure.

The Kenya Coffee Company has appointed a five-member team to create the company's Web site, and you're the team leader. After reviewing how FrontPage can be used, you decide to use the Corporate Presence wizard to begin building the Web site. In the Web site, you need to include a feedback form for viewer response and corporate contact information.

 NOTE For the purposes of this exercise, you will be creating a FrontPage Web without a Web server. The Kenya Coffee Company Web site will be created directly on your computer's hard drive. The only difference between this and using a Web server is the information you enter in the Web Server Or File Location box in the Corporate Presence Wizard dialog box.

You can also start FrontPage using the Programs Shortcut Bar.

Start a FrontPage wizard

In this exercise, you start FrontPage and select the Corporate Presence wizard to create a Web site for your company.

1 Click Start, point to Programs, and then click Microsoft FrontPage.

The Getting Started With Microsoft FrontPage dialog box appears.

If this folder did not exist, FrontPage would create it for you.

2 In the Create A New FrontPage Web area, click the From A Wizard Or Template option button, and then click OK.

The New FrontPage Web dialog box appears.

3 Click Corporate Presence Wizard in the Template Or Wizard box, and then click OK.

The Corporate Presence Web Wizard dialog box appears.

4 In the Web Server Or File Location box, type **C:\Office 97 SBS Practice\Lesson 12\FP Web**

This is the location of the folder that will store your Web files.

5 In the Name Of New FrontPage Web box, type **KenyaCC**

Your dialog box should look similar to the following illustration.

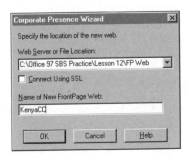

6 Click OK.

A message appears asking if you want to convert this folder into a FrontPage Web and add the necessary files and folders.

7 Click Yes.

The first dialog box of the Corporate Presence Web wizard appears. The wizard will create a Web site for you based on your answers to a series of questions.

IMPORTANT If you've installed the Office 97 SBS Practice files in a location other than drive C, enter the appropriate folder location.

Create a Web site using a wizard

In this exercise, you answer a series of questions to determine which kind of Web site the wizard will create.

1 Click Next.

The second dialog box of the Corporate Presence Web wizard appears.

2 Clear the What's New check box, and then select the Products/Services check box. Be sure that the Feedback Form check box is selected, and then click Next.

The third dialog box appears.

3 Clear the Mission Statement check box, and then select the Company Profile check box. Be sure that the Contact Information check box is selected, and then click Next.

The fourth dialog box appears.

4 Type **1** in the Products box, press TAB, type **1** in the Services box, and then click Next.

The fifth dialog box appears.

5 Be sure that the Pricing Information and both Information Request Form check boxes are selected, and then click Next.

The sixth dialog box appears.

6   Be sure that the Full Name, Company Affiliation, Telephone Number, FAX Number, and E-mail Address check boxes are selected, and then click Next.

The seventh dialog box appears.

7   Be sure that the Yes, Use Tab-Delimited Format option button is selected, and then click Next.

The eighth dialog box appears.

8   Select the Links To Your Main Web Pages check box under What Should Appear At The Bottom Of Each Page. Be sure that the Your Company's Logo, Page Title, Links To Your Main Web Pages, E-mail Address Of Your Webmaster, and Date Page Was Last Modified check boxes are selected, and then click Next.

The ninth dialog box appears.

9   Click the Flashy option button, and then click Next.

The tenth dialog box appears.

10   Be sure that the Custom option button is selected, be sure that the Background Color Pattern is Brown Texture 1, and then click Next.

The eleventh dialog box appears.

11   Be sure that the Yes option button is selected, and then click Next.

The twelfth dialog box appears.

A To Do List is an optional component that can be used by all authors of a Web site. A To Do List contains the tasks needed to complete the site; each task's assigned author, priority, and description; and the page or file linked to the task.

12   In the What Is The Full Name Of Your Company box, type **The Kenya Coffee Company**, press TAB, type **Kenya**, press TAB, type **5768 Coffee Drive Seattle, WA 98110**, and then click Next.

The thirteenth dialog box appears.

13   In the What Is Your Company's Telephone Number box, type **206-555-4321**, press TAB, type **206-555-1234**, press TAB, type **webmaster@kenyacoffee.com**, press TAB, and then type **info@kenyacoffee.com**, and then click Next.

The fourteenth dialog box appears.

14   Clear the Show To Do List After Web Is Uploaded check box, and then click Finish.

After a few moments, the structure of your newly created Web site will be displayed in the FrontPage Explorer window. Your screen should look similar to the following illustration.

Included Logo Page icon

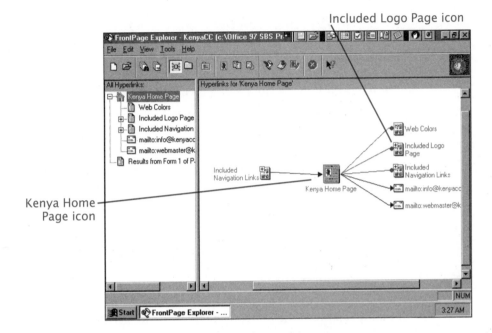

Kenya Home
Page icon

Adding Existing Information to a Web Site

For a demonstration on how to insert a file into an existing Web page, double-click the Camcorder Files On The Internet shortcut on your Desktop or connect to the Internet address on p. xxx.

FrontPage lets you insert files created in other programs into your Web pages. By inserting existing information, you not only reduce the amount of time spent creating your Web site, but you also prevent errors that could occur if you re-created the information. When you insert a file into a FrontPage Web, FrontPage takes care of converting the information into HTML. For example, a file created in Word is converted into rich-text format (RTF) and then into HTML when you click a single command.

When you insert files, you can insert them into existing Web pages or you can create new Web pages. On existing Web pages, you can simply insert the file contents at a designated point, or you can replace existing text or placeholder text with the file contents. You can add new Web pages that are blank, or you can use the templates and wizards in FrontPage to streamline the creation and design process. You can also add Web pages from existing Web sites. If you insert a file on a blank Web page within your Web site, the Web page contains only the file contents. The Web site format and colors must be applied manually to blank Web pages.

In The Kenya Coffee Company Web site, you want to use information from several existing files instead of retyping the information. These files include a recent press release to be used as the company profile, the annual report for the past year, and supporting financial information.

241

Insert a file into an existing Web page

In this exercise, you insert a file into your home page to replace the default placeholder text under Company Profile.

You can also click the Show FrontPage Editor button, and then on the File menu, click Open. In the Open File dialog box, click the name of the page you want to work with, and then click OK.

1 In the right pane of the FrontPage Explorer window, double-click the Kenya Home Page icon.

FrontPage Editor opens and the Kenya Home Page appears.

2 Select all the comment text under the Company Profile heading.

You will replace the comment placeholder text with text from a recent press release.

3 On the Insert menu, click File.

The Select A File dialog box appears.

4 Click the Files Of Type down arrow, and then click All Files (*.*).

5 From your Office 97 SBS Practice\Lesson 12 folder, click Press Release Excerpts, and then click Open.

FrontPage converts the file format to RTF and then to HTML, and inserts the file text into the Kenya Home Page. Your screen should look similar to the following illustration.

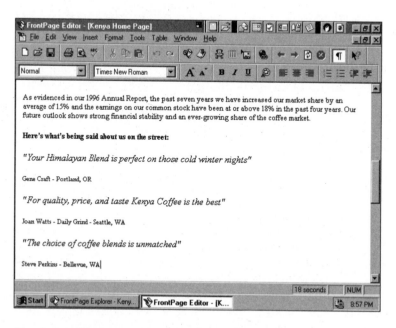

6 On the Standard toolbar, click the Save button.

Changes made to a Web page must be saved before they can become part of the Web site.

Save

⚡**WARNING** If you close a Web page without saving your changes, they will be lost.

Add a new Web page

To create a new blank Web page, you can click the New button on the Standard toolbar.

In this exercise, you add a new page to your Web site before inserting a file.

1 On the File menu, click New.

The New Page dialog box appears. The New Page dialog box contains a list of templates and wizards you can use to create new pages in your Web site.

2 Be sure that Normal Page is selected, and then click OK.

A new blank Web page appears.

Insert a document file into a new Web page

In this exercise, you insert a document file into a newly created Web page.

1 On the Insert Menu, click File.

The Select A File dialog box appears.

2 Be sure that All Files (*.*) appears in the Files Of Type box.

3 From your Office 97 SBS Practice\Lesson 12 folder, click Annual Report 96, and then click Open.

The text, tables, and graphics from the file are inserted in the Web page and appear as they did in the Word document.

4 On the Standard toolbar, click the Save button.

The Save As dialog box appears, allowing you to name the new page.

Save

5 Type **Annual Report 96** in the Page Title box, and be sure that annual.htm appears in the File Path box.

6 Click OK.

The Save Image To FrontPage Web dialog box appears.

7 Be sure that Images/annual1.gif appears in the Save As URL box, and then click Yes To All.

The text and images are saved to the Kenya Web site.

Insert a workbook file into a new Web page

In this exercise, you create a new Web page and then insert a workbook file as supporting financial information for the annual report.

243

New

The New button on the Standard toolbar adds a new blank Web page to your site. To add a new page from a template or wizard, click New on the File menu.

1 On the Standard toolbar, click the New button.

A new blank page is added to your Web site.

2 On the Insert Menu, click File.

The Select A File dialog box appears.

3 Be sure that All Files (*.*) appears in the Files Of Type box.

4 From your Office 97 SBS Practice\Lesson 12 folder, click Supporting Financials, and then click Open.

The contents of each worksheet in the Supporting Financials workbook is inserted into the Web page. Your screen should look similar to the following illustration.

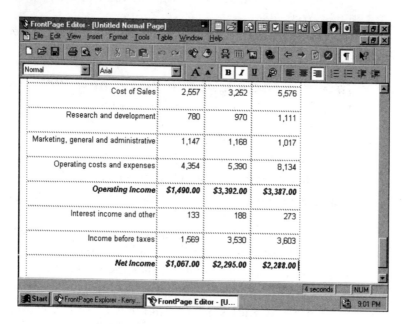

Save

5 On the Standard toolbar, click the Save button.

The Save As dialog box appears.

6 Type **Supporting Financials** in the Page Title box, and be sure that supporti.htm appears in the File Path box.

7 Click OK.

The text and numbers are saved to the Kenya Web site.

Linking Web Pages

To connect the information in your Web site, you use hyperlinks. Hyperlinks move the viewer within a single Web page, between Web pages, and to other Web sites. They even let people send you e-mail from your Web site—automatically. A hyperlink may also go to a multimedia file or a program. When you create hyperlinks, the challenge comes in creating a logical and clear system for the viewer.

Your hyperlinks should follow a general pattern throughout your Web site. For example, your home page should be the central location for the viewer. Topics that span several pages should have hyperlinks that move the viewer forward and backward in the topic, to related sites, and to your home page. All pages should have hyperlinks to the home page.

For clarity, hyperlinks should be limited to an image or one or two words. A viewer should clearly understand what type of information a hyperlink offers. Text hyperlinks are generally underlined and displayed as a specific color (blue is often used). The default display of hyperlinks can be customized using the Background Page Properties. Image hyperlinks do not have this distinction. Instead, the user must place the pointer over the image; if the pointer changes to a pointing hand, the image is usually a hyperlink.

If you insert or import a file that already contains hyperlinks, the hyperlinks will be integrated into the Web page. If an existing hyperlink is not operating correctly, it can easily be edited so it does.

The body of the Kenya Web site has been established. When you used the Corporate Presence wizard, several hyperlinks were already established for you. You now add additional hyperlinks to move viewers from the home page to the new pages and back again. You also edit an existing hyperlink from one of the inserted files.

Establish hyperlinks to the new Web pages

In this exercise, you create hyperlinks from the home page to the annual report and supporting financial workbook.

1 On the Window menu, click Kenya Home Page.

The Kenya Home Page appears in the FrontPage Editor.

2 In the Company Profile section, select the text "1996 Annual Report" in the third paragraph.

This text will become a hyperlink.

*Create Or Edit
Hyperlink*

3 On the Standard toolbar, click the Create Or Edit Hyperlink button.

The Create Hyperlink dialog box appears.

4 Be sure that the Open Pages tab is selected. In the Open Pages box, select Annual Report 96.

The hyperlink will connect to the Annual Report 96 page. The Hyperlink Points To information verifies which Web file the hyperlink is pointing to.

5 Click OK.

The text 1996 Annual Report appears in blue underlined text.

6 In the Company Profile section, select the text "financial stability" in the third paragraph.

This text will become a hyperlink.

Create Or Edit Hyperlink

7 On the Standard toolbar, click the Create Or Edit Hyperlink button.

The Create Hyperlink dialog box appears. The Open Pages tab is selected.

8 In the Open Pages box, select Supporting Financials.

The hyperlink will connect to the Supporting Financials page.

9 Click OK.

Your screen should look similar to the following illustration.

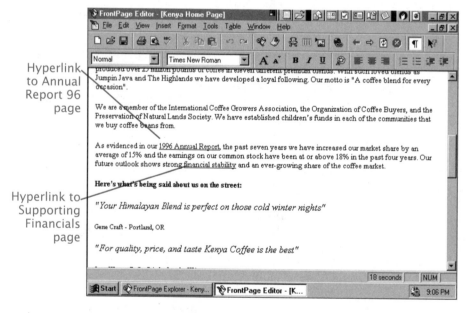

Save

10 On the Standard toolbar, click the Save button.

Edit an existing hyperlink

In this exercise, you edit the hyperlink from the Annual Report Web page to the Financial Workbook Web page.

1 On the Window menu, click Annual Report 96.

The Annual Report 96 page appears.

2 Select the entire hyperlink to the Supporting Financials under the Fiscal Statements 1996 heading, and then press DELETE.

3 On the Standard toolbar, click the Create Or Edit Hyperlink button.

The Create Hyperlink dialog box appears. The Open Pages tab is selected.

4 Click Supporting Financials, and then click OK.

The hyperlink is now directed to the Supporting Financials Web page instead of the file on your computer's hard drive.

5 On the Standard toolbar, click the Save button.

Create hyperlinks from new Web pages to the home page

In this exercise, you create a hyperlink from the Annual Report 96 page back to the Kenya home page.

1 Press CTRL+END, and then type Home.

The hyperlink to the Kenya home page will be placed at the bottom of the Annual Report 96 page.

2 On the Format toolbar, click the Center button.

The text "Home" is centered at the bottom of the page.

Center

3 Select the text "Home."

The selected text will become the hyperlink instead of the page name being inserted.

4 On the Standard toolbar, click the Create Or Edit Hyperlink button.

The Create Hyperlink dialog box appears. The Open Pages tab is selected.

5 Click Kenya Home Page, and then click OK.

The text "Home" appears as blue underlined text.

6 On the Standard toolbar, click the Save button.

View the structure of a Web site

In this exercise, you use FrontPage Explorer to view the structure of a Web site.

Show FrontPage Explorer

You can click on any of the pages in the left pane of the FrontPage Explorer to graphically view the hyperlinks to and from that page.

1 On the Standard toolbar, click the Show FrontPage Explorer button.

FrontPage Explorer opens.

2 In the left pane of the FrontPage Explorer window, click Kenya Home Page.

The hyperlinks to and from the home page are displayed graphically in the right pane of the FrontPage Explorer window. Your screen should look similar to the following illustration.

Links from the home page to Annual Report 96 and Supporting Financials

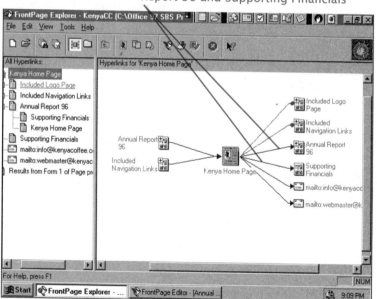

Formatting Web Pages

With all of the Office 97 programs, you have many formatting options. FrontPage is no different—you can change the font, font size, font attributes, color, and alignment of your Web page text. You can add symbols, images, tables, lines, and bullets to organize information. To make global changes, you can change the default format and colors of the entire Web site.

You have almost completed the Kenya Web site. To make sure the site has a consistent look, you apply the Web colors to the new pages that were added to the site, and change the font for the Supporting Financials page to add emphasis. You also place the company logo in the image placeholder so it appears on the home page of the Web site.

 NOTE When working on a real Web site, your next step after formatting would be to publish the Web site onto a Web server. To publish a Web site, click Publish FrontPage Web on the File menu. Fill in the information requested in the Publish FrontPage Web dialog box. FrontPage Explorer then copies your Web site from your Web server or file system to an intranet Web server or the World Wide Web server that you specify. If you are publishing to a server without FrontPage extensions, the Web Publishing wizard appears. Follow the instructions in each of the Web Publishing wizard dialog boxes.

Apply Web Colors

Depending on the Web browser being used to view your Web site, the Web site colors may differ slightly.

If you use a template or wizard when you initially create a Web site, the Web format and colors will automatically be applied when you insert a file in an existing Web page. If you create an empty Web site or add new blank Web pages, the default font and no color appear on the Web pages. In the case of an empty Web site, you can apply whatever Web format and colors you like. If you have added blank Web pages to a Web site that already has a format and colors, you will need to apply the same Web format and colors to the blank pages so that the Web site is consistent in appearance.

Apply your Web colors to a new Web page

In this exercise, you change the format of the new Annual Report 96 page to match the Web colors you defined earlier using the Corporate Presence wizard.

You can also click the Show FrontPage Editor button on the Standard toolbar, and then from the Window menu, click the page you want.

1   In the right pane of the FrontPage Explorer window, double-click the Annual Report 96 icon.

    The Annual Report 96 page appears in FrontPage Editor.

2   On the File menu, click Page Properties.

    The Page Properties dialog box appears.

3   Click the Background tab.

4   Click the Get Background And Colors From Page option button, and then click Browse.

    The Current Web dialog box appears.

5 Click index.htm Kenya Home Page, and then click OK.

The text "index.htm" appears in the Get Background And Colors From Page box.

6 Click OK.

The colors you defined for the Kenya Web site using the Corporate Presence wizard are applied to the Annual Report 96 page. Your screen should look similar to the following illustration.

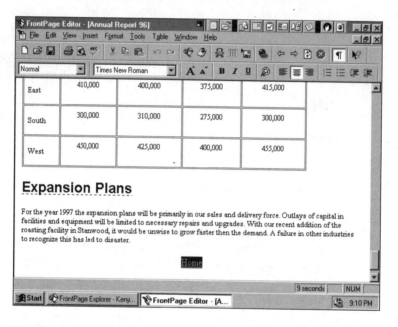

Save

7 On the Standard toolbar, click the Save button.

Apply Web colors to another new Web page

In this exercise, you apply the Kenya Web site colors to the Supporting Financials page.

1 On the Window menu, click Supporting Financials.

2 On the File menu, click Page Properties.

The Page Properties dialog box appears. The General tab is selected.

3 Click the Background tab.

4 Click the Get Background And Colors From Page option button, and then click Browse.

The Current Web dialog box appears.

5 Click index.htm Kenya Home Page, and then click OK.

6 Click OK.

The colors you defined for the Kenya Web site using the Corporate Presence wizard are applied to the Annual Report 96 page.

Save

7 On the Standard toolbar, click the Save button.

Adding Images to Web Pages

Images can be used to spice up your Web site. You can add images to convey a message, break up the text on a page, or to add a logo. Images can be added at any point on a Web page, or where there is a placeholder created by a template or wizard. If a Web site contains a placeholder for a company logo, you can insert a file containing a logo image into the placeholder.

Insert a company logo image

In this exercise, you replace the Company Logo placeholder on the home page with the Kenya company logo, which was created in a different program and saved as a file.

Show FrontPage Explorer

1 On the Standard toolbar, click the Show FrontPage Explorer button.

2 On the left pane of the FrontPage Explorer window, click Kenya Home Page.

3 In the right pane of the FrontPage Explorer window, double-click the Included Logo Page icon.

FrontPage Editor opens, and the Included Logo Page appears.

4 Click the "Company Logo" text.

Sizing handles appear around the text.

5 On the Insert menu, click Image.

The Image dialog box appears. The Current FrontPage Web tab is selected.

6 Click the Other Location tab, be sure that the From File option button is selected, and then click Browse.

The Image dialog box appears.

7 Click the Files Of Type down arrow, and then click All Files (*.*).

8 From your Office 97 SBS Practice\Lesson 12 folder, click kcclogo, and then click Open.

The Kenya Coffee Company logo replaces the logo placeholder.

9 On the Standard toolbar, click the Save button.

The Save Image To FrontPage Web dialog box appears.

10 Be sure that kcclogo.gif appears in the Save As URL box, and then click Yes To All.

View the logo in your Web site

In this exercise, you view the Kenya logo on the home page.

1 On the Window menu, click Kenya Home Page, and then scroll to the top of the page.

The text "Company Logo" still appears on the home page.

2 On the View menu, click Refresh.

After a few moments, the Kenya Home Page view is refreshed, and the logo appears. Your screen should look similar to the following illustration.

Kenya Logo image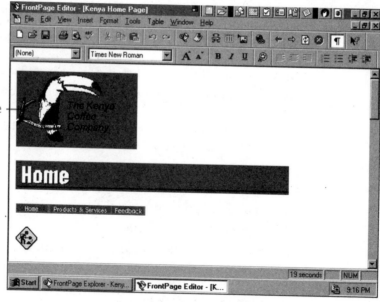

Save

3 On the Standard toolbar, click the Save button.

Formatting Web Page Text

As you add text to a Web site, you might have text that should be emphasized in some way, such as by changing the font. Changing font characteristics can draw the viewer's attention to a specific area or identify types of information. When changing font characteristics, be sure the change provides emphasis rather than detracting from the information being presented.

Format text

In this exercise, you change the font of the financial workbook text.

1   On the Window menu, click Supporting Financials.

2   On the Edit menu, click Select All.

    All the text on the Supporting Financials page is selected.

3   On the Format menu, click Font.

    The Font dialog box appears. The Font tab is selected.

4   In the Font box, click Times New Roman.

5   In the Size box, click 2 (10pt), and then click OK.

    The text appears as Times New Roman 10 pt. Your screen should look similar to the following illustration.

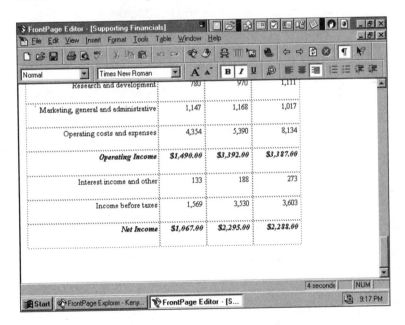

6   On the Standard toolbar, click the Save button.

NOTE   If you'd like to build on the skills that you learned in this lesson, you can do the One Step Further. Otherwise, skip to "Finish the lesson."

One Step Further: Creating a Marquee

Most Web browsers support advanced FrontPage features like marquees.

FrontPage comes with many special features that allow you to add zip to your Web site. One of these features is a marquee, a scrolling line of text that displays a repeating message. Marquees appear in places like Times Square and the New York Stock Exchange. You might use a marquee to make an announcement about a new product or a new addition to your Web site.

Add a marquee

In this exercise, you add a marquee to announce the release of a new product.

1 On the Window menu, click Kenya Home Page.

2 Select the comment text under the Contact Information heading.

3 On the Insert menu, click Marquee.

The Marquee Properties dialog box appears.

4 In the text box, type **Check out our new Bogota Blend and let us know what you think.**

5 In the Background Color box, be sure that the Default color appears, and then click OK.

The default color is the color you defined for your Web. The marquee appears on your home page. Your screen should look similar to the following illustration.

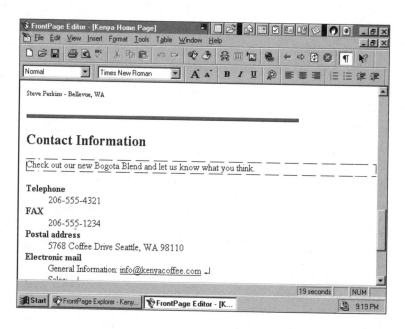

Save

6   On the Standard toolbar, click Save.

View a marquee

In this exercise, you view the marquee you added to the Kenya Home Page to see how it will appear when it is active on the Web.

Preview In Browser

If you use more than one browser, you can click Preview In Browser on the File menu. The Preview In Browser dialog box appears, letting you select which browser you want to use for previewing your Web site.

1   On the Standard toolbar, click the Preview In Browser button.

Your browser (or the default browser for HTML files that comes with FrontPage) starts, and the Kenya Home Page appears.

2   Scroll to the Contact Information heading, and view the marquee.

3   On the Kenya Home Page browser window, click the Close button.

The browser closes, and you return to FrontPage Editor.

NOTE   Some Web browsers cannot display marquees. A normal line of text will appear in place of the marquee if this is the case.

Finish the lesson

1   On the FrontPage Editor window, click the Close button.

If you are prompted to save changes to any of the Web pages, click Yes.

2   On the FrontPage Explorer window, click the Close button.

3   Close all open windows.

Lesson Summary

To	Do this	Button
Create a Web site using a wizard	In FrontPage Explorer, click the From A Wizard Or Template option button in the Getting Started With Microsoft FrontPage dialog box, and then click OK. Select a wizard, and then follow the instructions in each of the wizard dialog boxes. *or* In FrontPage Explorer, on the File menu, point to New, and then click FrontPage Web. Select a wizard, and then follow the instructions in each of the wizard dialog boxes.	
Add a new Web page	In FrontPage Editor, on the Standard toolbar, click the New button. A new blank Web page is created. *or* In FrontPage Editor, on the File menu, click New. Select a template or wizard in the New Page dialog box, and then click OK.	
Insert a file into a Web page	In FrontPage Editor, click where you want the file to be inserted or select the text that the inserted file will replace. On the Insert menu, click File. Select the file to be inserted in the Select A File dialog box, and then click Open.	
Create hyperlinks	In FrontPage Editor, click where you want the hyperlink to be placed or select the text or image that will become the hyperlink. On the Standard toolbar, click the Create Or Edit Hyperlink button. Select the tab that reflects the hyperlink source. Complete the information on the Create Hyperlink dialog box tab, and then click OK.	

To	Do this
Apply consistent Web page colors	Open the Web page you are applying the colors to in FrontPage Editor. On the File menu, click Page Properties. On the Background tab, click the Get Background And Colors From Page option button, and then click Browse. Select the Web site file and page you want to copy the colors from, and then click OK.
Add an image to a Web page	Open the Web page you are adding the image to in FrontPage Editor. Click where you want the image to be placed or select the text or image to be replaced. On the Insert menu, click Image. Click the Other Location tab, be sure that the From File option button is selected, and then click Browse. Select the image file, and then click Open.
Format text on a Web page	Open the Web page you are formatting in FrontPage Editor. Select the text to be formatted. On the Format menu or the Formatting toolbar, select the formatting option to be applied to the text.

For online information about	On the Help menu, click Microsoft FrontPage Help, click the Index tab, and then type
Using a Web wizard	*FrontPage*: webs
Integrating existing files	*FrontPage*: files
Creating hyperlinks	*FrontPage*: hyperlinks
Formatting Web pages	*FrontPage*: formatting, text

Review & Practice

Estimated time
30 min.

You will review and practice how to:

- Create hyperlinks.
- Create a Web site using a wizard.
- Integrate existing files into a Web site.
- Format Web pages.

Before you complete this book, you can practice the skills you learned in Part 5 by working through this Review & Practice section. You will create hyperlinks to move within a document and to automate access to the Internet. You will also create a Web site using a FrontPage Web wizard, add existing files to the Web site, and format Web pages.

Scenario

With your new skills, you've been asked to create a discussion forum for employees that will be used on the company intranet. You will add welcome text from a letter written by the Human Resources department, which outlines how the forum is to be used. The employee handbook will also be included as part of the discussion forum for reference.

Step 1: *Create Hyperlinks in a Document*

Before you add the employee handbook and letter from Human Resources to the discussion Web site, you add hyperlinks within the employee handbook and from the welcome text to the employee handbook.

1 Using the Office Shortcut Bar, open the Employee Handbook document from your Office 97 Practice\Review & Practice 5 folder. Save the file as **Kenya Handbook** in your Office 97 SBS Practice\Review & Practice 5 folder.

2 Create a bookmark on page 2 at the Absence from Work heading.

3 Using the text "Reporting absences" from heading 5.1 Employee Behavior, the second bullet, create a hyperlink to the Absence from Work heading.

4 Save and close the Kenya Handbook document.

5 From your Office 97 SBS Practice\Review & Practice 5 folder, open the Forum Welcome document. Save the file as **Kenya Forum** in your Office 97 SBS Practice\Review & Practice 5 folder.

6 Using the text "employee handbook" at the bottom of the document, create a hyperlink to the Kenya Handbook located in your Office 97 SBS Practice\Review & Practice 5 folder.

7 Save and close the Kenya Forum document. Close Word.

For more information about	See
Moving within and between documents	Lesson 11
Automating access to the Internet	Lesson 11

Step 2: *Create a Discussion Web Site*

To quickly create the discussion Web site, you use the Discussion Web wizard in FrontPage. You create the Web site on your hard drive until you're ready to publish it to a Web server.

1 Using the FrontPage Discussion Web wizard, create a Web site named **employee** in your Office 97 SBS Practice\Review & Practice 5\Dis folder. (Hint: allow FrontPage to convert the Dis folder into a new FrontPage Web.)

2 Complete the wizard dialog boxes by accepting all of the defaults. Be sure that the Submission Form contains all the features listed in the second wizard dialog box.

For more information about	See
Creating a Web site	Lesson 12

Step 3: *Integrate an Existing File into a Web Site*

Human Resources has a letter document that outlines how employees are to use the discussion forum. You insert the text from the letter into the Discussion Welcome page so it's the first thing the employees see when they enter the forum. You also add a new page and insert the excerpts from the employee manual.

1 Open the Discussion Welcome page in FrontPage Editor. Replace the generic text from "This is an on-line" to "loaded into this frame." with the Kenya Forum file located in your Office 97 SBS Practice\Review & Practice 5 folder, and save the changes. (Hint: Select All Files (*.*) in the Files Of Type box.)

2 Add a new Web page to the Discussion Web and insert the Kenya Handbook file located in your Office 97 SBS Practice\Review & Practice 5 folder.

3 Save the new Web page as **Employee Handbook**

For more information about	See
Integrating files in a Web site	Lesson 12

Step 4: *Formatting Web Pages*

The newly created Web pages need the same colors and fonts as the rest of the Web site. You apply your Web colors to the Employee Handbook page and do some text formatting on the Discussion Welcome page.

1 Apply the Web colors to the Employee Handbook page and save the changes. (Hint: Use the Page Properties command on the File menu.)

2 On the Discussion Welcome page, format the indented text as italic and save the changes.

3 Close the Discussion Web and FrontPage.

For more information about	See
Formatting Web pages	Lesson 12

Finish the Review & Practice

➤ Close all open windows.

Appendixes

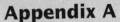

If You Are New to Windows 95, Windows NT, or Office 97

If you're new to Microsoft Windows 95, Microsoft Windows NT version 4.0, or Microsoft Office 97, this appendix will show you all the basics you need to get started. You'll get an overview of Windows 95 and Windows NT features, and you'll learn how to use online Help to answer your questions and find out more about using these operating systems. You'll also get an introduction to Office 97.

If You Are New to Windows 95 or Windows NT

Windows 95 and Windows NT are easy-to-use computer environments that help you handle the daily work that you perform with your computer. You can use either Windows 95 or Windows NT to run Office 97—the explanations in this appendix apply to both operating systems. The way you use Windows 95, Windows NT, and programs designed for these operating systems is similar. The programs have a common look, and you use the same kinds of controls to tell them what to do. In this section, you'll learn how to use the basic program controls. If you're already familiar with Windows 95 or Windows NT, skip to the "What is Microsoft Office 97?" section.

Start Windows 95 or Windows NT

Starting Windows 95 or Windows NT is as easy as turning on your computer.

In Windows 95, you will also be prompted for a username and password if your computer is configured for user profiles.

1 If your computer isn't on, turn it on now.

2 If you are using Windows NT, press CTRL+ALT+DEL to display a dialog box asking for your username and password. If you are using Windows 95, you will see this dialog box if your computer is connected to a network.

3 Type your username and password in the appropriate boxes, and then click OK.

   If you don't know your username or password, contact your system administrator for assistance.

Close

4 If you see the Welcome dialog box, click the Close button.

   Your screen should look similar to the following illustration.

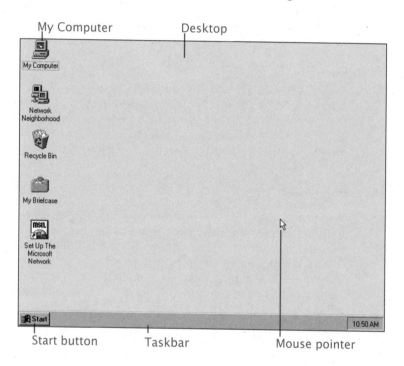

Using the Mouse

Although you can use the keyboard for most actions, it can be easier to use the mouse. The mouse controls a pointer on the screen, as shown in the previous illustration. You move the pointer by sliding the mouse over a flat surface in the direction you want the pointer to move. If you run out of room to move the mouse, lift it up, and then put it down in a more comfortable location.

You'll use five basic mouse actions throughout this book.

 NOTE In this book, we assume that your mouse is set up so that the left button is the primary button and the right button is the secondary button. If your mouse is configured the opposite way, for left-handed use, use the right button when we tell you to use the left, and vice versa.

When you are directed to	Do this
Point to an item	Move the mouse to place the pointer on the item.
Click an item	Point to the item on your screen, and then quickly press and release the left mouse button.
Use the right mouse button to click an item	Point to the item on your screen, and then quickly press and release the right mouse button. Clicking the right mouse button displays a shortcut menu from which you can choose from a list of commands that apply to that item.
Double-click an item	Point to the item, and then quickly press and release the left mouse button twice.
Drag an item	Point to an item, and then hold down the left mouse button as you move the pointer.

Using Window Controls

All programs designed for use on computers that have Windows 95 or Windows NT installed have common controls that you use to scroll, size, move, and close a window.

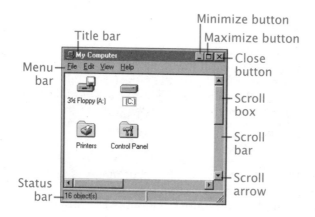

To	Do this	Button
Move, or *scroll*, vertically or horizontally through the contents of a window that extends beyond the screen	Click a scroll bar or scroll arrow, or drag the scroll box. The illustration above identifies these controls.	
Enlarge a window to fill the screen	Click the Maximize button, or double-click the window's title bar.	
Restore a window to its previous size	Click the Restore button, or double-click the window's title bar. When a window is maximized, the Maximize button changes to the Restore button.	
Reduce a window to a button on the taskbar	Click the Minimize button. To display a minimized window, click its button on the taskbar.	
Move a window	Drag the window's title bar.	
Close a window	Click the Close button.	

Using Menus

Just like a restaurant menu, a program menu provides a list of options from which you can choose. On program menus, these options are called *commands*. To select a menu or a menu command, you click the item you want.

 NOTE   You can also use the keyboard to make menu selections. Press the ALT key to activate the menu bar. Press the key that corresponds to the highlighted or underlined letter of the menu name, and then press the key that corresponds to the highlighted or underlined letter of the command name.

Open and make selections from a menu

In this exercise, you open and make selections from a menu.

You can also press ALT+E to open the Edit menu.

1   On the Desktop, double-click the My Computer icon.

The My Computer window opens.

2   In the My Computer window, click Edit on the menu bar.

The Edit menu appears. Some commands are dimmed; this means that they aren't available.

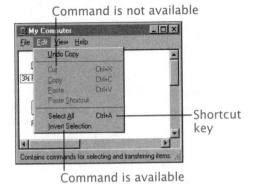

Command is not available

Shortcut key

Command is available

3   Click the Edit menu name to close the menu.

The menu closes.

4   Click View on the menu bar to open the View menu.

On a menu, a check mark indicates that multiple items in this group of commands can be selected at one time. A bullet mark indicates that only one item in this group can be selected at one time.

5   On the View menu, click Toolbar.

The View menu closes, and a toolbar appears below the menu bar.

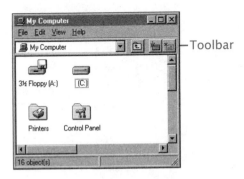

Toolbar

6   On the View menu, click List.

The items in the My Computer window now appear in a list, rather than as icons.

Large Icons

7 On the toolbar, click the Large Icons button.

Clicking a button on a toolbar is a quick way to select a command.

8 On the View menu, point to Arrange Icons.

A cascading menu appears, listing additional menu choices. When a right-pointing arrow appears after a command name, it indicates that additional commands are available.

9 Click anywhere outside the menu to close it.

10 On the menu bar, click View, and then click Toolbar again.

The View menu closes, and the toolbar is now hidden.

11 Click the Close button in the upper-right corner of the My Computer window to close the window.

TIP If you do a lot of typing, you might want to learn the key combinations for commands you use frequently. Pressing the key combination is a quick way to perform a command by using the keyboard. If a key combination is available for a command, it will be listed to the right of the command name on the menu. For example, CTRL+C is listed on the Edit menu as the key combination for the Copy command.

Using Dialog Boxes

When you choose a command name that is followed by an ellipsis (...), a dialog box will appear so that you can provide more information about how the command should be carried out. Dialog boxes have standard features, as shown in the following illustration.

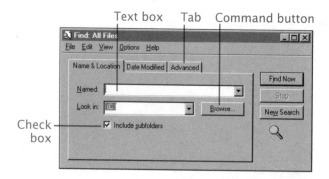

To move around in a dialog box, you click the item you want. You can also use the keyboard to select the item by holding down ALT as you press the underlined letter. Or you can press TAB to move between items.

Display the Taskbar Properties dialog box

Some dialog boxes provide several categories of options displayed on separate tabs. You click the top of an obscured tab to make it visible.

1 On the taskbar, click the Start button.

The Start menu appears.

2 On the Start menu, point to Settings, and then click Taskbar.

3 In the Taskbar Properties dialog box, click the Start Menu Programs tab.

Using this tab, you can customize the list of programs that appears on your Start menu.

4 Click the Taskbar Options tab, and then click to select the Show Small Icons In Start Menu check box.

When a check box is selected, it displays a check mark.

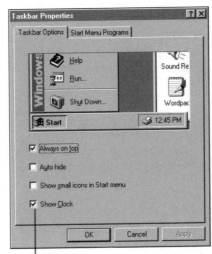

Click here. When you click a check box that is selected, you turn the option off.

5 Click the check box a couple of times, and watch how the display in the dialog box changes.

Clicking any check box or option button will turn the option off or on.

6 Click the Cancel button in the dialog box.

This closes the dialog box without changing any settings.

Getting Help with Windows 95 or Windows NT

When you're at work and you want to find more information about how to do a project, you might ask a co-worker or consult a reference book. To find out more about functions and features in Windows 95 or Windows NT, you can use the online Help system. For example, when you need information about how to print, the Help system is one of the most efficient ways to learn. The Windows 95 or Windows NT Help system is available from the Start menu. After the Help system opens, you can choose the type of help you want from the Help Topics dialog box.

To find instructions about broad categories, you can look on the Contents tab. Or you can search the Help index to find information about specific topics. The Help information is short and concise, so you can get the exact information you need quickly. You can use shortcut icons in many Help topics to directly perform the task you want.

Viewing Help Contents

The Contents tab is organized like a book's table of contents. As you choose top-level topics, called *chapters*, you see a list of more detailed subtopics from which to choose. Many of these chapters have Tips And Tricks sections to help you work more efficiently, and Troubleshooting sections to help you resolve problems.

Find Help about general categories

Suppose you want to learn more about using Calculator, a program that comes with Windows 95 and Windows NT. In this exercise, you look up information in the online Help system.

1 Click Start. On the Start menu, click Help.

    The Help Topics: Windows Help or Help Topics: Windows NT Help dialog box appears.

2 If necessary, click the Contents tab to make it active.

3 Double-click "Introducing Windows" or "Introducing Windows NT."

    A set of subtopics appears.

4 Double-click "Using Windows Accessories."

5 Double-click "For General Use."

6 Double-click "Calculator: for making calculations."

    A Help topic window opens.

7 Read the Help information, and then click the Close button to close the Help window.

Finding Help About Specific Topics

You can find specific Help topics by using the Index tab or the Find tab. The Index tab is organized like a book's index. Keywords for topics are organized alphabetically. You can either scroll through the list of keywords or type the keyword you want to find. You can then select from one or more topic choices.

With the Find tab, you can also enter a keyword. The main difference is that you get a list of all Help topics in which that keyword appears, not just the topics that begin with that word.

Find Help about specific topics by using the Help index

In this exercise, you use the Help index to learn how to change the background pattern of your Desktop.

1 Click Start, and then click Help.

The Help Topics dialog box appears.

2 Click the Index tab to make it active.

3 In the text box, type **display**

A list of display-related topics appears.

4 Click the topic named "background pictures or patterns, changing," and then click Display.

The Topics Found dialog box appears.

5 Be sure that the topic named "Changing the background of your desktop" is selected, and then click Display.

6 Read the Help topic.

Shortcut

7 Click the shortcut icon in step 1 of the Help topic.

The Display Properties dialog box appears. If you want, you can immediately perform the task you are looking up in Help.

8 Click the Close button on the Display Properties dialog box.

9 Click the Close button on the Windows Help window.

NOTE You can print any Help topic if you have a printer installed on your computer. Click the Options button in the upper-left corner of any Help topic window, click Print Topic, and then click OK. To continue searching for additional topics, click the Help Topics button in any open Help topic window.

Find Help about specific topics by using the Find tab

In this exercise, you use the Find tab to learn how to change printer settings.

1 Click Start, and then click Help to display the Help Topics dialog box.

2 Click the Find tab to make it active.

3 If you see a wizard, click Next, and then click Finish to complete the creation of the search index and close the wizard.

   This might take a few minutes. The next time you use Find, you won't have to wait for the list to be created. The Find tab appears.

4 In the text box, type **print**

   All topics that have to do with printing appear in the list box at the bottom of the tab.

5 In step 3 of the Help dialog box, click the "Changing printer settings" topic, and then click Display.

   The Help topic appears.

6 Read the Help topic, and then click the Close button on the Windows Help window.

Find Help in a dialog box

Almost every dialog box includes a question mark Help button in the upper-right corner of its window. When you click this button, and then click any dialog box control, a Help window appears that explains what the control is and how to use it. In this exercise, you get help on a dialog box control.

1 Click Start, and then click Run.

   The Run dialog box appears.

Help

2 Click the Help button.

   The mouse pointer changes to an arrow with a question mark.

3 Click the Open text box.

   A Help window appears, providing information about how to use the Open text box.

4 Click anywhere on the Desktop or press ESC to close the Help window.

   The mouse pointer returns to its previous shape and the Run dialog box appears again.

5 Click Cancel.

TIP You can change the way the Help topics appear on your screen. Click the Options button in any Help topic window, point to Font, and then click the size you want the text to be.

What Is Microsoft Office 97?

Microsoft Office 97 is an integrated family of programs that work seamlessly together to create professional documents and perform daily tasks. Office 97 comprises six individual programs: Microsoft Word, Microsoft Excel, Microsoft Binder, Microsoft PowerPoint, Microsoft Access, and Microsoft Outlook, plus the Office 97 shared components. With Office 97, you can copy, move, paste, link, embed, import, and export information between programs to integrate your work. For example, you do not need to retype or recreate tables and charts that you created in Excel in order to use them in a Word document or a PowerPoint presentation—you can easily integrate your tables and charts directly from Excel. With the power of integration among the Office 97 programs, your documents, workbooks, and presentations come alive as never before.

With more companies and individuals using the Internet, tools to access the Internet and communicate on the Internet are as necessary as a good word processor. Office 97 comes with built-in Internet capabilities that allow you to create and convert existing documents into HTML and create hyperlinks within documents, to other documents, and to sites on the Internet. Along with Microsoft FrontPage, you can integrate your Office 97 documents to create an attractive and professionally designed Web site.

Quit Windows 95 or Windows NT

1   If you are finished using Windows 95 or Windows NT, close any open windows by clicking the Close button in each window.

2   Click Start, and then click Shut Down.

    The Shut Down Windows dialog box appears.

3   Click Yes.

    A message indicates that it is now safe to turn off your computer.

 WARNING   To avoid loss of data or damage to your operating system, always quit Windows 95 or Windows NT by using the Shut Down command on the Start menu before you turn your computer off.

Adding Microsoft Office 97 Components

Microsoft Office 97 has many optional settings that can affect your ability to perform certain exercise steps described in a lesson. Use this appendix to determine which options need to be installed to complete the lesson.

 NOTE Each computer system is configured with different hardware and software; therefore, your screen display of icons, folders, and menu options might not exactly match the illustrations in this book. These system differences should not interfere with your ability to perform the exercises in the book.

Installing the Office Shortcut Bar

With a typical Office 97 setup, the Office Shortcut Bar will not be installed by default, unless you are upgrading from a previous version of Office and the Office Shortcut Bar was part of the previous Office startup. To install the Office Shortcut Bar, you may need access to the Office 97 installation disks. To install the Office Shortcut Bar after you have installed Office 97, perform the following steps.

1 On the Start menu, point to Settings, and then click Control Panel.

The Control Panel window opens.

2 Double-click Add/Remove Programs.

The Add/Remove Programs Properties dialog box appears. The Install/Uninstall tab is selected.

3 Click Microsoft Office 97, and then click Add/Remove.

The Microsoft Office 97 Setup dialog box appears.

4 Click Add/Remove.

The Microsoft Office 97–Maintenance dialog box appears.

5 Click Office Tools, making sure you don't clear the check box, and then click Change Option.

The Microsoft Office–Office Tools dialog box appears.

6 Select the Microsoft Office Shortcut Bar check box, and then click OK.

The Microsoft Office 97–Maintenance dialog box appears.

7 Click Continue.

After a few moments, a message appears stating that the setup was completed successfully.

8 Click OK.

The Add/Remove Programs Properties dialog box appears.

9 Click OK.

10 Close all open windows.

Start the Office Shortcut Bar for the first time

When you install the Office Shortcut Bar, it will not immediately appear unless you restart your computer or run the Office Shortcut Bar program from the StartUp menu. After you display the Office Shortcut Bar, it will appear each time you start your computer unless you exit the program. To display the Office Shortcut Bar for the first time without restarting your computer, do the following:

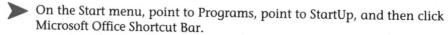 On the Start menu, point to Programs, point to StartUp, and then click Microsoft Office Shortcut Bar.

The Office Shortcut Bar program starts, and the Office Shortcut Bar appears at the upper-right area of your screen.

Installing Microsoft Query

With a typical setup of Office 97, the add-in program Microsoft Query is not installed. To install Microsoft Query after you have installed Office 97, perform the following steps.

1 If the Office Shortcut Bar is displayed, use the right mouse button to click the upper-left corner of the Office Shortcut Bar, and then click Exit.

   Microsoft Office 97 Setup will ask you to close the Office Shortcut Bar if you haven't already done so.

2 On the Start menu, point to Settings, and then click Control Panel.

   The Control Panel window opens.

3 Double-click Add/Remove Programs.

   The Add/Remove Programs Properties dialog box appears. The Install/Uninstall tab is selected.

4 Click Microsoft Office 97, and then click Add/Remove.

   The Microsoft Office 97 Setup dialog box appears.

5 Click Add/Remove.

   The Microsoft Office 97–Maintenance dialog box appears.

6 Click Data Access, making sure you don't clear the check box, and then click Change Option.

   The Microsoft Office–Data Access dialog box appears.

7 Select the Microsoft Query check box, and then click OK.

   The Microsoft Office 97–Maintenance dialog box appears.

8 Click Continue.

   After a few moments, a message appears stating that the setup was completed successfully.

9 Click OK.

   The Add/Remove Programs Properties dialog box appears.

10 Click OK.

11 Close all open windows.

Integration Techniques

There are many different ways to share information between Microsoft Office 97 programs. Although all of the Office 97 programs are designed to work in a similar manner, there can be slight differences in how each integration method is performed when working between programs. The following tables give you a comprehensive look at how to integrate information using each of the Office 97 programs.

Microsoft Access

To	Do this
Import a file from an Office 97 program to Access	*Excel*: Close the Excel file you want to use. In Access, on the File menu, point to Get External Data, and then click Import. Click the File Of Type down arrow, and then click Microsoft Excel. Locate the Excel file you are importing, and then click Import. Follow the instructions in each Import Spreadsheet Wizard dialog box.
	Word: Be sure that the information you want to import is in a delimited text format. Copy the information to a new file, name the file, and then close the file. In Access, on the File menu, point to Get External Data, and then click Import. Click the Files Of Type down arrow, and then click Text Files. Locate the Word file you

To	Do this
	are importing, and then click Import. Follow the instructions in each Import Spreadsheet Wizard dialog box.
Export an Access file to an Office 97 program	*Excel*: In Access, open the database containing the object you want to export, and click the name of the object. On the File menu, click Save As/Export. Be sure that the To An External File Or Database option button is selected, and then click OK. Click the Save As Type down arrow, and then click a Microsoft Excel version. Type a filename and location. Click Export.
	Word: In Access, open the database containing the object you want to export, and click the name of the object. On the File menu, click Save As/Export. Be sure that the To An External File Or Database option button is selected, and then click OK. Click the Save As Type down arrow, and then click Text Files or Rich Text Format. Type a new filename and select a location. Click Export. If an Export Text wizard appears, follow the instructions in each dialog box.
Copy information from an Office 97 program to Access	*Excel*: Use Copy and Paste buttons. If you copy more than one cell from Excel into a database table field, the cell information will be separated by the "[]" symbol.
	PowerPoint: Use the Copy and Paste buttons. If the information being copied will become a new database table, create the new table before pasting.
	Word: Use the Copy and Paste buttons. If the information being copied will become a new database table, create the new table before pasting.
Embed information from an Office 97 program in an Access database table field	*Excel*: In Access, create an OLE object field in the database you want to embed to. (For specific steps to create an OLE object field, see Lesson 8.) Use Copy and Paste buttons. (When you embed an Excel worksheet object, the entire workbook is embedded.)
	PowerPoint: Can only embed a new object or an existing file.
	Word: Use the Copy and Paste buttons.

To	Do this
Link information from an Office 97 program to an Access database table field	*Excel*: In Access, create an OLE object field in the database you want to link to. (For specific steps to create an OLE object field, see Lesson 8.) Select the information you want to link in the source program file. On the Standard toolbar, click the Copy button. Switch to Access. Place the insertion point where the information will be inserted. On the Edit menu, click Paste Special. Click the Paste Link option button. Click Microsoft Excel Worksheet Object in the As box, and then click OK.
	PowerPoint: Can only link an existing file.
	Word: In Access, create an OLE object field in the database you want to link to. (For specific steps to create an OLE object field, see Lesson 8.) Select the information you want to link in the source program file. On the Standard toolbar, click the Copy button. Switch to Access. Place the insertion point where the information will be inserted. On the Edit menu, click Paste Special. Click the Paste Link option button. Click Microsoft Word Document Object in the As box, and then click OK.
Link an Excel workbook to a database	In Access, open the database file the workbook information will be linked to. On the Tables tab, click New. Click Link Table, and then click OK. Click the Files Of Type down arrow, and then click Microsoft Excel. Locate the workbook file to be linked, and then click Link. Be sure that the Show Worksheets option button is selected, click the worksheet tab name, and then click Next. Select the First Row Contains Column Headings check box, and then click Next. Type the name of the new linked table, and then click Finish.

Microsoft Excel

To	Do this
Import a file from an Office 97 program to Excel	*Access*: Use Microsoft Query. (For specific steps in retrieving database information, see Lesson 6.)
	Word: In Excel, on the Standard toolbar, click the Open button. To locate the file you want to import, click the Files Of Type down arrow, click the file type you are importing or All Files, and then click Open. If Excel cannot convert the file format, try opening the file in Word and saving it in a file format (such as TXT) that Excel can open. Follow the instructions in each Text Import Wizard dialog box.
Export an Excel file to an Office 97 Program	Use importing in the Office 97 program you want to export the information to.
Copy information from an Office 97 program to Excel	*Access*: Use the Copy and Paste buttons.
	PowerPoint: Use the Copy and Paste buttons.
	Word: Use the Copy and Paste buttons.
Embed information from an Office 97 program in Excel	*Access*: Can only embed an existing file.
	PowerPoint: Can only embed a new object or an existing file.
	Word: In Word, on the Standard toolbar, click the Copy button. Switch to Excel. On the Edit menu, click Paste Special. Be sure that the Paste option button is selected. Click Microsoft Word Document Object in the As box, and then click OK.
	(If you are embedding another Excel worksheet object, the entire workbook is embedded.)
Link information from an Office 97 program in Excel	*Access*: Can only link an existing file.
	PowerPoint: Can only link an existing file.
	Word: In Word, on the Standard toolbar, click the Copy button. Switch to Excel. On the Edit menu, click Paste Special. Click the Paste Link option button. Click Microsoft Word Document Object in the As box, and then click OK.

Microsoft Outlook

To	Do this
Import a file from an Office 97 program to Outlook	In Outlook, on the File menu, click Import And Export. Click one of the import actions, and then click Next. Click the file type to import, and click Next. Click Browse, locate the file, click OK, and then click Next. Click the destination folder, and click Next. Click Finish. (Import supports Schedule+ or another program file, a personal folder file, or a Microsoft Mail file.)
Export a personal folder in Outlook to an Office 97 program	In Outlook, on the File menu, click Import And Export. Click one of the export actions, and then click Next. Click the folder to export from. Type the new filename and location or click Browse, and then click Finish. (Export supports a personal folder file or Timex Data Link Watch.)
Copy information from an Office 97 program in a mail message, calendar appointment, contact, task, or journal entry	*Access*: Use Copy and Paste buttons. *Excel*: In Excel, select the information you want to copy. On the Standard toolbar, click the Copy button. Switch to Outlook. Click in the text box. On the Edit menu, click Paste Special. Be sure that the Paste option button is selected. Click Formatted Text or Text in the As box, and then click OK. (Using the Paste button with Excel will embed the information.) *PowerPoint*: Use the Copy and Paste buttons. *Word*: Use the Copy and Paste buttons.
Embed information from an Office 97 program in a mail message, calendar appointment, contact, task, or journal entry	*Access*: Can only embed an existing file. *Excel*: In Excel, select the information you want to embed. Click the Copy button. In Outlook, on the Edit menu, click Paste Special. Be sure that the Paste option button is selected. Click Microsoft Excel Worksheet Object, and click OK. (When you embed an Excel worksheet object, the entire workbook is embedded.) *PowerPoint*: Can only embed a new object or an existing file. *Word*: In Word, select the information to embed. Click the Copy button. In Outlook, on the Edit menu, click Paste Special. Be sure that the Paste option button is selected. Click Microsoft Word Document Object in the As box, and click OK.

To	Do this
Link information from an Office 97 program in an Outlook message, appointment, contact, task, or journal entry	*Access*: Can only link an existing file. *Excel*: In Excel, select the information you want to link. Click the Copy button. Switch to Outlook. On the Edit menu, click Paste Special. Click the Paste Link option button. Click Microsoft Excel Worksheet Object in the As box, and click OK. *PowerPoint*: Can only link an existing file. *Word*: In Word, select the information you want to link. Click the Copy button. Switch to Outlook. On the Edit menu, click Paste Special. Click the Paste Link option button. Click Microsoft Word Document Object in the As box, and click OK.

Microsoft PowerPoint

To	Do this
Import a file from an Office 97 program to PowerPoint	In PowerPoint, click the Open button. Locate the file you want to import by clicking the Files Of Type down arrow, clicking the file type you are importing, and clicking Open. PowerPoint converts the file format and opens it. Save the file as a PowerPoint presentation. If PowerPoint cannot convert the file format, try opening the file in its source program and saving it in a file format (such as RTF) that PowerPoint can open.
Export a PowerPoint file to an Office 97 program	*Access*: Use the import feature in Access. *Excel*: Use the import feature in Excel. *Word*: In PowerPoint, open the file you want to export to Word. On the File menu, point to Send To, and then click Microsoft Word. The file is converted to a Word document.
Copy information from an Office 97 program to PowerPoint	*Access*: Use the Copy and Paste buttons. *Excel*: In Excel, click the Copy button. Switch to PowerPoint. On the Edit menu, click Paste Special. Be sure that the Paste option button is selected. Click Picture in the As box, and click OK. *Word*: In Word, click the Copy button. On the Edit menu in PowerPoint, click Paste Special. Be sure that the Paste option button is selected. Click Picture in the As box, and click OK.

To	Do this
	(Using the Paste button in PowerPoint with Excel and Word embeds the information.)
Embed information from an Office 97 program in PowerPoint	*Access*: Can only embed an existing file.
	Excel: In Excel, click the Copy button. Switch to PowerPoint. On the Edit menu, click Paste Special. Be sure that the Paste option is selected. Click Microsoft Excel Worksheet Object in the As box, and then click OK. (When you embed an Excel worksheet object, the entire workbook is embedded.) You can also use Copy and Paste.
	Word: In Word, click the Copy button. Switch to PowerPoint. On the Edit menu, click Paste Special. Be sure that the Paste option button is selected. Click Microsoft Word Document Object in the As box, and then click OK. You can also use the Copy and Paste buttons.
Link information from an Office 97 program in PowerPoint	*Access*: Can only link an existing file.
	Excel: In Excel, click the Copy button. Switch to PowerPoint. On the Edit menu, click Paste Special. Click the Paste Link option button. Click Microsoft Excel Worksheet Object in the As box, and then click OK.
	Word: In Word, click the Copy button. On the Edit menu in PowerPoint, click Paste Special. Click the Paste Link option. Click Microsoft Word Document Object in the As box, and click OK.

Microsoft Word

To	Do this
Import a file from an Office 97 program to Word	In Word, click the Open button. To locate the file you want to import, click the Files Of Type down arrow, click the file type you are importing, and then click Open. Word converts the file format and opens it. Save the file as a Word document. If Word cannot convert the file, try opening the file in its source program and saving it in a file format (such as RTF or TXT) that Word can open.
Export a Word file to an Office 97 program	*Access*: Use the import feature in Access.
	Excel: Use the import feature in Excel.

To	Do this
	PowerPoint: In Word, open the file you want to export. On the File menu, point to Send To, and then click Microsoft PowerPoint. The file is converted into slides based on heading styles.
Copy information from an Office 97 program to Word	*Access*: Use the Copy and Paste buttons.
	Excel: Use the Copy and Paste buttons.
	PowerPoint: Using the Copy and Paste buttons will create a hyperlink.
Embed information from an Office 97 program in Word	*Access*: Can only embed an existing file.
	Excel: In Excel, click the Copy button. Switch to Word. On the Edit menu, click Paste Special. Be sure that the Paste option button is selected. Click Microsoft Excel Worksheet Object in the As box, and then click OK. (When you embed an Excel worksheet object, the entire workbook is embedded.)
	PowerPoint: Can only embed a new object or an existing file.
Link information from an Office 97 program in Word	*Access*: Can only link an existing file.
	Excel: In Excel, click the Copy button. Switch to Word. On the Edit menu, click Paste Special. Click the Paste Link option button. Click Microsoft Excel Worksheet Object in the As box, and then click OK.
	PowerPoint: Can only link an existing file.

NOTE In addition to embedding information from an Office 97 program, you can also embed a new (program) object and an existing file. On the Insert menu, click Object. In the Object dialog box, use the Create New tab options to embed a new object, or the Create From File tab options to embed an existing file. You can also link existing files by clicking the Link check box.

Address Book A list containing all of the available addresses on your network, including those of other gateways and networks to which you can send mail. The Address Book consists of at least two address books: the global address list and your personal address book.

append An action that is used to add records from one table to another.

AutoFormat A feature used to format material with a predefined set of attributes.

AutoPick The process by which the schedules of selected individuals and resources are searched for the next mutually available meeting. *See also* Meeting Planner.

bookmark Selected text, graphics, or a location tagged with a reference name or tagged so that you can move quickly to the selection.

browser Software that can display information found in files posted on the World Wide Web. A browser can also play sound or video files if you have the necessary hardware.

cell The basic unit of a table or worksheet. The intersection of a row and a column forms one cell. You type text, numbers, or formulas into cells. Each cell is named by its position in the row (1, 2, 3) and column (A, B, C). For example, cell A1 is the first cell in column A, row 1.

cell comment A comment that explains or identifies information in a specific cell or range of cells.

Clipboard A temporary holding area in computer memory that stores the last set of information that was cut or copied (such as text or graphics). You transfer data from the Clipboard by using the Paste command. The information remains on the Clipboard until you cut or copy another piece of information, which then replaces the current contents of the Clipboard.

contact A person or organization that you correspond with.

copy To duplicate information from one location to another, either within a file, to another file, or to a file in another program. The copied information is stored on the Clipboard until you cut or copy another piece of information.

criteria The conditions that control which records to display in a query; the words or values used to determine the data that appears in a data list.

cut To remove selected information from a document so you can paste it to another location within the file, to another file, or to a file in another program. The cut information is stored on the Clipboard until you cut or copy another piece of information.

database A collection of data related to a particular topic or purpose, such as a database of customer information. Can also refer to a type of program, such as Access, that you can use to organize and manipulate detailed lists of information.

data source A document that contains customized information that varies with each version of a document.

default A predefined setting that is built into a program and is used when you do not specify an alternative setting. For example, a document might have a default setting of one-inch page margins unless you specify another value for the margin settings.

delimited The specific characters in text that are used to separate the data that should appear in separate columns. The delimiter characters can be commas, tabs, semicolons, or spaces.

Desktop The entire Windows 95 screen that represents your work area. Icons, windows, and the taskbar appear on the Desktop. You can customize the Desktop to suit your preferences and working requirements.

design template A template containing a color scheme, slide and title masters with custom formatting, and styled fonts that have been designed for a particular look.

destination A document or program receiving information that was originally generated in another program. *See also* source.

document Any independent unit of information, such as a text file, worksheet, or graphic object, that is created with a program. A document can be saved with a unique filename, by which it can later be retrieved.

drag-and-drop A mouse technique for directly moving or copying a set of information from one location to another. To drag an object, position the pointer over the object, hold down the mouse button while you move the mouse, and then release the mouse button when the object is positioned where you want it.

electronic mail Notes, messages, or files that are sent between different computers using telecommunication or network services. Also referred to as *e-mail*.

embed To insert an object from a source program into a destination document. When you double-click the object in the destination document, the source program opens and you can edit the object. *See also* link.

embedded object Data (such as text or graphics) that you can edit using the full resources of its source program while it is in a destination document. *See also* embed.

export The process of converting and saving a file to be used in another program. *See also* import.

field An area in a table or form where you can enter or view specific information about an individual task or resource. On a form, a field is an area where you can enter data.

filter A set of criteria you can apply to records to show specific tasks, records, or resources. The tasks, records, or resources that match your criteria are listed or highlighted so that you can focus on just the information you want.

file A document that you create or save with a unique filename.

file format The format in which data is stored in a file. Usually, different programs, such as Word or Excel, have different file formats.

folder A container in which documents, program files, and other folders are stored on your computer disks. Folders can help you organize your documents by grouping them into categories, as you would organize paper documents into file folders. Formerly referred to as a *directory*.

formula A sequence of values, cell references, names, functions, or operators that produces a new value from existing values. A formula always begins with an equal sign (=).

handles Small black squares located in the lower-right corner of selected cells or around selected graphic objects, chart items, or text. By dragging the handles, you can perform actions such as moving, copying, filling, sizing, or formatting on the selected cells, objects, chart items, or text.

HTML (Hypertext Markup Language) A language used by a computer programmer to prepare a document for viewing on the World Wide Web. You use a Web browser (such as Microsoft Internet Explorer or Netscape Navigator) to view HTML documents.

HTTP (Hypertext Transfer Protocol) A communications method used on the World Wide Web to transfer information found in HTML, VRML, and other documents.

home page The first page of a Web site, used as an entrance into the Web site.

hyperlink An object, such as a graphic, or colored or underlined text, that represents a link to another location in the same file or in a different file. Hyperlinks are one of the key elements of HTML documents. Typically, when you click a hyperlink, the file that appears in your browser changes.

icon A small graphic that represents an object, such as a program, a disk drive, or a document. When you double-click an icon, the item the icon represents opens.

import The process of converting and opening a file that was created in a another program. *See also* export.

Internet A worldwide network of thousands of smaller computer networks and millions of commercial, education, government, and personal computers. The Internet is like an electronic city with virtual libraries, storefronts, business offices, art galleries, and so on.

intranet   A self-contained network that uses the same communications protocols and file formats as the Internet. An intranet can, but doesn't have to, be connected to the Internet. Many businesses use intranets for their internal communications. *See also* Internet.

jump   A method of presenting information in which text is linked together so that the user can browse through related topics, regardless of the presented order of topics.

link   To copy an object, such as a graphic or text, from one file or program to another so that there is a dependent relationship between the object and its source file. *Link* also refers to the connection between a source file and a destination file. Whenever the original information in the source file changes, the information in the linked object is automatically updated. *See also* embed.

main document   A document containing standardized text or graphics that is merged with a data source to produce a merged document. A main document contains placeholder text to represent information that varies in the merged document.

Meeting Planner   A grid display in which you can view free and busy times for meeting attendees and other resources, and schedule a meeting during an available time. *See also* AutoPick.

merge field   The placeholder text in the main document that marks the location at which data is inserted when the main document is merged with a data source. In a data source, merge fields contain the data that is merged into the main document.

move   To transfer information from one location to another, either within a file, to another file, or to a file in another program.

object   A table, chart, graphic, equation, or other form of information you create and edit. An object can be inserted, pasted, or copied into any file.

Office Binder   A special Office program that you can use to assemble and publish files of different types as a single file. With Office Binder, you can create, edit, and print files from Word, Excel, PowerPoint, and other Microsoft programs, together in a single file divided only by sections.

OLE   A Microsoft programming standard that allows a user or another program to communicate with other programs, usually for the purpose of exchanging information. Drag and drop, and linking and embedding are examples of OLE features. *See also* link *and* embed.

paste   To insert cut or copied text into a document from the temporary storage area called the Clipboard.

PivotTable   An interactive worksheet table that summarizes data using a selected format and calculations.

protocol   A set of rules or standards that enable computers to exchange information with a minimum of errors.

query An Access database object that represents the group of records you want to work with. You can think of a query as a request for a particular collection of data.

record A set of information that belongs together, such as all the information on one job program or one magazine subscription card. A record can also refer to one row in a database. The first row of the database contains the field names. Each additional row of the database is one record. Each record contains the same categories of data, or fields, as every other record in the database.

ruler A graphical bar displayed across the top of the document window. You can use the ruler to indent paragraphs, set tab stops, adjust page margins, and change column widths in a table.

section A part of a document separated from the rest of the document with a section break. You can use sections to change the page setup, headers and footers, and column formatting in different parts of the same document.

section break A line that identifies the end of a section and the beginning of the following section. Section breaks are used to format different parts of a document, such as columns or headers and footers.

shortcut An object that acts as a pointer to a document, folder, Internet address, or program. If you double-click the shortcut, the object opens.

shortcut menu A menu of commands that appears when you click the right mouse button while your mouse pointer is on a toolbar, property sheet, control, or other screen element. The menu of commands depends on the element you click.

slide master The slide that holds the formatted placeholders for the titles, main text, and any background items you want to have appear on all slides in a presentation. If you make a change to the slide master, the change affects all slides in your presentation based on the master.

slide show The act of displaying the presentation electronically, using a computer. All tools, menus, and other screen elements are hidden during a slide show, and the slides expand to fill the screen.

source The document or program in which the data was originally created. *See also* destination.

style A named collection of text formatting choices, such as font, size, leading, spacing, and alignment, that can be applied to change the appearance of text. Body Text, Headline, and Subhead are examples of styles that are often used. Styles are common in word-processing programs and presentation programs. Styles are stored in a document or template.

table One or more rows of cells commonly used to display numbers and other items for quick reference and analysis. Items in a table are organized into rows (records) and columns (fields).

tag   Text, in angle brackets, used to represent HTML. Web browsers display text and graphic elements based on these tags. The tag itself is not displayed by the browser.

taskbar   The rectangular bar usually located across the bottom of the Windows 95 Desktop. The taskbar includes the Start button as well as buttons for any programs and documents that are open.

TCP/IP (Transmission Control Protocol/Internet Protocol)
An Internet standard for transferring data between networked computers.

template   A special kind of document that provides basic tools and text for shaping a final document. Templates can contain the following elements: text, styles, glossary items, macros, and menu and key assignments.

toolbar   A bar at the top of Windows-based programs that displays a set of buttons used to carry out common menu commands. The buttons displayed on a toolbar change depending on which window or view is currently selected. Toolbars can be moved or docked at any edge of a program window.

URL (Uniform Resource Locator)   An address to a specific resource, such as a World Wide Web page or gopher site. A URL defines the type of resource (such as FTP, HTTP, or gopher) to be accessed, the specific site where the information is stored, and its precise location in the site.

Web address   The path to an item, such as an object, a document, or a page. An address can be a URL (an address to an Internet site) or a UNC Network path (an address to a file on a local area network).

Webmaster   A contact person for a Web site.

Web page   A document on the Web, formatted in HTML. Web pages usually contain links that you can use to jump from one page to another or from one location to another. *See also* hyperlink, jump.

Web site   A collection of Web pages.

wizard   A tool that guides you through a complex task by asking you questions, and then performing the task based on your responses.

workbook   A Microsoft Excel document in which you can store other documents. A workbook can include multiple worksheets, modules, and charts.

worksheet   A set of rows, columns, and cells in which you store and manipulate data. Several worksheets can appear in one workbook, and you can switch among them easily by clicking their tabs with the mouse.

World Wide Web   A system for navigating the Internet by using hyperlinks. When you use a Web browser, a Web site can appear as a collection of text, pictures, sounds, and digital movies.

Index

A

Access. *See* Microsoft Access
actionable objects, 207–8
actuals, tracking in task lists, 106
address books
  adding contacts, 64–65
  e-mail address books, 129
  importing addresses, 63–64
  mail merging contact information, 63, 65–67
  routing Word documents, 194–95
  selecting address information, 66
addresses
  for Microsoft Press, xix
  hyperlink addresses, 223, 247
  including e-mail addresses in hyperlinks, 231–32
  relative and absolute file paths, 229
apostrophes ('), 140
appending data to database tables, 137–38, 142–45, 153
applications. *See* programs; *names of individual programs*
attachments in e-mail, 129
attendees for meetings, selecting, 168
audience for Web sites, 237
audiovisual Office demonstrations, xxx
AutoPicking meeting dates, 166

B

background colors on Access forms, 148–49
background graphics
  adding to slide masters, 196–98
  hiding on slides, 204
binders, 27–28
  adding files, 30–32
  adding sections, 32–33
  binder templates, 38–40
  checking spelling, 36
  creating, 28–30
  editing sections, 36
  headers and footers, 45–46
  naming, 30
  panes in, 28–29, 34

binders, *continued*
  placeholders for files, 32, 211–12
  previewing and printing files, 36–37
  rearranging sections, 34–35
  saving and closing, 30, 37
  saving sections as files, 33
  sharing on networks, 40–41, 42–43
  switching between sections, 34
blank records in databases, 154
blank sections in binders, 32
blank Web pages, 243
bold text formatting, 96
bookmarks, Word, 223, 224
bound objects, 171
breaking links, 84, 89–90
browsers, 229, 236

C

calculations in workbooks, 79
Calendar folder in Outlook, 166–71
Camcorder Files shortcut, xxiii, xxx, 223
canceling meetings, 173
cascading menus, 270
case-sensitivity in file search, 20
cells, workbook
  as hyperlink addresses, 223
  cell comments in workbooks, 99, 103–4
Certified Microsoft Office User Program, xvii
change history, shared workbooks
  accepting or rejecting edits, 104–5
  activating, 101
  merging changes, 109–10
  shared workbook overview, 100
charts, Excel
  charting PivotTable data, 127–29
  Chart Wizard, 127–28
  embedding in PowerPoint slides, 203–4
  linking to PowerPoint slides, 205–7
  resizing, 128–29, 204

charts, Excel, *continued*
  when to embed, 203
  when to link, 205
charts, organization, 75–77
charts, PowerPoint
  editing embedded charts, 77
  embedding in Word documents, 75–77
Chart wizard, Excel, 127–28
checking spelling in binders, 36
closing
  Access databases, 149
  binders, 37
  Excel workbooks, 9
  Microsoft Outlook, 22
  Office Assistant, 10
  PowerPoint presentations, 12
  programs, 9
  shortcut bars, 13
  Web pages, 242–43
  Windows 95 or Windows NT, 277
  Word documents, 9
colors
  Access form background colors, 148–49
  embedded text in slides, 189
  hyperlink colors, 230–32
  Web page colors, 249–51
combining changes in shared workbooks, 109–10
comma-delimited file format, 64
command buttons on toolbars, 16–18
commands on menus, 268–70
comma-separated values file format, 64
comments
  cell comments in workbooks, 99, 103–4
  creating reviewing toolbars for Word, 16–18
comparing
  workbook versions before merging, 109
  worksheet and databases before importing, 154–55
contact information. *See also* Microsoft Outlook
  creating in Word, 67–69

Index

Index

IMPORTANT—READ CAREFULLY BEFORE OPENING SOFTWARE PACKET(S). By opening the sealed packet(s) containing the software, you indicate your acceptance of the following Microsoft License Agreement.

MICROSOFT LICENSE AGREEMENT
(Book Companion Disk)

This is a legal agreement between you (either an individual or an entity) and Microsoft Corporation. By opening the sealed software packet(s) you are agreeing to be bound by the terms of this agreement. If you do not agree to the terms of this agreement, promptly return the unopened software packet(s) and any accompanying written materials to the place you obtained them for a full refund.

MICROSOFT SOFTWARE LICENSE

1. GRANT OF LICENSE. Microsoft grants to you the right to use one copy of the Microsoft software program included with this book (the "SOFTWARE") on a single terminal connected to a single computer. The SOFTWARE is in "use" on a computer when it is loaded into the temporary memory (i.e., RAM) or installed into the permanent memory (e.g., hard disk, CD-ROM, or other storage device) of that computer. You may not network the SOFTWARE or otherwise use it on more than one computer or computer terminal at the same time.

For the files and materials referenced in this book which may be obtained from the Internet, Microsoft grants to you the right to use the materials in connection with the book. If you are a member of a corporation or business, you may reproduce the materials and distribute them within your business for internal business purposes in connection with the book. You may not reproduce the materials for further distribution.

2. COPYRIGHT. The SOFTWARE is owned by Microsoft or its suppliers and is protected by United States copyright laws and international treaty provisions. Therefore, you must treat the SOFTWARE like any other copyrighted material (e.g., a book or musical recording) except that you may either (a) make one copy of the SOFTWARE solely for backup or archival purposes, or (b) transfer the SOFTWARE to a single hard disk provided you keep the original solely for backup or archival purposes. You may not copy the written materials accompanying the SOFTWARE.

3. OTHER RESTRICTIONS. You may not rent or lease the SOFTWARE, but you may transfer the SOFTWARE and accompanying written materials on a permanent basis provided you retain no copies and the recipient agrees to the terms of this Agreement. You may not reverse engineer, decompile, or disassemble the SOFTWARE. If the SOFTWARE is an update or has been updated, any transfer must include the most recent update and all prior versions.

4. DUAL MEDIA SOFTWARE. If the SOFTWARE package contains both 3.5" and 5.25" disks, then you may use only the disks appropriate for your single-user computer. You may not use the other disks on another computer or loan, rent, lease, or transfer them to another user except as part of the permanent transfer (as provided above) of all SOFTWARE and written materials.

5. SAMPLE CODE. If the SOFTWARE includes Sample Code, then Microsoft grants you a royalty-free right to reproduce and distribute the sample code of the SOFTWARE provided that you: (a) distribute the sample code only in conjunction with and as a part of your software product; (b) do not use Microsoft's or its authors' names, logos, or trademarks to market your software product; (c) include the copyright notice that appears on the SOFTWARE on your product label and as a part of the sign-on message for your software product; and (d) agree to indemnify, hold harmless, and defend Microsoft and its authors from and against any claims or lawsuits, including attorneys' fees, that arise or result from the use or distribution of your software product.

DISCLAIMER OF WARRANTY

The SOFTWARE (including instructions for its use) is provided "AS IS" WITHOUT WARRANTY OF ANY KIND. MICROSOFT FURTHER DISCLAIMS ALL IMPLIED WARRANTIES INCLUDING WITHOUT LIMITATION ANY IMPLIED WARRANTIES OF MERCHANTABILITY OR OF FITNESS FOR A PARTICULAR PURPOSE. THE ENTIRE RISK ARISING OUT OF THE USE OR PERFORMANCE OF THE SOFTWARE AND DOCUMENTATION REMAINS WITH YOU.

IN NO EVENT SHALL MICROSOFT, ITS AUTHORS, OR ANYONE ELSE INVOLVED IN THE CREATION, PRODUCTION, OR DELIVERY OF THE SOFTWARE BE LIABLE FOR ANY DAMAGES WHATSOEVER (INCLUDING, WITHOUT LIMITATION, DAMAGES FOR LOSS OF BUSINESS PROFITS, BUSINESS INTERRUPTION, LOSS OF BUSINESS INFORMATION, OR OTHER PECUNIARY LOSS) ARISING OUT OF THE USE OF OR INABILITY TO USE THE SOFTWARE OR DOCUMENTATION, EVEN IF MICROSOFT HAS BEEN ADVISED OF THE POSSIBILITY OF SUCH DAMAGES. BECAUSE SOME STATES/COUNTRIES DO NOT ALLOW THE EXCLUSION OR LIMITATION OF LIABILITY FOR CONSEQUENTIAL OR INCIDENTAL DAMAGES, THE ABOVE LIMITATION MAY NOT APPLY TO YOU.

U.S. GOVERNMENT RESTRICTED RIGHTS

The SOFTWARE and documentation are provided with RESTRICTED RIGHTS. Use, duplication, or disclosure by the Government is subject to restrictions as set forth in subparagraph (c)(1)(ii) of The Rights in Technical Data and Computer Software clause at DFARS 252.227-7013 or subparagraphs (c)(1) and (2) of the Commercial Computer Software — Restricted Rights 48 CFR 52.227-19, as applicable. Manufacturer is Microsoft Corporation, One Microsoft Way, Redmond, WA 98052-6399.

If you acquired this product in the United States, this Agreement is governed by the laws of the State of Washington. Should you have any questions concerning this Agreement, or if you desire to contact Microsoft Press for any reason, please write: Microsoft Press, One Microsoft Way, Redmond, WA 98052-6399.

The
Step by Step
Practice Files Disk

The enclosed 3.5-inch disk contains time-saving, ready-to-use practice files that complement the lessons in this book. To use the practice files, you'll need Microsoft Office 97 and either the Microsoft Windows 95 operating system or version 3.51 Service Pack 5 or later of the Microsoft Windows NT operating system.

Most of the *Step by Step* lessons use practice files from the disk. Before you begin the *Step by Step* lessons, read the "Installing and Using the Practice Files" section of the book. There you'll find a description of each practice file and easy instructions for installing the files on your computer's hard disk.

Please take a few moments to read the license agreement on the previous page before using the enclosed disk.